The imperial curriculum

The colonial experience has played an enormous role in shaping today's perceptions of race. Central to the construction of racial images was the British system of imperial education; a field which to this day remains an under-researched area.

The Imperial Curriculum presents the first comparative analysis of racial attitudes in the formal schooling of both Britain and its former dominions and colonies. The various contributions examine the issue right across the British imperial experience – with case studies ranging from Canada, Ireland, East and South Africa, through the Indian subcontinent to Australia and New Zealand. The book breaks new ground in its consideration of racial indoctrination from the perspective of both colonizer and colonized. The central theme throughout is that a racial hierarchy was taught through both curriculum and text in schools throughout the former British Empire.

In covering nineteenth-century Ireland to present-day South Africa, *The Imperial Curriculum* is notable for its historical as well as geographical breadth and should therefore appeal to students of the history of education, race and ethnicity, and imperial and social history.

J.A. Mangan is in the Faculty of Education at Strathclyde University. He is the author of numerous books and articles including *Athleticism in the Victorian and Edwardian Public School* (Cambridge University Press: 1981) and *The Games Ethic and Imperialism* (Viking/Penguin: 1986) and is the editor of *'Benefits Bestowed'?: Education and British Imperialism* (Manchester University Press: 1988) and *Making Imperial Mentalities: Socialisation in British Imperialism* (Manchester University Press: 1990).

The imperial curriculum

Racial images and education in
the British colonial experience

Edited by
J.A. Mangan

London and New York

First published 1993
by Routledge
11 New Fetter Lane, London EC4P 4EE

Simultaneously published in the USA and Canada
by Routledge
29 West 35th Street, New York, NY 10001

© 1993 J.A. Mangan

Phototypeset in 10pt Times by
Mews Photosetting, Beckenham, Kent
Printed and bound in Great Britain by
Mackays of Chatham PLC, Chatham, Kent

British Library Cataloguing in Publication Data
A catalogue reference for this book is available from the British Library

ISBN 0–415–06883–5

Library of Congress Cataloging-in-Publication Data
has been applied for

ISBN 0–415–06883–5

Contents

Figures and tables

Contributors

Kathryn Castle is Principal Lecturer in History, University of North London. She is presently completing a book on the image of non-Europeans in British history textbooks and childrens periodicals.

Terry Lilly is Senior Lecturer, Crewe and Alsager College of Higher Education. He taught geography in schools and now lectures in Geography and Environmental Studies. He has engaged in research at the Centre for Southern African Studies, University of York.

John Coolahan is Professor of Education, Maynooth University College, Ireland. He is past President of the Educational Studies of Ireland and is on the Scientific Committee of the Association for Teacher Education in Europe (ATEE). Publications include *Irish Education: Its History and Structure* (1981) and *The ASTI and Post Primary Education* (1984).

Colin McGeorge is Senior Lecturer in the Education Department of the University of Canterbury, Christchurch, New Zealand. Publications include a number of articles on the history of New Zealand education.

Stewart Firth writes on the history of the Pacific Islands besides researching into the history of Australian education. He has published articles on social values in New South Wales schools before 1914 and on the celebration of Empire Day in Australia. He was a co-author of *Papua New Guinea: A Political History* (1979). His *New Guinea under the Germans* was published in 1982, and in 1987 he published *Nuclear Playground*, a nuclear history of the Pacific. Most recently he has co-edited a translation of German documents on Nauru under the title *Nauru, 1888–1900, by Wilhelm Fabricius* (1992). He is now an Associate Professor in the School of History, Philosophy and Politics, Macquarie University, Sydney.

Robert Darling has specialised in Australian history. He is the author of *Eric Campbell and the New Guard* (Sydney: Kangaroo Press, 1983), *Sudan to Vietnam* (Sydney: Shakespeare Head Press, 1987) and, most recently, *Understanding Australian History* (Melbourne: Heinemann Educational, 1992). He is presently Head Teacher of History, Evans High School, Sydney.

Jo-ann Archibald of the Sto:lo Nation, is an Instructor and Advisor to the Ts'kel First Nations graduate students in the Faculty of Education, University of British Columbia. At present she is researching Coast Salish orality.

Anthula Natsoulas is Associate Professor of Secondary Education, University of Toledo, Toledo, Ohio. Formerly a Fulbright Scholar in mathematics education in Cyprus. Publications include *Mathematics education: Trends for the future* (1992), 'Taxicab conics' in *Journal of Computers in Mathematics and Science Teaching* (1989) and 'Mathematics education in Greece' in *School Science and Mathematics* (1988).

Theodore Natsoulas is Professor of African History, University of Toledo, Toledo, Ohio. Publications include *Hellenic Presence in Ethiopia* (1977) and articles on Ethiopia and Kenya published in the *International Journal of African Historical Studies, Northeast African Studies*, the *Journal of Asian and African Studies*, the *Journal of Religion in Africa*, and the *Journal of African Studies*.

P. Godfrey Okoth is Associate Professor and Head of the Department of History, Makerere University, Kampala, Uganda. Publications include *United States of America's Foreign Policy Toward Kenya* (1992). He is also Editor of the *Makerere Historical Journal* and former Editor-in-Chief of *Ufahamill: The Journal of the African Activist Association*, UCLA.

Swiesh Chandra Ghosh is Professor of History of Education, Jawaharlal Nehru University, New Delhi. Publications include *The Social Condition of the British Community in Bengal, 1757–1800* (1971), *Dalhousie in India, 1848–56* (1975), *Indian Nationalism* (1985), *Education Policy in India since Warren Hastings* (1989), *Freedom Movement in India, 1857–1947* (1991), and three volumes of *Educational Records of the Government of India* edited between 1977 and 1992.

Keith Watson is Professor of Education, University of Reading. Publications include *Educational Development in Thailand* (1980), *Education in the Third World* (1983) and *Multicultural Education: Debate, Policy and Teacher Education* (1989). He is also Editor-in-Chief of the *International Journal of Educational Development*.

Peter Kallaway is Associate Professor of Education, University of Cape Town, South Africa. Publications include *Apartheid and Education* (1984); *Johannesburg: Images and Continuities: A History of Working Class Life through Pictures* (with P. Pearson) (1986): *The Bible and the Slate: Missionary Education in Southern Africa* (forthcoming).

Introduction

This collection of essays explores faint trails in the history of cultural imperialism as yet barely trodden. A caveat for the too demanding – space precludes geographical, conceptual and empirical comprehensiveness. It is simply not possible to discuss every colonized territory, subject people or relevant theme. Readers no doubt will have their specialist areas of interest. Some will be catered for here; some will not.

Nevertheless within the space available there is a *deliberate* diversity of region, peoples and subject. The hope here is to start a hillside of academic hares and to stimulate the fuller pursuit of enquiries into the relationship between imperialism, culture and curriculum in the belief that the past is part of the present – to a degree often unrealized: 'The power of past images should not be underestimated. They remain impressed on a culture as a palimpsest, shaping and colouring all the images that evolve at later dates'.[1]

Curiously the issue of racism in British imperial education as yet has not been adequately explored in academic monographs, articles or essay collections. Increasingly, however, there is discussion of the topic in academic journals, edited works and pamphlets by, for example, Stephen Ball, Chris Mullard, Kevin Lillis and J.A. Mangan.[2] It is interesting to note the dates of the appearance of these articles and chapters. This suggests that the time is ripe for a more extensive and systematic consideration of the issue. While the literature on racism is now extensive, there are sizeable and important omissions in the many publications available. In particular, despite frequent assertions about the need to understand the historical roots of racism, no sustained attention has been paid to the role of the imperial curriculum and, within the curriculum, to the school textbook in the promulgation of racial stereotypes, the creation of ethnocentric attitudes and the 'labelling' of colonial peoples.

This collection of essays is the first of its kind on the topic of racism, education and imperialism and focuses on the function of education, curriculum and textbook in shaping imperial images of dominance and deference. It is a comparative historical analysis and draws on recent work of scholars from (and about) Africa, Australia, Britain, Canada, India, Ireland, Malaya (and Singapore) and New Zealand. The subject matter is new, the spread of former imperial territories is unique and the book constitutes the *first comparative analysis* of racial attitudes in the formal schooling of motherland, dominion and colony.

In addition, the book considers the issues of racial indoctrination through curricular policy and chosen textbook from the perspective of *both* colonizer and colonized. It takes account, in other words, of the view of imperialism from below as well as above; a too frequently neglected perspective.

It is hoped that the book will have a wide readership in the English-speaking world including general historians of imperialism, political historians, social historians, historians of education, historians of former dominions and colonies, anthropologists and sociologists with an interest in education and general educationalists and curriculum specialists. Above all, it is hoped that the book will be of special interest to those working in the field of equal opportunity, race relations and antiracism.

In an area of study that provokes intense reactions and strong feelings it is important to stress that the emphasis is academic not polemical. It has been rightly argued that we must guard against research on colonialism that is substantially an emotional anticolonial diatribe. This volume will attempt to examine the careful use of education, curriculum and textbook in the creation of racial images in order to explore efforts to create attitudes of dominance and deference within an imperial context. To this end open-minded scrutiny is a basic requirement. Equally it is a requirement to ensure that the coverage is culturally and regionally specific, and deals with 'local' imperial dissimilarities as well as similarities arising from a general imperial framework. In addition, contributors pay attention to the following fundamental issues: the nature, purpose and process of indoctrination, the extent of the success of this indoctrination and the extent to which it was conscious and unconscious, intentional and unintentional. This, in turn, requires a careful consideration of purpose as distinct from implementation, dissemination as distinct from assimilation and the receptivity, respectively, of colonist and colonized.

J.A. Mangan's chapter (chapter 1) deals with the general purpose of stereotypes as explanations for and justifications of racial inequality, and considers within the framework of formal education the formulation of, and rationale for, a range of stereotypes arising out of altruistic and ulterior attitudes associated with political imperatives, cultural myopia, spiritual idealism and racial prejudice.

Both Kathryn Castle and T. Lilly (chapters 2 and 3) look at images of the colonized in the school textbooks of metropolitan Britain. Castle has three aims: to examine the 'types' of Indian represented to the young Britain, to explore the self-serving nature of such imagery and the part it played in ensuring loyalty to the concept of imperialism, and to consider the formulation of image in the context of specific situations in British society, such as the Indian Mutiny, which sharply shaped racial attitudes both at the time and in later decades. Therefore she addresses the issues of both continuity and change asssociated with image depiction, and the extent to which it served the self-perceived needs of imperial Britain. Lilly, for his part, reveals bias in the earliest published geographical surveys at the beginning of the nineteenth century, a bias extended into the twentieth century given the long shelf-life of school textbooks. He argues that the influence of geography in the school curriculum in terms of racial imagery, was 'widespread and lasting', and the role of the geography textbook as formulator and reflector of racial prejudice was substantial.

John Coolahan (chapter 4) begins the survey of racial imagery in the colonies and dominions. He deals with school textbooks in Ireland – Britain's oldest imperial territory. As he reveals, in the interest of unity, textbooks stressed the bonds which unite the people of the British Isles and deemphasized cultural, religious and linguistic differences (p. 55). These textbooks contrasted sharply with the insulting image of the Irish in the popular press, racialist pamphlets and political cartoons. Coolahan offers, therefore, a study of contrasts. In addition, he analyses the depiction of 'other peoples' in the school textbooks used in Irish schools which indulged freely in stereotypic images of inferiority. Finally he assesses the potency of this positive and negative imagery in socializing the young.

With Colin McGeorge (chapter 5) the focus shifts to New Zealand, Maori and Pakeha. Here, as will be seen in the next chapter on Australia, initially the emphasis in curriculum and textbook was on the development of New Zealand within the framework of the issues of race and imperialism. Past depiction of the Maori within the schools was complimentary but selective – admired images of a past and primitive heroism. Smooth assimilation of the Maori into 'Western culture' was stressed and attempted. Today, suggests McGeorge, the current proposal that the syllabus should include *taha Maori* (the Maori side of things) reveals both a complacency with past heroic depiction and a discomfort over the former concern with 'a cabinet of ethnographic curiosities' (p. 78). It should not be overlooked, argues McGeorge, that Pakeha imagery of the Maori, despite its apparent benevolence had as its fundamental purpose the legitimizing of expropriation, settlement and assimilation.

Robert Darlington and Stewart Firth (chapter 6) demonstrate both the pervasiveness and cohesiveness of the imperial message of 'a hierarchy of races' in the dominions. It reached out with some success into the Australian schools before the Great War. Subsequently in the inter-war period the message, despite some attention to pacifism and internationalism, remained largely unchanged. Australian schoolchildren learnt that what was important was the preservation and expansion of the British race (pp. 86–92). This message despite subsequent changes in educational policy, curriculum and textbook, has continuing grave consequences for the Aborigine.

Jo-Ann Archibald's view of curriculum policy (chapter 7) associated with the indigenous peoples of Canada under colonial rule, is stark and condemnatory. Formal schooling served only as confirmation of racial stereotyping. It was shot through with racist attitudes and actions which were self-fulfilling and remained racist in conceptualization and implementation until the middle of this century.

Theodore and Anthula Natsoulas (chapter 8) argue that the history of educational provision for the African in colonial Kenya was determined by the requirements of the three European 'interlopers': administrator, missionary and settler. The interlopers' image of the African both determined and was determined by imperial needs. These needs demanded an education for the African that ensured 'cultural migration', and economic, social and political subordination. However the African resisted, and attempted to adapt, both stereotypes of native ability and rationalization of the consequent educational system.

P.G. Okoth (chapter 9) offers a discussion of the imperial curriculum in Uganda from the perspective of those 'underneath'. He sees it as both a deliberate mechanism designed to brainwash the Ugandans into discarding their own cultures and embracing 'superior' Western culture, and an ethnocentric instrument for the civilizing of the allegedly 'primitive' peoples of Africa. Racist and paternalistic curricular policies, he claims, fostered a culture of dependency, inferiority and self-doubt.

Keith Watson (chapter 10) traces the curricular policies of successive British imperial administrations in colonial Malaya and Singapore. They were policies founded on subscription to the differing perceptions of the various communities – Malays, Chinese, Indians and Europeans. Policies, curricula and textbooks had, in common, patronizing attitudes and explicit favouritism. Both were to have a lasting impact on Malay society, resulting in an absence of multiracial harmony and the creation of racial resentments. Watson scrutinizes the ethnocentric racial emphasis in imperial educational provision and discusses the consequences of this for Malayan society.

Suresh Chandra Ghosh (chapter 11) deals with the British 'superiority complex' explicit in curriculum and textbook in imperial India and its unforeseen consequences – a diet of English education among the Indians had raised 'a fighting cock' while it was expected to raise an enormous 'hen' (p. 193). He explores the nature of educational indoctrination and the unexpected influence of this indoctrination on the Indian people.

Peter Kallaway (chapter 12) is concerned with various manifestations of racism in education in South Africa: racism between the white groups (English speaking and Afrikaans/Dutch speaking) and between white and black. According to Kallaway racial stereotypes and ethnocentric myths were basic elements in the educational curricular policies of the British in South Africa both before and after the Boer War, while the Christian National Education of the Afrikaner put great emphasis on the Boer struggles and victories and their defence of their national, linguistic and cultural identity. This approach was accentuated after the Second World War in the wake of the political ascendancy of the Purified National Party. For their part, the blacks have been badly served in the writing of South African history, states Kallaway. Their task was to believe and internalize the white colonialists' myths about themselves and thus read themselves out of history. In short, the historical functions of schooling, the curriculum and textbooks were the product of white rule and aimed at establishing domination. The task for the future, he argues, is is to provide a history syllabus 'which embraces the need for a strategy for nation-building' (p. 208).

This volume is essentially an investigation into the making and breaking of confident identities – individual and corporate; a fundamental role conscious and unconscious, it is argued here, of cultural imperialism and imperial culture. However the volume has several dimensions: it is at one and the same time an analysis of 'ruling discourse', a study of educational ideologies in action, an investigation of attempted racial socialization, a case-study of period ethnocentricity and above all an inquiry into the role and nature of imperial image-construction.

J.A. Mangan
Glasgow

1 Images for confident control

Stereotypes in imperial discourse

J.A. Mangan

The main theme of this chapter is the role of British imperial education in the creation of 'appropriate' racial images. A major purpose of this education was to inculcate in the children of the British Empire appropriate attitudes of dominance and deference. There was an education in imperial schools to shape the ruled into patterns of proper subservience and 'legitimate' inferiority, and one in turn to develop in the rulers convictions about the certain benevolence and 'legitimate' superiority of their rule. Imperial education was very much about establishing the presence and absence of *confidence* in those controlling and those controlled. Once colonial territories were established this process began in classrooms. Here imperial confidence, and lack of it, was as often as not a matter of purposeful image construction.

Ashis Nandy writes of two generations of British colonialists: initially, bandit kings – rapacious conquerors of the colonies; and latterly, philosopher kings – liberals, modernists, and believers in progress.[1] This later colonialism, he asserts, colonized minds in addition to bodies, released forces within the colonized societies that altered their cultural priorities for ever, and transformed the concept of the West from a geographical and temporal entity to a psychological reality; with the result that 'the West is now everywhere, within the West and outside; in structures and in minds.'[2] Certainly the European forced his way into the worlds of other peoples with epistemological models, representative symbols, alien forms of knowledge and patterns of action which he defined. In turn, these peoples had to reconstruct their worlds to embrace the fact of white domination and their own powerlessness.[3]

This chapter is concerned with the second stage of British colonization, and with cultural agents and agencies within the framework of formal education which supported, resisted and adapted themselves to image construction in the British imperial culture. A large part of imperial image construction was concerned with the creation of positive and negative stereotypes. These stereotypes existed to manipulate reality so as to reflect imperial values, ambitions and priorities and to promote them as proper, necessary, and constructive: imperialism required a carefully crafted image of the colonizer and colonized. Image creation has a crucial place in the dialectics exalting the colonizer and humbling the colonized. The created image was a rationalization without which the presence of the colonizer was inexplicable.[4]

The focus of this chapter is cultural. It is concerned less with the psychological influence of image construction on the individual and more with the potential of image construction for shaping the cultural consciousness of groups by offering them, through stereotypic image depiction explanations of relationships, descriptions of group capacities and patterns of expected behaviour. Within cultures the creation of stereotypic images is a means of rationalizing, legitimating and controlling human action. Arguably all cultures need stereotypes to help them structure their universe, to make static and manageable the 'flux of reality', to establish the appearance of reasonable, self-evident truths, to create an ordered, controlled world. For these reasons all cultures have their functional stereotypes. They are the purposeful products of the history of the culture that perpetuates them: 'None is random: none is isolated from the historical context'[5]. At any given time cultural stereotypes reveal the ideological concerns of a culture. Its 'icons of representation', set hard in firmly-held mental constructions, are invariably determined by its ideological preconceptions. The adequacy of these icons is determined by the basic needs they serve rather than by the complexities they embrace. Indeed, too much complexity can result in too much confusion: 'The yearning for rigidity is in us all. It is part of our human condition to long for hard lines and clear concepts. When we have them we have either to face the fact that some realities elude them, or else blind ourselves to the inadequacy of the concepts.'[6]

In response to the basic need to organize the world in familiar and controllable patterns cultures employ 'root-metaphors': explanatory models that allow their members to make acceptable sense of the world.[7] They learn to perceive the world in terms of historically determined sets of these metaphors. Among other things such stereotypic constructions facilitate an accommodating 'perceptual blindness' protecting the group from information likely to produce stress. They permit a mental myopia which offers insulation from corporate cognitive dissonance. In the late Victorian and Edwardian period of British imperialism the irony of a metropolitan democratic tradition co-existent with imperial despotic practice, produced an outstanding example.[8] Of course, the incongruities of such myopia seldom provide perfect protection from irony. While the stereotype offers, at any one time and in any one location, a secure sense of identity, at other times and places the same stereotype may be contradicted and confronted: the colonial stereotype was an insecure representation, as anxious as it was assertive.[9]

Every culture then possesses ideological imperatives that shape its representative stereotypes. In turn these arise out of a culture's need to have control over its world. Here is the crux of the matter: no matter how this control is constructed, whether as political power, social status, religious persuasion, or economic domination, invariably it establishes an appropriate vocabulary and a set of verbal images depicting significant *difference*. It is this difference that threatens order, security and control.[10] It must be successfully accommodated. Stereotypic depictions function as accommodating symbols in the discourse of the group; symbols that provide the foundation for secure solidarity.[11] Stereotypic images, carefully constructed and equally carefully defined, are, therefore, mechanisms of control linked to structures in the society which provide stability, power and status. One of these structures is the education system. The curriculum within the formal education system as a source of image depiction is an ideal source also for the study of both the stability and the fluidity of stereotypical concepts. A major function of the school curriculum is to provide a culture with an effective system of control. In this essential role incidentally, curriculum must be understood in the broadest sense of that term. All structured systems of image representation, in no matter what medium, should be viewed as 'curriculum' for the study of stereotypes.[12]

It has been suggested that historians have tended to ignore the phenomenon of 'national character' and have preferred to deal with aggregates rather than images: 'with functional interests rather than fantasy selves'.[13] They have not felt the need to discuss 'the caricatures in popular art, the character types of novelist, playwright or poet. Likewise they have been indifferent to symbolic landscapes so much a part of idealization of national character.[14] These caricatures are paradigmatic figures for popular purpose. They are not seen as valuable by historians. They are not part of 'the world of empirically verifiable facts. They isolate character traits where the historian would want to contextualize them. They seize on the eccentric and elevate it to the grotesque'.[15] Consequently, positive mythical stereotypes reinforcing corporate self-esteem and negative mythical stereotypes reinforcing conceptions of vice have been left, to a large extent, to the antiquarian and folklorist, despite the fact that they 'exercise an enormous hold on the popular imagination'.[16] This is an unfortunate academic legacy. It is a basic task of the social historian to consider, certainly within the framework of the education system, the relationship of these culturally constructed stereotypes to their time, to the conventions they symbolize, and to the purposes they serve.

In fictional and non-fictional studies, it has been observed, there is a common imperial stereotype of the 'native' which exists in such widely different localities as Ireland and Indonesia, Algeria and Antigua, Burma and Bechuanaland. It is a global phenomenon of imperialism. The characteristics attributed to the 'native' are extraordinarily uniform.[17] To usefully employ a baking metaphor, they all appear to be cut with the same pastry cutter! Furthermore in the world of past imperialism, more often than not in pursuit of an understanding of its stereotypes and their origins, the historian is confronted with an Manichean allegory: 'a field of diverse yet interchangeable oppositions between white and black, good and evil, superiority and inferiority'.[18] While it is certainly not the whole truth, the definition of the conqueror and conquered relationship as a 'Manichean' struggle is not simply a metaphoric but is a literal representation of a profound struggle: 'the dominant model of power in all colonial societies is the Manichean opposition between the putative superiority of the European and the supposed inferiority of the native. This axis in turn provides the central feature of the colonialist cognitive framework'.[19] To borrow a sharp aphorism: the Manichean allegory is the central trope of imperialism.[20]

Abdul R. JanMohamed has argued that the ideological functions of colonialist fiction in the dominant phase of imperialism should be understood not simply in terms of its intended and actual effects on the native but in terms of the imperialist's ideology, politics and culture. The purpose of constructed racial difference, of the imperial fixation and fetishization of native savagery and evil, for example, should be considered in terms of its political culture and its associated ideological imperatives.[21] A significant feature of colonialist fiction, JanMohamed states, is the nature of its audience; as imperialists administer the resources of the conquered country so colonialist discourse 'commodifies' the native into stereotyped subject and uses him as a 'resource' for colonialist fiction. The imperial writer commodifies the native by negating his individuality so that he is perceived as a generic phenomenon that can be exchanged for any other native. Once reduced to his exchange-value in the colonialist simplifying system he is fed into the Manichean allegory, which functions as the currency for the entire colonialist discursive system. In short, the writer's task is to reproduce the native in a seemingly infinite variety of images, the apparent diversity of which, however, is determined by the simple machinery of the Manichean allegory. There is a profound symbiotic relationship between the discursive and material practices of imperialism: 'the discursive practices do to the symbolic linguistic presence of the native what the material practices do to his physical presence: the writer commodifies him so that he can be exploited more effectively by the administrator.[22] Exploitation is the reality beneath the rhetoric. This rhetoric offers an overt benevolent ambition for colonialism: to 'civilize' the savage, while the covert, malevolent purpose of colonialism is to exploit the colony's natural resources thoroughly and ruthlessly.[23] This ulterior aim of colonialism is to be found in partnership in colonial literature with a fixation on the savagery and evil of the native in order to justify imperial occupation, control and exploitation: 'If such literature can demonstrate that the barbarism of the native is irrevocable, or at least very deeply ingrained, then the European's attempt to civilize him can continue indefinitely, the exploitation of his resources can proceed without hindrance, and the European can persist in enjoying a position of moral superiority.[24]

The imperialist, certain of his political, cultural and moral superiority, rarely questioned the validity of the values of his own society or attempted to understand 'the worthless aleatory of the colonized'.[25] The pendulum was hopelessly jammed on the side of prejudice. Imperial literature affirmed its own ethnocentric assumptions, certainties and images. It projected them onto the culture of the colonized. In this process selective depiction of inferior, often degenerate, images were an effective means of maintaining a sense of moral difference and distance. In this way they were also instruments for creating and destroying cultural confidence. In British imperialism the 'allegorical mechanism of Manicheanism' permitted literature to establish significant metaphysical differences:

> The ideological function of this mechanism, in addition to prolonging colonialism, is to de-historicize and desocialize the conquered world, to represent it as a metaphysical 'fact of life' before which those who have fashioned the colonial worlds are themselves reduced to the role of passive spectators in a mystery not of their making.[26]

Furthermore, by allowing the imperialist to denigrate the native in a variety of ways, the literary allegory permitted the imperialist to build his stock of moral superiority ever higher allowing him 'to accumulate surplus morality', which was further invested in the denigration of the native in a self-sustaining cycle.[27] In this way, stylized figures rather than real people were created which then became archetypal depictions.[28] This process created for the dominant, settled conditions of order, stability and control through the mechanism of *distancing*:

> In the Manichean world of the colonizer and the colonized . . . distance tends to become absolute and qualitative rather than relative and quantitative. The world is perceived in terms of ultimate, fixed differences . . . The economic, social, and political hierarchical organization of the colonial society turns into a quasi-feudal world, which finds its appropriate literary forms in the adaptable categories and hierarchically valorized structures of allegory and racial romance.[29]

To reinforce this 'quasi-feudal' imperial structure, imperial ideology and fiction formed a symbiotic relationship: ideology shaped the fiction and the fiction, in turn, formed the ideology.[30] The purpose of colonial discourse, therefore, is to depict the colonized as racially degenerate to justify conquest and to establish appropriate systems of control, administration and instruction.[31] To this end it employs derogatory metaphors and similes to do frequent, malific and wilful injustice to reality, and sets them in loud and confident antiphons of superiority. However there is a further point of substance to consider. It has been said of India, but it is true for all of the colonies, that for the rulers colonial exploitation was an incidental and regrettable by-product of a philosophy of life that was in harmony with perceived superior forms of political and economic organization; consequently to rule they had to construct bulwarks against a possible sense of guilt produced by disjunction between their colonial actions and domestic practices. Conflicting moralities had to be rationalized. The rulers could not afford to be moral cripples: this destroyed the *confidence to control*. Thus colonialism without a civilizing mission was no colonialism at all.[32] There was strong rhetorical enforcement of this mission. To this extent colonialism was a contrived moral doctrine:

a rubric of imperial moralist similes and metaphors which arose out of the *creation* of a set of human images, which gave rise, in turn, to appropriate political, economic, social and educational policies and practices. In fact, the imperialist over-compensated for his moral conundrum: he imputed to himself feelings of omnipotence and permanence – at home and abroad. Britannia not only ruled the waves: for its inhabitants it also ruled the future of human consciousness.[33] And to an extraordinary extent this is still true: 'Western culture ... for all its loss of self-confidence, continues with remarkable resilience to fashion human societies throughout the globe in many aspects of its image'.[34]

To avoid mass cognitive dissonance, to preserve self-esteem, to rationalize control, to justify policy, colonial stereotypical discourse contributed to the institutionalization of racial ideologies that were knowingly discriminatory, biased, mythical: by 'knowing' the native population as 'fallen astral spirits' prejudicial, discriminatory and authoritarian forms of political control were considered correct, relevant and appropriate. The colonized were, in this way, deemed to be both the cause and effect of the system and imprisoned in an interpretative cycle.[35] A moralistic ideology of amelioration resulted – the Civilizing Mission or the White Man's Burden. And paradoxically despotic forms of political control co-existed with liberal philosophical beliefs; thus the barracks stood by the church which stood by the schoolroom, while the cantonment stood hard by the civil lines.[36]

No better illustration of 'interpretative imprisonment' can be found than that of the imperial myth of the Dark Continent. Britain and Africa represented the opposing poles of a single system of values variously phrased as light opposed to darkness, civilization to savagery, good to evil. Africa was the 'continent of dark negation'.[37] African 'darkness' was often deliberately exaggerated to justify the missionary's presence, to win support for his efforts, to ennoble his purpose and to explain lack of success in winning converts.[38] Descriptions of Africa laid conscious stress on 'barbarism, superstition, treachery, cunning, paganism, sexuality, and general moral depravity,[39] to point up the panacea: the Christian message and European civilization.[40] However, it was not simply the African who was to be redeemed: 'The assumption was that all the cultures the missionaries encountered were under the control of the Evil One. "Heathen" societies were the domain of Satan in all their aspects ... All that was embraced by the term "culture"'.[41] The heathen, if not the devil, was certainly his neophyte. The British missionary movement, with very few exceptions, accepted that non-Christian societies stood in need of a comprehensive regeneration. They needed to be transformed by 'civilization'.[42] Mostly with a Panglossian optimism and an insensitive naivety the missionary set about the task.

If Roger Bastide is to be believed there was another form of 'interpretative imprisonment' at work. The stereotyped imagery of the missionary was predictable and anchored in the long heritage of the symbolism of colour. He was simply adding surface layers of paint to an old canvas. One manifestation of this was the Aryanization of Christ which was in strict accordance with the logic of colour symbolism.[43] The most significant Christian bifurcation, states Bastide, is that of black and white; white expresses the pure and black the impure.[44] Thinking is so enslaved to language, he asserts, that the link between associated ideas operated automatically when white man met black man. The consequence was inevitable: 'The Victorian (and Edwardian) looked upon the Negro as the photographic negative of the Anglo-Saxon, and they seemed to get a clearer perception of their own supposed racial uniqueness from the inverted image of the the black man'.[45] And once black skin was designated as a sign of moral inferiority individuals became interchangeable corporate ciphers.[46]

In addition to the requirements of imperialism and a historical symbolic legacy, a mid-nineteenth century biological ideology helped establish a pecking order of humanity for the imperialist.

> In the mid-nineteenth century, a new vigorous racist ideology challenged the humanitarian traditions of the anti-slavery movement, and preached a new doctrine of racial supremacy. Growing out of the armchair investigations of the new science of anthropology, and reinforced by the romantic speculations of historians seeking in folk myths the elusive qualities of the national character, this new ideology of racism, which declared that moral and intellectual as well as physical traits were biologically determined, confused cultural and physical characteristics, and gave 'race' an all-inclusive meaning so that it became, in the minds of its exponents, the most significant determinant of man's past, present and future.[47]

However, Victorian racial attitudes owed more than a little to a further influence. Douglas Lorimer has argued strongly and convincingly that consideration of the racial attitudes of English men 'securely at home and untouched by personal experience of the Empire', reveals that domestic as well as imperial influences moulded the racial attitudes of the Victorians.[48] The intellectual history of scientific racism, the needs of imperial rule and symbolic tradition do not fully explain Victorian racial attitudes. Changes occurred in part out of 'new attitudes towards social status emerging within English society'.[49] More important for the growth of racism than the biological ideology of an intellectual minority was 'the ease with which the personal experience of class relations within England could be translated into racial terms'.[50] As the Victorians become more and more preoccupied with the pursuit of gentility, they became more and more concerned with excluding those of doubtful status. Racially and historically the Negro was identified with both servitude and savagery. As a consequence he was now allocated to 'the brutish and perpetually lower orders'. Only Anglo-Saxons could be gentlemen.[51] In this way, the colour question became a matter of class. Indeed, racism often functions 'as a displaced or surrogate class system, growing more extreme as the domestic class alignments it reflects are threatened or erode. As a rationalization for the domination of "inferior" peoples, imperialist discourse is inevitably racist; it treats class and race terminology as covertly interchangeable or at least analogous. Both a hierarchy of classes and a hierarchy of races exist; both are the results of evolution or the laws of nature ... the "conquered races" of the empire were treated as a new proletariat – a proletariat much less distinct from slaves than the working class'[52] And just as the social class fantasies of the Victorians often expressed the fear of falling into the abyss of poverty so the minatory myth of the Dark Continent contained 'the submerged fear of falling out of the light, down the long coal chute of social and moral regression', and so the missionaries thrust into the heart of darkness to discover lust, depravity, cannibalism and devil worship.[53] Unsurprisingly, the prevailing image of the African, and other native peoples,[54] more often than not, became one of a self-indulgent indolent wallowing in heathen superstition. In fact, over four centuries of British literature on Africa 'the continuities are far more striking than the changes, since they are the result of the unifying and constant force of ethnocentricism'. This ethnocentricism has preserved to the present 'a persistent fantasy: the civilized Briton in confrontation with savage Africans in an Africa that never was'.[55]

The missionaries' view of African laziness did not inexorably denote biological racism. Frequently it was more a manifestation of cultural chauvinism and religious bigotry. Whereas racism implied that inherent biological differences made some superior to others, cultural chauvinism simply recognized the obvious fact that in some respects some cultures were superior to others. And European culture was greatly superior, cultural chauvinists would assert, largely because the European worked harder; most, if not all, missionaries had internalized the Protestant Ethic, which placed industry next to godliness.[56] African 'indulgence' led many missionaries to believe the African was incapable of benefiting from a literary education. In their view he was incapable of conceptual assimilation and could not be taught any type of bookish knowledge; his perceptive faculties were strong, but his reflective and imaginative faculties were undeveloped. A black who proved himself capable of literary pursuits was peremptorily dismissed as 'a fraud or a black with impure blood'.[57] A bold, tight negative pattern of general non-ability was woven in which loose individual threads were systematically pulled-out. This is a fine example of Memmi's 'remodelling of the colonial image', which, in his view, consisted, in the first place, of a series of negations: 'The colonized is not this, is not that.'[58] The arrested development of the African required vocational education; to combat depravity, to instill Christian virtues and to inculcate a sense of the dignity of labour.[59] This plea for an education suited to native capabilities, the warnings against a literary education for Africans, the praises heaped on model farms which promoted native industriousness was 'part of the rhetoric of African educational policy reports well into the twentieth century'.[60]

It is interesting to reflect on the influence of the transmission, explicit and implicit, of missionary impressions of African cultures on the African and the consequent image of himself that he discerned in the missionaries' often benevolent but invariably patronizing attitude. Over educational systems, institutions and curriculum for the African hovered a spectre of native inadequacy that projected an image of fundamental inferiority and a mirror image of superiority. A vast network of racial mythology, states Phillip Mason, exists arising from the desire to keep dividing categories between dominant and subordinate groups rigid and permanent, and once such categories are established and one group believes it is dominant, and another is subservient, both will act in accordance with these allotted roles and in time their picture of each other to some extent becomes true: 'this is the familiar case of the self-fulfilling prophecy, and there is no need to enlarge on it further'![61]

Africans now speak confidently for themselves. The writer Ngugi wa Thiong'o, like Patrick Brantlinger earlier, has argued that 'colonialism was a manifestation of the imposition of one class upon another'.[62] For Ngugi imperial and post-imperial education was not 'an accident of content, time, place and persons'. Rather the 'sad, undeniable truth is that the content in our syllabi, the approach to and presentation of the literature, the persons and machinery for determining the choice of texts and their interpretation, were all an integral part of cultural imperialism, and they are today an integral part of the total lingering effects of that imperialism in the neo-colonial era'.[63] While the colonialist saw an absence of African literature under colonialism as evidence of an African incapacity for creativity, Africans themselves perceived the lack of encouragement or opportunity from colonial educators as a symbol of colonial domination.[64] Ngugi has allocated to literature a critical significance in imperial *and* post-imperial education. And it had a key role in colonial strategy: it not only debased the black, his experience and his world but also exposed him to the concept of class, and therefore to racial and cultural values.[65] In the interests of imperialism he was doubly exploited: as a member of a race and as a member of a class.[66] For this reason, in Ngugi's view, it was imperative that the African should seize back the right to make his *own* definitions of valid knowledge and finally deny the iconic memory of the imperial experience.

As Ngugi has suggested the past has survived into the present. Abena P.A. Busia writes of the continuing 'Myth of Africa': a long literary tradition which owes 'its survival to its remarkable ability to adapt itself to the needs and tastes of changing British society'. In Busia's view there are two distinct literary traditions of novels of Africa: adventure and political romance. The first was an iconographic vehicle for demonstrating the English gentleman's moral courage; the second was a stylized setting for a spiritual drama of European self-discovery. In both, the historic idea of Africa as the 'dark continent' has changed little: this permanence gives currency to a continuing myth. Novels of past *and* present try to 're-order the world of Africa in the name of justice, peace and sanity'.[67] The European imagination has a staple ingredient; an Africa in moral disarray. This provides the opportunity for evangelism and ethnocentrism which are part and parcel of the baggage of the white hero.

One form of imperialism has been replaced by another. Throughout both Africans remain passive. They play little part in controlling the major elements of the drama in this continuing theatre of ideological confrontations between good and evil. Meanwhile the relationships of dominance and subservience survive and the African remains a menace, always, like the contents of Pandora's box, threatening to jump out. Literary stereotypes have been remarkably permanent for the simple reason that the choice of images in literature reflects cultural perceptions.[68] Consequently fiction has consistently perpetuated the fantasy of the Englishman in confrontation with Africa. Englishman and African, as in a morality play, remain respectively the stylized exemplars of civilization and savagery. And the African image remains the negative reflection of the Englishman's self-image.[69]

Whatever present literary fashions exist, derogatory sterotypic literary imagery was a colonial constant. The racial kaleidoscope was stuck fast and the patterns displayed were persistent and predictable. It was no different for Asia: 'Colonialism replaces the normal ethnocentric stereotype of the inscrutable Oriental by the pathological stereotype of the strange, primal but predictable Oriental–religious but superstitious, clever but devious, chaotically violent but effeminately cowardly.[70] Images could be a little more subtle but not much. Asians, like Africans, were childlike or childish. The martial races of India, and Africa, possessed the positive, childlike attributes of good savages; the truculent, effete, non-martial races displayed negative, childish attributes.[71]

Frances M. Mannsaker links explanation of the role of the stereotype in imperial fiction with the world of schoolboy fiction and the classroom of the imperialist schoolboy. Mannsaker observes of the imperial boys adventure story, widely read in the public schools of Victorian and Edwardian Britain, that the native characters are invariably 'type figures' lacking individuality; not that they are necessarily inaccurate, unconvincing or even undifferentiated as racial representatives but they function as types. This role type, she suggests, contributes towards a 'curious sense that the natives do not properly exist. They never surprise'.[72] They are drawn within clearly defined parameters and maintain a consistent and distinctive relationship with the white man. They exist to demonstrate the heroism of the white hero. The adventure is always imbued with moral purpose. Acts of heroism contain fundamental messages of proper superiority: 'Basically, adventure is simply in *being* the rulers'. Mannsaker draws an interesting conclusion from these literary conventions:

> It is at least plausible to suggest that writers who were themselves of the empire establishment found in the boys' adventure stories a set of conventions which could readily be used to carry their explanations of the British imperial role. They inherited from their schooldays a language which offered a description of the British national character as active, moral and heroic, and which, translated into the business of governing the empire,

provided an apparently convincing justification for its continuance. But at the same time, the particular image of the white hero this required was largely dependent upon the reverse image of the native as either savage and uncivilized or child-like and unsophisticated.[73]

It has been suggested that there is no need to treat African imperial fictional and non-fictional material separately since both are governed by the same conventions, and differ only in respect to greater or lesser consistency and integration.[74] The same would seem to hold true for general imperial writing.

Now what seems to be true of imperial fiction inside and outside classrooms seems equally true of the *curriculum* of imperial schooling. It served precisely the same purpose of creating generalized and simplistic 'archetypes' in the interests of the colonizer. At one level it was a curriculum to perpetuate control; by stereotype. It should never be overlooked that the school curriculum is an integral and significant part of the culture of society and an effective source of political power. The fundamental significance of the curriculum is its demonstration of political authority.[75] The curriculum, to adapt M.F.D. Young, is a specific medium for expressing political relationships. It reflects the distribution of power in society.[76] The study of the history of the curriculum, it has been suggested, has the capacity to transform our understanding of educational events by posing fundamental questions and pointing towards hitherto unconsidered educational agendas for study. In fact, its capacity is more potent, extensive and significant. It can throw light on the agents and agencies of political influence. In a colonial context it can throw a harsh light on the role of imagery in the process of domination![77] It has also been observed that unquestioning acceptance of the form and content of the curriculum denies understanding of nature of political priorities and associated forms of attempted social control. This is even more to the point.[78] The colonial curriculum was a means of establishing and perpetuating political inequalities. If hegemony in society is the power to shape group consciousness; in education it is the power to define 'Valued knowledge'[79] which in turn, also shapes collective awareness.

John MacKenzie has demonstrated how the composite curriculum – history, geography, religion and English, increasingly brought imperialism to the centre of British school studies by the end of the nineteenth century.[80] He also reveals the extent to which the school system was the handmaiden of the larger society the central concerns of which were patriotism, militarism, adulation of the monarchy and imperial expansion as central concerns. A 'congruence of simple thought ... and direct action' resulted. History and Geography were honed down 'to a series of stark and simple statements about "development", "progress", and "racial superiority".'[81] Schoolchildren were not to be 'confused' by complexity. Seeley was the great exemplar of simplicity. For him history was a means of moral indoctrination. Through his influence, as one teachers' manual later described it, 'the history of England was "a series of unavoidable wars", from which pupils could learn patriotism, good citizenship and moral training.'[82] These wars led to an improvement of the human condition through 'The civilizing effects of state, technology and Christendom'.[83] Great men led the way and their deeds were fully recorded for the young. There was a further 'congruence between the imperial world view and the use of personalities in moral training'[84] and the 'ideal hero combined piety, adventure and military prowess in the tradition of Christian militarism created in the 1860s and 1870s, which reached its apotheosis with Gordon'.[85]

The inevitable outcome of such conditioning by continuous, simplistic propaganda was a surge of self-confident superiority made all the more certain by the equally repetitive and simplistic depiction of black, brown and yellow 'races'. School texts were replete with demeaning racial assertions: Africans were self-indulgent children 'sunk in tropical abundance'; Asians were impotent representatives of civilizations in decline.[86] And as MacKenzie has pointed out influential school texts with these messages had an astonishing shelf-life surviving from the 1890s to the 1960s:[87]

> Thus the imperial and patriotic mould, formed at the end of the nineteenth century, was not broken until at least the late 1960s and 1970s ... A late nineteenth century world view continued to be transmitted long after an elite literary culture had moved on. The formulation of history syllabuses and historical method, even more significantly of the geography equivalents, occurred just at the time when they were likely to be most susceptible to the imperial core ideology. A generation of imperial thinkers at the end of the century influenced the imperial idealists of the Edwardian period and set up ripples through manuals of teaching method, Board of Education handbooks for teachers, and school texts, which, periodically agitated by the two World Wars, survived at least until the 1950s and 1960s. In these ways the ideas on the uses of history promulgated by Seeley, Stubbs, and others survived for decades until a revolution in the writing and teaching of history took place in the late 1960s. The result was a world view similar to that of classical China.[88]

Textbooks as ideological statements are a commonplace of educational history. School knowledge is a political assertion. It attempts to establish the parameters of acceptable knowledge, impose ideological boundaries, determine the range of permissible interpretations, point the way to action – and, both overtly and covertly, create images of self-belief *and* self-doubt. School knowledge plays its part in portraying and establishing approved perceptions of other cultures, and in defining subsequent relationships. In short, the curriculum, and textbooks within the curriculum, promote and sustain political ideologies *inter alia* through the careful presentation of human images. Within imperial schools it was this complicity of power, knowledge and image which constituted the basic fabric of colonialism;[89] a collusion of control and curriculum which dispensed images of ability *and* disability.

It is, of course, relatively easy to ascertain the racial images projected through curriculum and textbook, and more difficult, if not impossible, to assess the way in which the messages in school materials was transmitted by teachers, and how images of superiority and inferiority were reinforced by manner, word and action. The curriculum proposed is a long way from the curriculum implemented. It is far from easy to chart the perilous translation from curriculum as blueprint to curriculum as action[90] especially in any consideration of its relatively sophisticated role in image dissemination rather than as a means of unsophisticated enculturation through compulsory subjection to a set curriculum. Nevertheless an attempt should be made if only in the most general terms.

Stephen Ball has sensibly challenged the crude assumption of colonial 'imposition' – the enforced cultural incorporation of the natives through compulsory schooling for three reasons: the indigenous peoples demanded Western educational institutions; the whole history of colonial schooling was marked by the confrontation between rival social and political groups with separate and conflicting vested interests – colonial authorities, missionaries and various groups of native peoples; sociological analyses of colonial schooling set essentially in an economic analytical frame contain a profound misreading of the objectives of British colonial educational policy.[91]

Ball discusses at length three competing curricular policies, based on radically different assumptions about the nature and purpose of schooling: the Evangelical curriculum, the adapted curriculum and the academic curriculum. He deals, in some detail, with the motives of, and attitudes towards education, of European and African. He is much concerned with the ostensible utilitarian purposes of the curriculum as a civilizing tool, as source of labour, as an instrument of control (a means of achieving political hegemony among the elite and a means of achieving the educational exclusion of the masses). But he has nothing to say about the projected image of the African, explicit and implicit, in the proffered curricula. It is a nice illustration of not seeing the wood for the trees!

He does discern however, an imperial ideology at work throughout Africa and elsewhere; an ideology of racism based on the perceived intellectual inferiority of the native. Such a perception, of course, involves the projection of an essentially negative image. Ball, as many others, fails to consider adequately the construction of this image as a potent, consistent and systematic part of his discerned imperial ideology. He does discuss the African response to the imperialist's legitimation of an education based on his perceived needs of African society, the extended process of development towards self-government and the requirements of economic productivity in the colonies. The Africans, Ball observed, 'came to see the social, economic and material advantages of the colonizer as founded on their access to and control of education. For some this was a realization related to the potential for personal advance. For others, education was seen to be the key to mass political consciousness. In each case, the process of education was identified with the skills of literacy.'[92] This vision, of course, had to confront the problem of negative image projection. None the less, the colonized were frequently keen to take advantage of Western education. In the colonized world it was the route to relative wealth, status and power, or the route to retaining them. Of course, enthusiasm for Western education varied from culture to culture. Berman has an interesting dicussion of variation of response in Africa.[93] He also provides examples of Africans, fully aware of the restrictions imposed by the limited education made available to them by missionary and administrator, demanding full access to all forms of educational provision: 'Western education became the most obvious tangible symbol of European power. Education was, therefore, synonymous with the type of education provided in the metropolitan country; deviations from the pattern were not acceptable'.[94] The Africans realized only too well that the 'reward system in colonial Africa was not geared to the manual occupations but to white collar positions, which had been reserved almost exclusively for the European elite'.[95] They appreciated that vocational education was a means of perpetuating colonial servitude, low status occupations and inferior image: education for subservience. Therefore despite the problems of self-confidence engendered by missionary denigration of African customs and lifestyles, many Africans accepted the education of the missionary for their own ends. In pursuit of these ends 'temporary apostasy seemed justified'.[96] Many, however, were critical of the missionary. They saw no difference between the missionary and the administrator. Indeed despite areas of disagreement, there was considerable 'commonality of interests between missionaries and colonial officials'.[97] Among other things *both* projected an essentially negative image of the African. Consequently, as the Kenyan nationalist Tom Mboya observed, the creation of a spirit of pride and confidence in the African was largely *his* own responsibility.[98]

As Mboya has implied there is good reason to believe that the rhetoric of imperialism with its assured depiction of images of competence and incompetence had a profound impact and imposed a corporate responsibility on the colonized, not simply because of the collusion between power, pedagogy and pedagogue and the conformity and certainty of imperial ideological conviction but also because of the authority within the colonial classroom to define cultural perspectives and cognitive perceptions within the framework of one 'symbolic universe' and through the linguistic symbolism of the dominant.

In order to understand the effectiveness of imperial power in this respect it is crucial to reconstruct its concept of imperial 'truth'.[99] This truth was uncomplicated. For late Victorian (and later) British middle and upper classes 'dominant over a vast working class majority at home and over increasing millions of "uncivilized" peoples of "inferior" races abroad, power was self-validating. There might be many stages of social evolution and many seemingly bizarre customs and "superstitions" in the world, but there was only one "civilization", one path of "progress", one "true religion". "Anarchy" was many tongued; "culture" spoke with one voice'.[100] The power of this imperial culture to dominate, legitimate, authorize, validate and demote was considerable in classrooms and elsewhere.[101]

In consequence, in the schoolroom, on one side there appeared to be an acquiescent silence and on the other 'a deluge of ruling discourse'.[102] Hardly surprising: 'a man who has language . . . possesses the world expressed and implied by that language . . . Mastery of language affords remarkable power.'[103] Victorian imperialism (and its education) was characterized by a monopoly of discourse. There was a one-way linguistic traffic: the European bible to the native but seldom if ever the native 'bible' to the European. Unless they became virtually 'mimic men' not merely the Africans but all the colonized were stripped of articulation. The outcome was the creation of the voiced and the silent.[104] And there is a post-imperial legacy: 'Discourse – that most subtle yet inescapable form of power in its imperial guise persists' in the terms 'First World' and 'Third World', 'advanced' and 'backward' societies, and in the media stereotypes of modern Africa.[105]

For the colonized the discourse of Western education created a crucible for the re-working of cognitions and evaluations. Within the school the native intellect was submitted to pressures to translate experience into an alien language. Adjustments, adaptations, and syncretisms had to be worked out.[106] An excellent example of this process at work is provided by M.J. Ashley.[107] He has discussed the different universes of belief of white and black in the Eastern Cape of South Africa in the early nineteenth century and the consequent clash of ideologies: specific definitions of reality attached to power. In his analysis of this confrontation he makes effective use of Berger's and Luckman's concept of 'symbolic universes – the integration of all the meanings attached to individual biographies and social institutions into one over-arching body of theoretical explanation'[108] which make sense of individual experience and social institutions.

The missionaries were confident agents of proselytization for their 'universe'. They demanded subscription to new definitions of reality and denied the validity of alternatives or assigned them an inferior status. According to Ashley, education was the significant means by which to intervene in the process of transferring legitimacy of ideological perspective from one genera-tion to the next. In the process of education, literacy was a vital element. It made possible individual maintenance of a new symbolic universe through independent access and removed the individual from the enclosed world of oral tradition. As Ashley says: 'Missionary education was doing more than purvey knowledge or teach skills. It was an important part of the missionary effort to effect a transfer of pupils from one universe to the other'.[109] Ashley sees missionary doctrines and educational themes to do with the degenerate black heathen as ideology because of their close association with the political pursuit of power and control of the Colonial Government at the Cape. For the politician the missionaries were one means of ameliorating the savage disposition. Ultimately military force was the final effective colonial instru-ment of subjection, but it was preceded by a cultural assault on the universe of the black which fortified white belief in supremacy and placed black culture on the defensive from which it has still not recovered.

African resistance, however, was pervasive and persistent. It relied on the techniques of nihilation (denying the worth of the missionary universe) and therapy (pressure on actual or potential deviants to remain within orthodox definitions of reality). From the earliest stages of this confrontation the school had a historic role as a focal point of conflict between symbolic awareness. Ashley points out that the missionary 'universe' was a distinctive segment of the larger and more loosely assembled 'universe of modernity' within which the consciousness of Britons existed.[110] And in the later nineteenth century this total universe of modernity was responsible for the violation of traditional socialization by Western formal education, through the formal curriculum and its integration and transmission by the missionary teacher. The confident dominance of Western ideology and the associated progress of its institutional forms including education, depended on the migration of black cultures from the security of their traditional universe to the British universe of modernity. The missionary educationalist played a key role in this cultural migration, for his spiritual salvation was part and parcel of a native commitment to British civilization with its superior social, economic and political forms. Civilization had the stamp of divine approval upon it.

Since formal education, as Ashley argues, offers an important location for processes of cultural legitimation being a major source of the inductive machinery offering explanations of the nature of reality, it was an important means of transmitting new forms of knowledge, cognitive styles and theological explanations linked wth imperial and racial theories. The resistance of the African to the new universe stimulated the British to construct arguments for the failure of their universe to win widespread acceptance. Evolutionary racial theories, increasingly available from the mid-nineteenth century, offered acceptable and reassuring explanations of native rejection, evolutionary backwardness. This also provided a comfortable explanation of the superiority of the European and the inferiority of the native cultures. This construction, of course, was a *general* imperial phenomenon: throughout the empire 'natural scientists joined theologians in constructing a new reality in which race was of central importance'.[111] The choice available to the colonized was either petrification or catalepsy – if they were faithful to their culture they were considered primitive and if they were unfaithful to it they were considered poseurs. Either way they were unequal. The ideology of imperialism effectively consigned the native to a subservient position.[112]

Education in the history of South Africa, and of course, elsewhere in the empire, was a powerful instrument of this hierarchical allocation: 'Native peoples were seen as destined to compose the lower orders of society ... As in the case of their counterparts in Britain and the Empire, they were to be taught the principles of Christianity, self-control and moral discipline, ... household care, agriculture and handicrafts.'[113] Most importantly in the face of failure to achieve collective cultural migration the confidence of the colonialist was retained through the creation of theories for this failure and the further creation and expansion of an education system to put theory into practice; a process which constituted a second assault on the cultures of the colonized which consistently, explicitly and implicitly, attacked their self-image. Perhaps even more significantly, this largely successful assault saved the colonizer from the humiliating role of 'imperial inadequate' incapable of convincing the morally inferior of the superiority of the colonizers' moral universe. In this way the colonizers' own self-image was sustained and that of the colonized reduced. And in this assault, the teacher, *pleno jure* in the classroom was a cultural mediator and through manner, word and action assisted in the transformation of both corporate universe and self-image.

In summary, there was a persistent stereotypic image *and* mirror-image in the British imperial culture of the second-half of the nineteenth and first-half of the twentieth centuries. Metaphorically speaking, an imperial printing plate with a well-defined picture existed with identical copies in wide circulation throughout the empire: a inferior native and a superior European.[114] A shared imperial ideology transmitted throughout a common culture by means *inter alia* of a general education system produced remarkably consistent image projection over space and time. This is not to deny ideological variation, regional emphasis, sectional difference, individual deviance or collective resistance, but it is to assert the general existence of a firmly held set of images, if necessary, independent of fact, extraordinarily resistant to change, easy to assimilate, sustained with certainty and potent in effect, which served important ethnocentric purposes.

In the cultural context of educational expectations, related performances, and self-fulfilling prophecies there was, therefore, a considerable and persistent obstacle to the development of the confidence of the colonized. Looming over educational system, institution and curriculum was the heavy shadow of stereotypic image. Structure, institution and curriculum met its demands creating and consolidating an imperial consciousness on the part of the colonizer and colonized which, to a remarkable degree, has survived colonialism. All of which leads directly to the assertion that consideration of the potency of image creation, projection and assimilation should be a central concern of studies of imperial socialization in the interest of a full understanding of the impact, past and present, of the phenomenon of imperialism.

2 The imperial Indian
India in British history textbooks for schools 1890–1914

Kathryn Castle

It was an interest in the origins and function of racial stereotypes which first brought my attention to the British history textbook. How, and by what agencies, were ideas about race transmitted to the rising generation in a period of British history when the imperial ethos was at its zenith? The original study was wide ranging, examining not only the images of India, but also of Africa and China, in school and popular reading materials. In the propagation of racial ideas textbooks were only part of a network of learning and leisure activities which mutually reinforced concepts of nationalism, character formation, and racial myths.[1] They were, however, to play an important and, I believe, distinctive role. Textbooks gave to the information they imparted to young minds the legitimacy of historical fact and analysis, and required for at least some of the recipients, the retention and display of this knowledge for teachers and examiners.

That education, and in particular history, should play an important role in securing youth's adherence to national goals was an idea voiced by public figures, the historical establishment and educationalists of the era.

> In former years the burdens of Empire or of the State fell on the shoulders of a few – now the humblest child to be found on the benches of a primary school will in a few years time be called upon to influence the destinies of not only fifty four millions of white, but also three hundred and fifty millions of coloured men and women, his fellow subjects scattered throughout five continents of the world. Such overwhelming responsibilities have never before in the history of this world fallen upon any people. If the white men and women of the British Empire are idle, soft, selfish, hysterical and undisciplined, are they likely to rule well?[2]

> Unless the younger generation is more thoroughly taught the eternal principles of History and Patriotism, the Britain of the future must be a declining power.[3]

If the fate of the nation was seen to rest upon an awareness of the nation's history, the Board of Education felt the need to elaborate upon this crucial interaction between the past and receptive young minds. A successful history lesson would also prove invaluable in building the individual's character.

> Without laboured exhortation they will feel the splendour of heroism, the worth of unselfishness and loyalty to an ideal, and the meaning of cruelty and cowardice. The influence of their lessons in history will be at work long after the information imparted in them has been forgotten.[4]

The History textbooks written in these years were to assume these tasks with notable enthusiasm. Publishers printed the textbooks supplied by a new generation of academic authors, with a speed prompted by the profit of an expanding market. If the burgeoning school population was to become literate, they would do so partly through the historical readers and texts which carried to the young lessons in history, citizenship and character formation. All classes in society would benefit from the message. From senior texts to the simplest readers the imperial past provided lessons on nationality for both potential rulers and for the newly-educated masses. In a period when fears of external threats, national degeneracy and class antagonisms created anxiety within British society, a consensus about the past seemed essential. Where better to search for it than in the history of the British Empire in India?[5]

Were the authors of the history textbooks conscious of the demands which history was to fulfill? It would seem that they were. While obviously some texts were more overtly patriotic than others, the majority shared the assumption that the story of British expansion abroad would demonstrate what was best in Britain's national character. The influential historian, S.R. Gardiner, showed, perhaps unwittingly, that there could be an inherent conflict in the service of both history and Empire.

> This work precludes all expression of my own views ... especially is this rule to be observed in a book addressed to those who are not yet at an age when independent investigation is possible.[6]

While Gardiner did approach certain events in the history of India with a more measured view than many of his contemporaries, he shared with them, despite his disinterested disclaimer, the common celebration of the 'peace and civilization which it was the glory of British statesmen to introduce into India'. Nor could he resist describing the Empire as 'a great movement which has filled the waste places of the world with children of the English race'. *MacMillans History Readers* of the same year were more explicit in seeking a 'proper' response from the younger pupil to the story of the 'Expansion of England'. While the reader was advised to consider the 'wonderful development of the Anglo Saxon race' they were also reminded that it would be a 'still greater thing to do our best to preserve that fabric from harm'. In 1905 Walker and Carter's *Local Examination History* balanced the strength of the Empire against the warning of racial 'decay', asserting that it was the former which allowed Britain to 'raise her head among the nations'. Arthur Innes' *History of England* directly appealed to the student to use his/her

Imagination and reasoning powers ... to enable him to realise how
the British race has become at once the most free and the most law
abiding in the world, how the British nation achieved the greatest Empire
the world has known, and what manner of men ... to whom we owe these
things.[7]

While textbook authors of the era may have thought that they were providing
a 'disinterested inquiry' into Britain's imperial past, their own words illustrate
how clearly history had been marshalled to support a hegemonic view of race
and Empire. It is within these controlling priorities that India and the Indian
peoples found a place in the history textbooks of the era.

The image of India and her peoples emerges both through what is included
in the texts and what is omitted, through general observations on the 'condition'
of India and the assessment of individual figures, and through the comparisons
which were inevitably drawn between English actions and character and those
of the 'alien'. The image of India which emerged was both ethnocentric,
enhancing the cultural superiority of Great Britain, and racist, assuming the
critical differences between British and Indian to rest not only on environmental
differences but on inherited biological factors. When the textbooks were tested
against R. Preiswerk's useful guidelines on identifying racism in school texts,
they passed with ease the vast majority of indicators, including ethnocentric
perspectives, racist images of other groups, and a set of racist themes and
objectives used to justify and explain the relationship between groups. While
this is not a surprising conclusion, none the less, testing against such criteria
does help to illustrate that school histories of the era were not only excessively
nationalistic, but important in delineating and propogating racial stereotypes
of subject races.[8]

Before examining the images offered by the texts, having established the
intention of the authors, school authorities and many public figures to transmit
such ideas to the young, one should consider if the message found its audience.
Enough evidence exists to make the reasonable assumption that it did. Reports
from the school inspectorate at the time show that historical readers were
very popular in the lower forms of schools, and a prominent feature of such
readers was stories from Empire. The combination of storytelling and stirring
deeds from history would make them attractive to the child and similar to
the content of the juvenile publications in mass ciruclation at the time.[9]
Inspectors' comments also show that the textbooks examined here were in
use in many schools, often recommended by the Board of Education. And
the teaching of history in the upper standards was frequently, in the inspectors' view, overly dependent on memorization from such set texts, reflecting
the demands of the examining boards. An examination of the questions set
by London, Oxford and Cambridge examining boards in the years from 1890
to 1914 show that students were expected to understand the growth of British
power in India, the significance of the battle of Plassey, the Seven Years War,
and the achievements of Clive and Hastings.[10] One Examiners' Report from

July 1908 gives an interesting insight into what children did remember from their history lessons on Clive.

> The salient points only should be given. Picturesque details of Clive's youth, or grim statistics as to the Black Hole of Calcutta, should not crowd out the effects of Arco and Plassey. Clive was often confused with Hastings.[11]

It would seem, then, that children did read the junior and senior history texts which have been examined here for their images of race and perhaps often conflated the more interesting details with out of school reading. Methods of instruction and examination promoted a reliance upon the history reader and textbook, while for the pupils there were a number of considerations which would encourage their retention of the material. That pupils read 'stirring tales from history' in the popular press would have helped the material come alive for all ages. Readers often directly replicated such tales. For the older student of history the setting of questions on British involvement in India occurred on both British and Imperial history papers, encouraging the utility of such knowledge for exam results. Exam prizes themselves were often the stirring imperial fiction of authors like G.A. Henty or W.H. Kingston.[12]

One of the most important considerations in the history textbooks treatment of British India was the selection of events to illustrate the historical relationship between the two nations. Most writers conformed to a similar pattern of historical development, beginning with the establishment of the East India Company, moving to the struggle for supremacy with the French in the eighteenth century, emphasizing the years of the Indian Mutiny, and finishing with the relative tranquility and good government of the post-Mutiny era of consolidation.[13] The student was encouraged to view India's 'history' as beginning with her recognition by the Western world. Discussion of the state of India in the eighteenth century was included only in the context of the opportunities afforded for the penetration of the European powers. George Carter's description of the Moghul Empire 1707 was a characteristic example of the historian's attitude toward the usefulness of indigenous Indian history: 'It was a disordered state . . . with an entire absence of anything like patriotism and unity, an easy prey to a foreign invader'.[14]

Authors presented India in a state of anarchy and confusion with a population ravaged by the constant warfare of constituent states, indeed hardly a nation at all by European standards. It was precisely this disorder which invited the imposition of foreign control and justified its expansion.[15]

Some texts did offer the pupil general information on the races which inhabited the subcontinent, but again the knowledge of Indian peoples was directly linked with the evolution of British rule. Osmund Airy, in his description of India, asserted that 'our Empire in India had been possible because the inhabitants were not one race, but many races'.[16] Diversity was viewed not as a rich cultural asset, but as a riot of competing linguistic and religious groupings. Students taught to appreciate the orderly emergence of the Anglo-Saxon states of Western Europe must have felt their distance from 'the Hindoos of 3,000 castes, with the worship of innumerable gods and endless diversity of ritual'.[17] The Indian peoples might also be divided for the student into categories such as the non-Aryan, the Aryan invaders and the Hindu, whose racial characteristics were assessed in relation to the Anglo-Saxon norm. York-Powell and Tout in 1900 described the non-Aryans as 'flat nosed savages', the Aryans as a 'primitive civilization' and the Hindu as 'a mixture' of other two.[18] In 1912 Warner and Marten contributed the following analysis of Indian racial diversity.

> The inhabitants of a vast continent speak 50 languages and vary in colour from the light brown of northern Pathan to the black of southern Tamil; and they are divided into races which, in the words of a recent viceroy, differ from one another 'as much as an Esquimaux from a Spaniard or Irishman from Turk'.[19]

From this 'vast mass of different elements' they argued, a 'stationary civilization' had emerged where 'no cohesion or unity was possible'.[20] In these remarks, which usually prefaced the section on the growth of British India, the textbook did little to encourage either sympathy, tolerance or understanding of India and its peoples. They were not only a strange and disordered state, but clearly inferior to the progressive, Anglo-Saxon community of the reader. Only occasionally in the junior readers can one find the older image of a 'romantic' India which had been current in the eighteenth and early nineteenth century. It was in the context of storytelling that the 'great and mysterious empire of India which has always exercised a fascination over men's minds' might still find expression.[21] In the textbooks of this era, however, as in British society at large, tolerance or fascination with the land of mystery had given way to the more pragmatic considerations of progress, order, and control. In the presentation of racial, social and religious characteristics on the eve of British intervention in India, the textbooks displayed the ethnocentric and racial arrogance of the age. Students could hold little respect for a nation which worshipped 'animals such as the cow, and the monkey, or of anything unusual, such as a peculiarly shaped stone or tree'.[22]

The instability of India and the insecurity of her populations was underscored in the texts by the characterization of indigenous peoples who resisted the European advance into their territories. While Bright offered a rather vague image of the Mahrattas 'dreaming of restoration of their national greatness', the majority of historians agreed with S.R. Gardiner, that they were no more than 'freebooters on a large scale', and an 'imminent danger' to both British and native interests. Meiklejohn in 1901 stated that 'they were disturbers of the peace of India, and had therefore to be put down'. Oman noted that they were 'finally crushed in 1817–18'.[23]

Some respect was accorded to pre-Mutiny native rulers, however hostile, who represented a recognizable code of military or civil conduct. Haider Ali, ruler of Mysore in the eighteenth century and a Muslim, was one such figure.

York-Powell and Tout provided an explanation for the textbooks' admiration of the 'Master of Mysore':

> a tall, robust, strong active man of fair and florid complexion a bold horseman a skillful swordsman and an unrivalled shot . . . a Mohammedan, but tolerant and kindly to his Hindu neighbours . . . the old soldier held his own until his death in 1782.[24]

Much like the Sikh leader, Ranjit Singh, 'Lion of the Punjab', Haider Ali was respected as a formidable opponent, and presented as the exception in leaders of his era, accepting the need for religious alliances rather than conflicts. Also, crucially, the textbooks admired the fact that he recognized the potential threat of the British power throughout the subcontinent, and that his death in 1782 effectively removed the hope of effective resistance. The textbooks' description of his 'qualities' clearly illustrated the ethnocentric and racial standards in operation. The 'good' Indian was light-skinned, athletic, brave in battle, fair and tolerant, in fact, remarkably English.

The Sikhs consistently earned admiration for their warlike qualities despite opposing the British in two bitter wars of the nineteenth century. A textbook published in 1893 explained why they earned such a place in the British affections.

> They were a religious sect who maintained the abolition of caste, the unity of the godhead, and purity of life, and were distinguished for the steadiness of their religious fervor.[25]

Warner and Marten in 1912 found that the 'steadiness and zeal' of the Sikhs could be compared with 'Cromwell's famous Ironsides'.[26] This was one of the very rare instances in which any foreigners were accorded the status of shared characteristics with the British, and showed the unique position occupied by the Sikh in the history of British India. Certainly part of the approval rested upon this group transferring their loyalty to the British, and most texts emphasized their steadfast behaviour in the 1857 Mutiny as proof of their allegiance to the Empire. These 'loyal' troops, like Haider Ali, found acceptance for a way of life which distanced them from the majority of their fellow Indians.[27]

The general impression conveyed was of a cacaphony of peoples in anarchic chaos. However the texts might favour a worthy opponent in battle or demonstrate that the most disciplined of Indian nationalities gravitated to the British cause, these exceptions did not nullify the conclusion that the Indian subcontinent needed the order and peace of foreign rule. Gardiner summed up what many of the textbooks suggested in their references to the 'state of India' in the course of gradual British expansion.

> England cannot but perceive that many things are done by the natives of India which are in their nature hurtful, unjust or even cruel, and they are naturally impatient to remove evils that are evident to them.[28]

The characterization of the Indian peoples as exploited static masses crushed by the greed and military ambitions of their native leadership was a common feature in the textbooks across the twenty-five years of the study. This belief underpinned the students' understanding of the need for British intervention, by creating an image of the subcontinent as quite different from the European model of a single sovereign state. India was presented as a nation whose native power structure was not only incompetent, but of doubtful legitimacy by European standards.

> The nawabs and viziers ... held sway merely because they themselves or their grandfathers, had been successful soldiers who had overthrown competitors; they had no established dynastic rights like the monarchs of Europe.

The choice in India was, quite simply, between 'outrage and misery' or 'peace and settled government'.[29] This was the Indian environment in which authors placed the 'great events' and 'heroes' of the British rise to power.

It was within an environment both alien and potentially dangerous that the careers unfolded of Robert Clive and Warren Hastings. Their importance to this study lies in the textbooks' treatment of their interaction with India, and what this told the pupil of the nature of India and her peoples. The treatment of these two figures illustrated some of the difficulties faced by historians in following the guidelines of the Board of Education *Suggestions for Teachers* published during this period.

> The teacher should place in relief those actions of his heroes and heroines which exhibit their highest qualities but should take care not to raise them too far by the omission of their faults and shortcomings.[30]

In the historical readers and the texts for the lower forms the need for simplicity and compression tended to work to enhance the heroic qualities of the two figures. If only a few sentences were to be included it sufficed to describe Clive as 'England's champion', her 'deliverer' or 'hero', or to mention his victory at Plassey and 'avenging' of the Black Hole. While Hastings was less directly associated with stirring deeds and therefore appeared less often in the readers, the texts for lower forms did encapsulate his career in descriptions of his 'glorious service' or through a single image. J.R. Green's junior text asserted that 'after a century of great events Indian mothers still hush their infants with the name of Warren Hastings'. These brief and uncritical references to the two men suggested a rather simple 'mastery' over the Indian environment. To Clive was attributed both the reactions of native troops who 'fled in terror' at his advance and 'a touching devotion' from his own sepoys. Hastings presented a strong and just figure, a statesman towering over the intrigues of corrupt local leaders. They were presented as heroes not only to the British, but also to the inhabitants of the areas they brought under British control. Here the Indian was clearly co-opted in the elevation of the men to heroic status.[31]

The role of India was rather more complex, however, in the texts which dealt with the controversial aspects of Clive's and Hastings' careers. Throughout the period senior texts did introduce the student to the accusations levelled against both men in their lifetimes. What is notable over the twenty-five years is how the authors of the texts, whatever reservations they may have had of the methods employed by the men, attribute culpability for their actions. Few writers offered a very positive view of the East India Company, acknowledging the uneasy mix of profit and good government, and they associated both Clive and Hastings with the positive move away from Company rule. However, when dealing with the possibility of corruption and irresponsibility in the Englishmens' dealings, it became clear, particularly toward the end of the period, that it was India itself which shouldered a large portion of the blame. Both Clive and Hastings were seen to have paid a heavy price for their long periods of service – infection with the corruption and venality which was endemic in the 'nature' of India. Clive was doomed by 'the oriental falsehood and treachery to which he stooped', by 'the laxity and unscrupulousness of Indian politics'. Carter observed that 'the shock was so great that he went mad, and died shortly afterwards'.[32]

Hastings was accused by Gardiner of 'soiling the English name' by 'lending troops to an Eastern potentate . . . certain to abuse a victory won by their arms'. The corrupt influence of native princes was seen as the main contributory factor in Hasting's errors of judgement. Innes summed up the moral of Hastings' flawed career.

> He unfortunately allowed methods to be employed which were a matter of course in oriental warfare and oriental courts, but were thoroughly repugnant to European ideas. The lesson had not yet been learned that in dealing with peoples whose moral standards are different from those of Europe, the white man must hold to the white standard that is not only the right course, but the course that pays best in the long run.[33]

It became clear by the end of the period in question, even in the senior texts, that there was a growing reluctance to tarnish the reputation of Clive and Hastings by holding them or the 'British character' responsible for their actions. Increasingly it was the Indian who was to blame, tempting them with riches, embroiling them in unwonted intrigues, and undermining their natural code of conduct. This interpretation of the career of Clive and Hastings produced an image of the Indian as immoral, dangerous, untrustworthy and also somehow dirty, soiling reputations and causing good men to end their days in suicide or alienation. This was a heavy burden for India to bear, and certainly decreased any possible sympathy which the young Briton might have had for a population exploited by both local and British profiteers. Clive's and Hastings' 'crimes' were reduced to 'misdemeanours'. Historical judgement acquitted them in a context of provocation beyond reasonable limits. Any tarnish upon their reputations was seen to be the mark of contact with India and her peoples. Their experience could certainly carry the message that it was wise to distance oneself from contact with the Indian, the reality of British administration in India during the late nineteenth and early twentieth centuries.[34]

In contrast with the treatment of Clive and Hastings, the textbooks offered few examples of Indian leaders from the history of British India whose character and actions merited anything but critical assessment. There were a few exceptions, as has been noted earlier, but one could argue that the inclusion of exceptions to the rule did little to soften the impact of the significant 'villains'. It was these figures who helped to place in 'relief' the British heroes, and served to illustrate that 'meaning of cruelty and cowardice' highlighted by the 1914 Board of Education circular. The characterization of Siraj-u-doulah and Nana Sahib was centred upon their association with 'outrages' perpetrated against the British, respectively the 'Black Hole of Calcutta' and the siege of Cawnpore. For the vast majority of texts, it was these Indian leaders who personified the 'oriental methods and morals' which could be set against British character and conduct.[35]

In the late nineteenth century the story of the 'Black Hole' remained alive within the popular imagination, fuelled by the memoirs of J.Z. Holwell, commander of the garrison of 170 British soldiers left at Fort William in June of 1756. Historians of the late twentieth century acknowledge the significance of the event and its impact upon public perceptions, citing Holwell's account as one 'which would ignite generations of British schoolboys with passionate indignation and outrage against the "uncivilized natives" of India'. M.E. Chamberlain, writing of the British image of India, explained the impact of the event as 'living on in English folk memory, the first in a long series of incidents which were to have totally different meanings for the two sides'. Within the modern perspective, both British and Indian historians have re-evaluated the role of Siraj-u-doulah, showing that 'he himself had neither ordered such torture nor been informed of it'. A more balanced view makes of him 'neither the monster of English legend nor the hero of some later Indian nationalist propaganda'.[36]

By the time of the writing of these textbooks nearly one hundred and fifty years had elapsed since the incident of the Black Hole, yet there seemed little desire on the part of the authors to reassess the image of the Indian held responsible for a deliberate and conscious atrocity against British lives. As little information was given on the context of his rise to power in Bengal, or civil and military considerations which informed his actions, Siraj's behaviour in relation to the British was presented as having no rational motive whatsoever. His actions in directing forces to Fort William were portrayed as those of 'a cruel young man who hated the English', or as a 'youth with monstrously inflated ideas of his own power and importance [who] decided to pick a quarrel with the British'. While some texts used more restrained language in their treatment of the young nawab, the seemingly irrational basis of his sudden 'decision to seize British property at Calcutta' was not clarified.[37]

Adjectives used to describe Siraj-u-doulah were indicative of the short-comings of Indian leadership. He was portrayed as 'weak', 'cruel', 'debauched', 'effeminate', 'despotic', 'stormy', 'treacherous', 'vicious' and 'monstrous'.[38] As his actions and character were often mentioned in direct proximity to Clive, the 'avenger', the student must have noticed the comparison, if only to forgive Clive his difficulties in dealing with such corrupt and immoral beings. Even those texts which restrained from calling him a bloodstained ruler, saw him as unmanly and subject to the tempestuous and petulant behaviour of the 'pampered prince'. Whether it was his immaturity or cruel nature was not made clear when historical readers exercised the story-tellers licence in relating his laughter at the death throes of innocent British victims.[39] Siraj-u-doulah was not discredited merely for his opposition to the British, but for characteristics which were seen as particularly Indian, the potential for treacherous cruelty, emotional and moral laxity, a lack of manliness, and a disregard for the value of individual human life. His image was to pass into the popular consciousness, along with Nana Sahib, as the prototype of the unacceptable Indian leader, an image partly fostered by his presentation in the history textbooks.

Nana Sahib was also to enter the texts at a particularly emotive period of history, the discussion of the course of the Indian Mutiny. His historical significance was limited to his role in the 'massacre' at Cawnpore, where 400 British subjects had surrendered to him, had been guaranteed safe passage, and were subsequently killed by Nana Sahib's troops. Like the Black Hole before it, the murder of British men, women and children at Cawnpore sparked off a wave of revenge and reprisals, and exacerbated the racial enmity between European and Asian.[40] Again there was no attempt to place the Indian's opposition to the British within a context of conflicting attitudes toward British policy. Nana Sahib's loss of status through the doctrine of 'lapse' did not enter the texts. Only Gardiner went as far as to explain 'his hatred of the British on account of the wrongs which he conceived himself to have suffered'. Airy diminished his motivation to the 'refusal of a pension'. Many texts referred to no more than his 'dire treachery'.[41] The language which described Nana Sahib was similar to that attached to Siraj-u-doulah, but if anything he was perceived as more evil in his cold-blooded betrayal. The historical readers frequently featured the horrors of Cawnpore, a scene of 'Englishmen and women slaughtered like sheep . . . hacked and mutilated'. Nana Sahib became a 'monster', the 'fiend in human shape'.[42] To this mutineer was credited a 'slaughter of innocents', and as the sole representative of Indian leadership mentioned during the discussion of the rebellion, he became a potent symbol of the dangers encountered and dispelled by the British victory at arms.

In the cases of Nana Sahib and Siraj-u-doulah, the textbooks gave credence to the popular images from newspaper reports and the popular press, and confirmed rather than dispelled the racial enmity which concentration on such episodes exacerbated. Both the emotive language used to describe the two Indian leaders, the omission of a context for their actions, and the absence of a counterbalance of 'good Indians' made of them the stereotype of the

Indian ruler. Students' attempts to hold on to the image of a Haider Ali, would be reminded that 'all else pales before the horrors of Cawnpore'.[43]

Much like the general descriptions of Indian disunity and lack of progress, the image of Indian leadership worked to justify the expansion of British rule on the subcontinent. None appeared, as did the English, concerned with peace and stability for the masses. Justice and good government were concepts deemed alien to their minds and impossible to obtain within their jurisdictions. It was only in the post-Mutiny era, of 'quiet, steady work' by British officials, that native rulers, in tandem with English advisers, were described as 'working well for their people'. Pacified princes and loyal Sikh and Gurkha regiments represented the proof of the advances which could be secured under the Raj. The *Oxford Survey of the British Empire* noted in 1914 that native princes who had benefited from British education were 'practically English gentlemen', in no sense more so than in opposing the unrest of the Indian National Congress. Hawke in 1911 stressed that the princes 'trust the British government as an impartial protector'. A number noted that it was the focal point of the British monarchy which provided the unity which had for so long been absent from India.[44]

While few texts wished to disturb this view of *Pax Britannica*, there was some mention of new voices within India, raised both in the vernacular press and emerging nationalist movements. While not credited with the stature of leaders, nor individually named, these figures were clearly viewed as troublemakers, intent on leading the Indian people astray with 'silly and seditious' ideas. Oman feared the emergence of a 'half educated literary proletariat', and toward the end of the period texts acknowleged that at some point in the future the stirrings of nationalism might have to be recognized and accommodated.[45] For the vast majority of texts throughout the period, however, it was the Anglicized and tame princes whom they wished to designate as partners in Empire, separated in time and divided by culture from their disloyal predecessors or contemporary critics. Students learned from the history textbook's assessment of the past and present nature of Indian leadership a crucial part of the argument for the validation of Empire. Whether in discredited opposition or in enlightened partnership the textbook image of indigenous Indian leadership worked to justify their subjection to Western power.

No incident in the history of the British in India so hardened the hearts and minds of the English toward their Indian subjects as did the Indian Mutiny of 1857–58.[46] If the Black Hole and Cawnpore represented the duplicity of Indian leaders, it was the mutiny which shook the Empire to its core, and presented the spectre of collective betrayal. Historical readers retold the events of Cawnpore and Lucknow while the textbooks devoted considerable attention to the origins, action and aftermath of the conflict. First-hand accounts of the Mutiny had become available to the British public soon after the event, conditioning public anger and outrage. Reinforcing and reflecting these established attitudes, the history texts stretched their language to its emotive limits. Authors were reduced to the admission that words were inadequate to fully convey such awful happenings. Granville was just one of those who confessed a failure to encompass the 'innumerable outrages'.[47]

Notwithstanding a shared sense of the horrors of the rebellion, and a patriotic pride in the eventual success of British arms, the textbooks did exhibit significant differences in their treatment of the mutineers over the years of this study. Historians writing in the period from 1890 to the turn of the century adopted a more balanced approach to the causes of the Mutiny and a more objective assessment of the conduct of the war and its immediate aftermath. J.F. Bright's multi-volume *History of England* published early in the period reflected both the author's Liberal sentiments and this tendency for earlier texts to take a more judicious stand on the plight of the native soldier.

> The sepoy was not only a soldier but a member of a nation ... liable to be influenced by the social and political feelings of those around him ... brave men fighting after the nature of their kind for a national liberty which they loved or for a religion in which they devoutly believed.

He was also critical of the English reprisals, describing the executions as 'apparently indiscriminate ... a batch of 12 executed merely because their faces turned the wrong way'. Bright charged his countrymen with showing 'in a cruel fashion ... their incapacity for understanding the rights or feelings of those opposed to them'.[48]

Even the readers of the early years admitted English errors of judgement, Macmillan's popular series questioning 'the deliberate attempt by the English to force some to sacrilege'. Charlotte Yonge's history pointed to the impact of British arrogance toward the native.

> The British did not take pains, as a rule, to show friendly courtesy to the grave and dignified Hindoos, often of high rank ... and though the native might cringe and obey, he laid up hatred in his heart.[49]

Gardiner in 1892 asserted in his senior text that 'the British government had not shown itself sufficiently careful of their feelings and prejudices'. Airy in 1893 stated that for the sepoy the loss of caste was 'the most dreaded calamity'. Other texts of the 1890s noted the dismay of the Indian peoples at the loss of their native leaders, and accepted that the doctrine of lapse had 'given great offence to the people of India'.[50]

By the early 1900s, however, the tone was becoming harsher and the judgements more uncompromising. York-Powell and Tout described a Bengal army 'pampered and spoiled by foolish indulgences'. Legitimate grievances were more often displaced by descriptions of 'the punctilious Brahmin and the bigoted Muselman who came to believe that new ammunition was greased ... the fears of a suspicious race were not easily allayed'. A sense of incipient nationalism became the work of rumour and mischief, and now unselfconscious soldiers were misled by seditious elements within their midst. Oman concluded in 1904 that 'a foolish rumour set the army in a flame'. A sense of the

Indian 'case' was balanced by the credulous sepoy's 'misunderstanding' of the British good intentions. While earlier histories had accepted the short-comings in Dalhousie's policies, particularly the annexation of Oudh, Innes in 1907 told the student that 'its kings had been warned over and over again, that if they did not mend their ways their dynasty would be deposed'.[51]

Warner and Marten's senior text in 1912 placed the cause of the breakdown firmly in the Indian camp, concluding that 'Western reforms mystified and unsettled the Indian mind, and natives thought the world was being turned upside down'. Much of the blame for the rebellion was now placed, not on mistaken British policy decisions or misguided implementation, but on the character and actions of the Indian subject. Earlier textbooks' willingness to engage with the issue of a defiling of religious beliefs by the greased cartridges, for example, became increasingly relegated to a ridiculous notion or attributed to 'audacious and subtle falsehoods'.[52]

As the character of the Indian peoples came to bear more directly the blame for Mutiny, so the suggestion of excessive reactions by the British troops or administrators began to disappear from the textbooks. The earlier works had accepted that the conditions of the time created the possibilities of unacceptable behaviour by British soldiers, 'a ferocious if natural desire for revenge'. Gradually, however, the accounts of mutineers blown out of cannons were replaced by such terse statements as 'the treachery and cruelty of the sepoys was punished with ruthless severity'. Keatinge and Frazer in 1911 only observed that 'the tragedies of the Mutiny made it impossible for the British to be altogether merciful'.[53] The removal of overly emotive language and descriptions from the textbooks might be viewed as a positive develop-ment. However, the deletion of 'excesses' applied only to the British actions, leaving the Indian mutineer isolated in his recourse to cruel and unnatural behaviour.

The textbook historians' treatment of the Mutiny did change over the time period of this study, and within their revisions the image of the Indian altered as well. A consideration of the possible reasons for the hardening of attitudes towards mutineers and the increasingly uncritical assessment of British actions suggest that the histories of this period were clearly responsive to the needs of Empire. Representations of the Indian became dependent upon a version of history which supported national interests, including the legitimacy of British rule in India. By the early 1900s it became increasingly important to reassure the student of Empire that it was still 'the most remarkable fact in modern history'.[54] Writing within a period which included the Boer War, fears of national degeneracy, and challenges to national stability from other European nations, it was perhaps natural that historians would want to emphasize the stability and strength of British rule abroad. Within these national considera-tions there was increasingly little room to consider the Indian as aggrieved, discontented, angry or exploited. The same texts which dismissed the Indian case in the Mutiny years also discredited the rise of Indian nationalism or stirrings in the native press after the turn of the century. While emphasizing the loyalty of Indian princes the texts were also presenting discontent, whether of the 1850s or the present, as 'misunderstandings', 'irrational fears', and 'sedition'. The overriding concern was with the safety of Britain's position in India. It became less important to learn from the errors of the past than to eradicate them. In the process the image of the Indian lost a fragile claim to a rational and independent voice. As the image of legitimate discontent waned that of the treacherous troublemaker and the duped sepoy took the field. As British heroism and good intentions became the most significant facts of the Mutiny, subjects who failed to recognize their own best interests assumed responsibility for the resort to armed conflict. In the *Oxford Survey of the British Empire* published in 1914 it was admitted that a concentration on the 'heroism of the British' meant that a study of the incident 'added to rather than diminished British prestige'.[55]

While this may have been the case, and undoubtedly was the purpose, Britain's gain was history's and the Indian's loss. While the image of India and her peoples had always been co-opted in the texts to support the intervention of the British, this process became extraordinarily self-serving by 1914. That textbooks adjusted their view of the Indian to fit these external considerations can be seen in the treatment of the Mutiny, where even mild suggestions of rational response to legitimate grievances were eliminated. A conflict of interests or a study of policy became a struggle of national characters, in which the behaviour of the Indian attested to his inadequacy, immaturity and duplicity. If the rebellion had proved a nascent spirit of nationalism, forged in reaction to British policy, the India of disorder and chaos which had legitimized European expansion was challenged as a permanent factor of Indian life, and perhaps with it the longevity of outside rule. If the textbooks acknowledged a maturing of Indian political judgement, by leader or follower, this too might question the security of Empire. In this era few textbooks suggested that the Indian might have an independent view of his/her best interests that differed from that of the 'civilized' world. Authors echoed the view from India, expressed by Lord Curzon at the turn of the century.

> We cannot take the natives up into the administration. They are crooked and corrupt. We have got therefore to go on ruling them and we can only do it with success by being both kindly and virtuous. I daresay I am talking rather like a schoolmaster; but after all, the millions I have to manage are less than schoolchildren.[56]

It is important to remember here that the history textbooks were written for children in their formative years. In the textbooks' own words, the rising generation must carry on the work begun by their forefathers, this 'noble work for civilization' which the Indian Empire represented.[57] It is arguable that the authors knew no more of the Indian than they represented, that their own knowledge of the Empire rested upon the ethnocentric history they had themselves studied and credited in their works.[58] In their assessment of Indian character and actions they were doing no more than echoing the prevalent ideas of the time, the delivered dogma of scientific racism, the racial hierarchies of the evolutionists and Spencerians, and the progressive idea of history.[59] While all this is undoubtedly true, and epochs create the history suitable for their times, the texts legitimized a view of India and her peoples which long outlived the needs of Empire. Not only did the images enter the public consciousness through the generation educated in the years before the First World War, but the outlines of the imperial Indian reappeared in the reprinted texts for decades afterward, and influenced their successors.[60]

In this sense, the era covered by these history textbooks and readers can be regarded as seminal in creating and reinforcing racial stereotypes of the Indian peoples. At one end of the spectrum were the 'exceptional' Indians, those admired for their militaristic discipline, like Haider Ali and the Sikhs, or the post-Mutiny elite of Anglicized princes. These were figures admired for qualities which approached the Anglo-Saxon ideal. Unlike the majority of Indians, the Sikh could be trusted. This had been proven in the Mutiny and later in their service in the ranks of imperial defence. The princes of post-Mutiny India shared a class identification with British administrators, perhaps educated at the same public schools, and openly demonstrated their loyalty to the British sovereign. The textbooks celebrated their positive role in modern India as proof of their enlightenment and the essential justice of British rule.

The texts also showed the other face of India, those who attempted to contest progress and shared the darker characteristics, both physical and spiritual, which called for suppression, proving in Sir Charles Oman's words, that 'the British bayonet was still needed'.[61] Many of these images centred upon the 'villains' of India, Siraj-u-doulah and Nana Sahib, representing the duplicity and treachery which might be present or activated in the Indian character. The tradition of princes or chiefs who exploited their peoples, pursued violence with a ruthless regard for human life, and operated on the principle of power without responsibility helped to excuse the excesses of the East India Company, accounted for the 'lapses' of Clive and Hastings, and dismissed a new generation of troublemakers under the modern Raj. In the world view of the late nineteenth and early twentieth centuries, barbarism must give way to the forces of progress. Only by displacing this aspect of India and substituting the British model of just and good government could the subcontinent hope to advance from 'infancy to political manhood'.[62]

The 'teeming masses' of India were caught between the acceptable elite and the self-serving native leaders. Most texts agreed that they were imprisoned in the strange religions and customs of a pre-civilized society. Poverty and ignorance, assisted by the caste system, made for an essentially conservative and static peasantry. Historians suggested that their loyalties were volatile, as centuries of exploitation and primeval religious practices had contained them in the grip of childlike emotions and superstitious beliefs. They were the focus of the 'quiet and steady work' of the *Pax Britannica*, in which the British dispensed education, hospitals, roads, railroads, irrigation and sanitation for the improvement of native life. This India was the 'vast responsibility' which textbooks emphasized as a major feature of the imperial relationship. The backward races of the subcontinent were presented as slowly being introduced to the wonders of the modern world. York-Powell and Tout reflected the textbook view of India's populace under the Raj.

> This enormous mass of human beings now enjoys a peace and prosperity such as was never known in India before . . . in the great industrial cities the stationary stage of civilization has almost been outgrown.[63]

India was the 'pride' of the Empire, and the student of history was expected to feel no less. The Empire was presented as an unmixed blessing in the lives of the vast majority of Indian subjects, both in the past and the present. There was, however, little mention of the vital economic relationship between the subject nation and Great Britain, beyond vague allusions to the 'riches of India' or the importance of 'trade' in the twentieth century. There is no doubt that the forces of profit and loss did not sit comfortably with the Empire of stirring deeds, noble British leaders and the foundations of *Pax Britannica*. The textbooks acknowledged this in their treatment of the East India Company, Clive and Hastings. The control exercised by the British was held to be 'beneficent'. The emphasis on Britain's investment in the Empire avoided the troubling consideration that Indians were in any sense deprived of the freedom of self-determination. Control was neutralized into acceptable notions of guardianship or parental responsibilities, relations which the readers of the text could readily understand. Reducing the majority of Indians to a childlike status helped to persuade the pupil that Britain's role was essentially protective, safely distanced from any suggestion of coercion or exploitation. In the end, however, the Indian was left both without power and without value. There is no suggestion that the labour of the Indian contributed in any way to the strength of the Empire, and the impression created is that the natives were only the passive recipients of British benevolence. There was no suggestion that the English needed the Indian, indeed were dependent upon his production of wealth for the continued power of Empire. Students might have been excused for believing that the strength of Empire rested solely upon the extension of British ideals, rather than upon the profits of colonial trade.[64]

This was the history of an imperial age, and as J.H. Plumb has observed, 'where the service of the past has been urgently needed, truth has ever been at a discount'. The image of India which these authors chose to present did little to teach the student of the reality of the Indian subcontinent, but were arguably successful in imparting to the rising generation an image of India central to the support of Empire, and helpful in reasserting the strength of British national character. From the history textbooks, the pupils found a reinforcement of the views held and disseminated by other important influences in their lives, including juvenile magazines and comics of the era. The comparison between the Indian world and the familiar world of Britain was uniformly unfavourable, and the knowledge acquired served to diminish the students' sympathy and understanding for difference and diversity. History became a partner in the controlling ideology of the age, removing an independent existence from the 'subject races', and independent thought from the youth of Great Britain. In this respect the imperial Indian becomes an indicator of the insecurity and anxiety of the period. The touchstone of racial stereotyping can be a useful point around which to establish national unity in the face of internal division and external threats, just as displacing undesirable characteristics onto the 'other' can reassure the individual. Eurocentric history placed power not only in the hands of the adult masters, but also in Santayana's 'schoolboy masters of the world'.[65]

By exploring the creation of the imperial Indian in these school history textbooks a number of lessons emerge for the contemporary historian, educationalist and individual. For the historian there is the knowledge that the demands of government, nation, and his/her own training may inculcate a bias which works against the best ideals of the discipline itself. For the educationalist in a multi-cultural society this era illustrates the dangers of following an excessively nationalistic curriculum, particularly one which emphasizes the links between national identity and the learning of history. For the individual it remains a task to finally unlearn the racial myths disseminated into the public consciousness by these textbooks and their successors. The origins of the imperial Indian may now seem safely in the past, but the influence of these images has been tenacious and long-lived, far byeond the empire they were created to serve.

3 The black African in Southern Africa
Images in British school geography books

T. Lilly

The role of the school textbook as an aid to learning and its influence upon thoughts, opinions and attitudes cannot easily be demonstrated. It is only one source of reference of many that may act upon a child's perception of the world. It can be argued that storybooks, pictures, comics and, nowadays, film and TV are more pervasive influences. The oft repeated Tarzan films and the later 'Zulu' and 'Zulu Dawn' have much to answer for as shapers of children's attitudes to Africans. In the past, these alternatives to formal learning were less common, allowing the schoolbook a proportionately greater role. The logical premise has to be that a textbook placed in front of a child for a year or more always has some potential to persuade and it is clearly the duty of the teacher to work from such a premise, ensuring that the influence is as benign as possible.

The message of schoolbooks is fairly obvious at one level and seldom challenged by the child except passively when boredom leads to rejection. At another level is the hidden message, sometimes conveyed subtly by selection of words, by association, by picture or even by omission. The message will be more significant if there are few alternative sources. This was usually the case when the subject was distant places and peoples. Not only did the child lack direct experience but so did the teacher. Alternative secondary sources on a place like South Africa were few until quite recent times. It can be surmised that the school textbook was an influence upon the teacher as well as the pupil. In a subject whose long-held ambition was to teach the 'world geography' fashionable until the 1960s there was little time to go outside the one reference available to any given class of pupils. If the textbook was biased then both teacher and child were at its mercy.

School geography books are a product of their age and are likely to reflect the current ethos of their time. Their persistence through several editions plus a lengthy shelf life can project this ethos well beyond their own time. A twenty- to thirty-year run has been common for the most 'successful' texts.[1] Their authors were teachers and lecturers and they themselves largely depended upon secondary sources which they interpreted. In the space available, often a few pages, they had to be highly selective, identifying the appropriate information for the age group targeted. Authors were as much the victims of the received wisdom of their age as their readers, yet writing for the British education system they were fairly free to indulge their own ideas and beliefs. The market, however, was a conservative one not looking for anything too radical and the seller was a commercial firm hoping to tap the potential sales of over one million copies such as recorded by Stamp's *The World*.[2]

With hindsight it is easy to criticize, but it is necessary, for the need is not only to understand why and how attitudes on race might have been inculcated but also to promote alertness to any persistent racist imagery. The school texts that are referred to in this review are a sample of those that have been used in schools. The proportion they represent of the total is unknown, but it is a major one, giving a good indication of trends over the time considered. Although the analysis looks back to an earlier inspiration for the imagery projected the date 1850 is a satisfactory starting point for analysis of the texts.

In 1844 a school inspector wrote 'no good school books on geography exist'. In 1847 another inspector stated

> The manuals of geography employed by the teachers are various. They are merely the sources of their own information, and not generally placed in the hands of children . . . but a very superior manual, just published by Mr James Cornwell . . . will most probably come into extensive use, and effect a great improvement.[3]

Cornwell was indeed to establish a new approach to the subject. He moved away from simple statement of facts about place and product and introduced commentary on the people. It made for a livelier text, but did little to promote sane attitudes on race. His book was published at the beginning of an expanding publishing period for geography texts, increasing as elementary education was expanded by Parliament from the 1870s. Cornwell's thinking on his subject was not new. He was following in a long tradition as was clear in many views he expressed. Such books can only be appraised properly by reviewing them in the context of the school system in which they existed, the school subject which they served and the time and society of which they were a part. These moulded the book which then did its bit to move thinking along either a regressive or progressive line.

Views and attitudes held by people of any nation have remote origins. South Africa was unknown to all the British until the sixteenth century and remained unknown to the vast majority until the nineteenth century. First reports would have come back from sailors and settlers, but as most of these reports were not from English-speakers, language would limit their promotion in Britain. In so far as attitudes to southern Africans were held they would be conditioned by those formed about Africans generally in an earlier age. These earlier impressions have been appraised by Jordan.[4] He emphasized the reaction of the English to actual and perceived differences of appearance and custom between themselves and the Negro. It was easy to transfer pre-formed judgements to the southern part of the continent.

By the time of serious British involvement in South Africa the institutions of slavery clouded all thinking. One significant consequence of British participation in the trade was a substantial resident population in England of people of African origin or ancestry, perhaps 15,000 in 1770. Contact with these was one way for the Briton at home to learn directly about Africans, but most it must be supposed learned of them from hearsay or written word. The written words too often promoted the 'caricatures' identified by Walvin.[5]

When the serious 'educational' books were written they were produced by authors already conditioned by generations of conformity to the idea of an African different and inferior, contrasted with the ascendant British.

By the late eighteenth century there was a serious interest in Africa. The unknown interior was a curiosity to many of that age and there was an increasing audience for information about it. The 95 members of the African Association in 1790 were enthusiastic followers and promoters of attempts to discover more. The Association's formation in 1788 was by nine members dedicated to encouraging advancement of knowledge and trade and its members soon represented the spectrum of aristocratic, professional and businessmen of that time.

The eighteenth-century writers produced great tomes for the libraries of the elite. Impressive in size and intention was Bankes's *Geography*.[6] It extended to 972 pages on the 'History and description of the whole world' and 104 of these pages were addressed to Africa. Following an initial acknowledgement of past fame: 'It has given birth to eminent divines, heroes and poets', Bankes quickly countered this laudation '. . . but the natives are now degenerated to such a degree, as to become odious to a proverb'. He chose South Africa as the first region to be detailed under its then title of 'Caffreria, or the Country of the Hottentots', a place its readers were told that was '. . . neglected through the insuperable indolence of the natives'.[7] Such language and images were to be repeatedly offered to students for the next 180 years.

Bankes's *Geography* was published in 1787. Its influence might be deemed as small. Few could have afforded this luxurious leather-bound volume, yet those who could afford it were the powerful and influential of their day and the tome was there as a reference for later works. The received message was that Africa was curious and its peoples worthy only of contempt. Many of the recipients of the message would leave Britain – as sailors, explorers, missionaries and colonists of the nineteenth century – leaving for Africa with their ideas already formed. Those who meanwhile stayed at home and wrote the schoolbooks would turn to such texts as their sources, echoing or plagiarizing them. The echo would continue down the centuries. One hundred and fifty years after Bankes wrote, an author named Bygott would write 'the natives are averse to sustained work'.[8] Most overtly negative comment ceased from the mid-1930s, although damning with faint praise remained common. There were some authors who made distinct efforts at positive images, even if a little patronizing. As early as 1898, Bird wrote of the Bantu as 'tall and well grown, brave and intelligent'.[9] By the 1950s most books avoided personal comment and if anything was written it was so bland as to be almost meaningless as in 'The Bantu has maintained his vigour'.[10]

When the earliest school texts were printed, the formal education system still had a long way to evolve. The late 1700s to the early 1800s was a time of neglect and often decay, yet this was against a background of social and economic change in which radical ideas incorporated philosophies on education which were to reverberate through the next hundred years. For most children in 1800 it mattered little that Rousseau was already admired or that Adam Smith and Malthus favoured publicly provided education. The poor who comprised more than three-quarters of the British population were for the most part deprived of significant schooling. Advances in literacy were evident. The better-off could pay for school although what they bought was often questionable. Information on who actually was subjected to the earlier geography textbooks is fragmentary. It had to be a fairly small percentage of the nation's children. Typical was probably the experience of Thomas Dunning referring to his elementary schooling in about 1825: 'I had very little time for writing or arithmetic, and none for grammar or geography'.[11]

By the time that David Livingstone was travelling through Africa the evidence is of a stronger position for schoolroom geography, presumably encouraged by the active interest that exploration itself generated.[12] Some specific figures were produced by the 1851 census on education in England and Wales on the percentage of scholars instructed in different subjects in day schools. Fourth on the list after reading, writing and arithmetic appears geography: 30.6 per cent of male and 25.6 per cent of female scholars are recorded as attending this subject.[13] Evidence of the ambition and achievement of such instruction is conveyed vividly in Inspector's Reports for the 1840s. The children might be able to 'tell the names of every known tribe of barbarians in Africa'.[14] Within what was in fact a criticism there is this clear pointer to the nature of most school geography of the time. Its main purpose was to inculcate the learning of lists of names – of places, landforms and peoples. This in itself was of doubtful merit, but if it did little good, it equally did little harm. A list of tribes was fairly innocuous. It was the introduction to the list that could be full of racist taunts.

British geography was learned from the tales of travellers, but as an academic subject it was strongly fed by the earth sciences. In the order of concerns in a typical textbook, peoples were often given scant attention. When mentioned they were seen as agents of economic and commercial processes, the producers of commodities. It is not the intention here to consider the adequacy of geographers' treatment of South Africa as a region, but rather to focus upon that aspect which many authors would have seen as peripheral to their main task. People and policies were often dealt with in a passing reference: yet even the briefest comment can be ill-judged and potentially harmful when dealing with a sensitive social environment. When the inspectors quoted employed the adjective 'barbarian' they had with one word bolstered the racial imagery of the time. Their second word, 'tribes', reinforced it further. Implicit in such words are all the ideas that are manifest in a racially prejudiced society. A cautious interpretation is needed. Words that now cause offence or are deemed clearly pejorative may have been less so in their earlier usage. Thus when the Greeks employed their word that we write as barbarian they meant someone differing in language and culture. It has potential for use as an abusive form and has come to connote cruelty and coarseness. Its use in Victorian English is open to semantic debate. It could be used more to describe than deliberately offend. Much depended on the way the word was used and what it supported in its context. When the first report of the African Association referred to African nations 'consigned to hopeless barbarism'[15], the word 'hopeless' set the tone. When David Livingstone used it freely it was more to denote a 'scale of social development from barbarism to civilization'.[16] His more thoughtful use of the word was in the framework of sentiments that argued that 'The African is a man with every attribute of human kind'.[17] Others less sensitive than that astonishing traveller could use the same word with much more arrogance, as when the explorer Richard Burton, a few years after Livingstone, wrote of the Wanika as a 'futile race of barbarians'.[18] The textbook writer could pick and choose whatever view appealed and perhaps with less care as to context than was desirable.

The writings of the explorers were there to feed any prejudice that the less well travelled might exhibit and their authority was hardly to be contradicted. However, what impresses is a prevailing ambivalence. It is there in Livingstone's writing and even in the more dogmatic Stanley's who did much to promote the 'darkest Africa' epithet with his books of that title.[19] He headed a section 'My Reverential Feelings for the Pygmy'. Having captured a man and woman at Avatiko he methodically measures them and makes clear that his veneration derives from their descent as 'outcasts of the earliest ages . . . eternally exiled by their vice, to live the life of human beasts'. Yet, he credits them with souls and 'finer feelings inert and torpid through disuse, they were there for all that'.[20]

Schoolbook writers were offered confusing images by their mentors, but there was some choice. They could have emphasized 'reverence' but until well into the 1900s the choice was mostly of the negative image. A further factor in influencing this must have been the vigorous debates and the events of the last forty years of the nineteenth century. These largely worked to reinforce European prejudices. Darwin's theories on natural selection could easily be adapted to support and justify white dominance and the expansion of white rule. Alfred Wallace who spurred on the publication of 'Origin of Species' put out a view forcibly in 1864:

> The intellectual and moral, as well as the physical qualities of the European are superior; the same powers and capacities which made him rise in a few centuries from the condition of the wandering savage . . . enable

him when in contact with the savage man, to conquer in the struggle for existence and to increase at his expense.[21]

Others like the journalist Mackay would write with equal conviction and with greater insult.[22] As the scramble for Africa sent the Foreign Office officials far and wide they went to the continent already primed with thought and language. Some, like Duff, fed it back in familiar enough form, describing Africans as 'not very markedly distinguished from the higher orders of beasts by any quality of the heart or brain.[23]

How could any scribe of a schoolbook challenge such mighty pens? In South Africa one event in particular did give pause for thought. If half a British regiment could be wiped out by Zulu at Isandlhwana it would not do to emphasize that the victors were 'indolent' – savages perhaps, but lazy ones would not be worthy opponents, and would suggest less than an heroic last stand by imperial troops. Most writers on South Africa made some interesting distinctions between types of people. The battle of 1879 received much attention in the British press and ultimately in the schoolbooks where it was not only historians who felt some accord was due the Zulu. The geographers were forward with admiring phrases: 'a fine warlike race' (1891);[24] 'tall, well grown, brave and intelligent' (1898);[25] 'dark brown, powerful, handsome race' (1902).[26] It seemed as though the southern African was to be higher placed than compatriots further north with attempts to see them as different, 'nobler specimens of humanity than the true negro' (1893).[27] However, there was a narrower view derived from their success at slaughtering the unfortunate South Wales Borderers. Such an event could be interpreted as clear evidence of savagery, or a state akin to it – one referred enigmatically to the 'half savage'.[28] However, a frequently used adjective was 'fine', as in 1891, 'The Zulu are a fine warlike race'.[29] Sometimes it was exchanged for 'noble' or 'sturdy' but it was still used in 1963: 'finest is the Zulu'.[30] The authors dropped the idea just as the film makers picked it up and sent their fine black warriors yelling into schoolchildrens' minds, with no portrayal of the individual warrior as a person.

School pupils did not inevitably receive only the one image from their books. It was possible to be subjected to quite contradictory ones, but as most would see only one book the choice lay with the teacher.

The Zulu presented the authors with an enigma and each resolved it according to their own understanding. Further attempts to subdivide black people into categories, who were then represented as possessing particular traits, led to many confused distinctions. Negroes were put forward as different to Bantus and Kafirs as a sub-branch of the Bantus. Usually they followed old obsessions with classifications of race based upon physical characteristics. As recently as 1970 Coysh and Tomlinson's *Africa* devoted three pages to 'Racial groups'[31] with details of physical traits emphasized just as they were in the early 1900s. The later books of the 1970s abandoned this approach. Hickman refers to race only in the context of political divisions[32] and White entitles a section 'Indigenous Inhabitants'.[33]

In the older books there was a near consensus on groups whose physique or culture allowed confident identification – usually in ignorance of subtle societal differences. In South Africa there were perceived to be two very easily recognized peoples unique to that region, dubbed as Hottentot and Boeschman by the Afrikaner. These Khoi–San peoples were normally condemned with a passion that now seems paranoic. It is difficult to account for, beyond the fact that they were a nuisance to the settlers. No condescending remarks about virtues softened the antagonism. The first colonial governor of the seventeenth century Cape started the fashion with a venemous reference to 'black stinking dogs'.[34] Cornwell lashed out at them in his new school textbook:

> The Hottentot perhaps rank the lowest amongst men . . . The Bushmen are the most degraded . . . appearance and filthy habits, excite invincible disgust.[35]

Children were still being told they were 'perhaps the most degraded of all known people' in 1935,[36] whilst others had added 'ape-like', 'little intelligence', 'incapable of civilization', 'lowly savage' to the abuse. 'Primitive' was the common prefix and having first appeared in 1921, it was still in use in 1971 when second formers were invited to 'Find out all you can about the primitive race called the Bushmen'.[37] The only author to use this title but qualify it was an American in 1961 who wrote: 'The word points out that although their civilization is not modern, they nevertheless do have a civilization of their own.[38] Some saw them only in terms of exploitation: 'dishonest and unreliable . . . these characteristics are a hindrance to rapid settlement.[39] As another remarked 'the Dutch did not find them useful'.[40] Very few of the books could now be judged to have done anything but develop prejudice towards this branch of humanity. Not until 1978 were the titles Khoikhoi and San employed (a necessary recognition of their proper names for themselves) and the impact of European settlers upon them fairly described.[41]

There are many difficulties that an analysis of this kind encounters as value judgements interfere with objectivity. It is easy to recognize gross distortion or prejudice and to appreciate the careful attempt to convey a full and balanced picture. Less easy to appraise is the choice of phrase and the innuendo. These can act more insidiously upon a child's perception, even though the author intended no racist taunt. In a book in 1923 the Bushmen were referred to as 'a race of yellow skinned dwarfs'.[42] In 1974 they were described as 'short and light skinned'.[43] Both authors are essentially saying the same thing. The image portrayed is quite different. The second description avoids the racist imagery of the 1920s. Role reversal helps underline the persistence of a problem. To describe the British similarly it could be said that they are fat and pink skinned. If that were all that were written about us in a San school textbook we would have some right to take offence. So generalized, superficial and yet personal comment also leaves the reader ignorant of all but the most irrelevant.

Analysis is further complicated by the tendency of some to present contradictory images in different sections of a book or even within the same paragraph. Sometimes odd words or phrases disfigure what otherwise was a respectable text. Quotation out of context may give an unfair impression of the overall tone of a book. The main concern has been to examine trends over time. In the books selected for appraisal each decade is well represented after the 1880s, except for the 1940s when war disrupted publication. It is noticeable that the 1930s was a particularly active period for publications on Africa although most books were not confined just to that continent, even though regionally specific books appeared in the 1920s. In their attempts to cover a wider world, often literally 'The World', they gave little scope for a fair synthesis of the small part that is South Africa. The picture they represented evolves, but not in a strictly sequential way, for the individuality of authorship disturbs any easy chronological account.

One interesting change that can be plotted on a time graph is the use of names for peoples. If an image is in a name then choice of that name is important. Some names were not previously considered to convey the offence that is now recognized. The textbooks appear to have avoided the word 'nigger'. When the child went home from school to the story books and comics it was there in print – in the Rider Haggard novels, the Jack Harkaway serials and the first comics.[44] The word 'savage' has been avoided by all but one geography author since the 1890s, which is perhaps surprising since a figure as well known as Gordon Childe, the anthropologist, still used it in 1954 to describe Palaeolithic man and those he saw as their modern counterparts.[45] The one geography author who used it incorporated it in his title, in a junior school book that began life in 1911 and went on to its sixth edition in 1932, suggesting an unfortunate popularity and a lengthy malevolent influence upon those of impressionable age reading their *First Book of Geography*.[46]

The word 'kaffir', originating as a name for peoples on the eastern frontier, has had a longer life than it should have, lingering on in a 1970s book in the guise of 'kaffir corn' (sorghum).[47] 'Native'(s) appeared rather late but was very popular in the 1930s, continuing in use into modern books.[48] 'Bantu' is ever popular, am ambiguous all-embracing word of harmless origins, meaning people. It has been used by half the authors over the period 1890 to 1975. Its promotion by the South African government made it a word with unfavourable connotations. 'Negro' spans the whole period under review until 1970. The prolific writings of a well-known academic, Dudley Stamp, exemplify its use 'the Negroes are for the most part backward and lazy as well as being frequently quarrelsome'.[49] Typically, having chosen their collective noun, most authors presumed to offer comment upon the appearance, character, temperament and intellect of Africans. At last 'African' was used. It made an interesting first appearance in 1935 but became popular only after 1950. It was a safer, less prejudicial term, but not without its own ambiguities in respect of white residents with a long ancestry on the continent.

The origins of the people classified by such names led authors into further distortions. In doing so they have often helped in what Laurence has described as 'South Africa's selling of a mostly fictitious version of its racial history'.[50] He relates this to the basic historical deception that promotes the idea of white and black arriving in the south of the continent at the same time, a presumption which can then be tied to a justification of apartheid's land distribution policy. The promotion campaign had its effect for books in school use in the 1970s gave this version of history.[51] Statements echoing Afrikaner history have included: 'Zulus at that time advancing from the north';[52] 'thinly peopled by negro hunter herdsmen, of Bantu stock, who were only just moving down this way themselves';[53] 'While the Europeans had been expanding from around the Cape another group of people were moving into southern Africa from the North'.[54]

Differing approaches to presentation of people as a work force illustrate further facets of the textbook as image former. The labour force has a highly controversial place in South Africa's history and economic and social life. Geography books have been particularly concerned with economic production. The black labour force was often written of simply in employers' terms which in South Africa meant neat racial divisions. Examples include: 'mostly natives employed, cheap labour is an advantage';[55] 'use cheap native labour';[56] 'Their wages are rather high'.[57] Some acknowledged why they were seeking work, most notoriously to pay tax imposed on huts.[58] These authors were amongst an interesting group who were highly critical in their observations of a racially based economy at an early date. Even in 1917 Wallis wrote that men were herded together inside compounds 'and have little freedom'.[59] Change was envisaged in 1922, 'Soon the black man, instead of being slave to the white will be his fellow worker'.[60] By the 1930s condemnation was forthright: 'it is wrong to treat him as a mere pawn . . . The native is South Africa's cheap drudge'.[61]

It is of particular significance to appraise how the mine labour force was presented for nearly every geography book at all levels mentions gold and diamond mining. There is the practice of housing workers (always blacks) in compounds to explain, or ignore. Detail, stress and choice of words again become critical as measures of racial imagery. The compounds, first established in 1887, set the dilemma of straight reporting versus persuasive comment. Some chose a dull informational approach merely announcing that labourers are housed in compounds. Most recognized that a British child would have little idea of what this meant so they tried to describe, often using analogy. In this way compounds became compared to anything from a holiday camp to a prison. Between 1917 and 1972 the following images were offered: 'surrounded by corrugated iron fences'; 'enclosure'; 'necessary precaution against theft'; 'small towns'; 'villages'; 'great camps'; 'special housing'; 'barracks'; 'hostels'. Inside the compound it was the facilities: 'food and medicine'; and fun: 'open spaces for dancing' that were given emphasis. Only in books from the 1970s has sufficient information been given to enable children to form their own opinion. Wicks, in 1973, started his chapter: 'As the door of the pit-head closed . . . Edward Kawinga began to wish he had never left his village'.[62] At last the detail raised some of the human problems which by 1980 could also be vividly portrayed in the colour photographs of Mack's *Zulu*.[63]

Nineteenth-century authors found nothing worthy of comment about the social and political treatment of black people. More surprisingly Heaton, in 1908, alerted readers to the problem that was to dominate the century ahead:

> The problem before South Africa lies not in her climate or her resources but in the wise government of so heterogeneous a population . . . The Kaffir is perhaps the greatest problem to the white ruler . . . he claims the firm and patient rule of his British superiors.[64]

From then on some aspect of white policy and practice is mentioned and commented upon by 60 per cent of the writers.

The 1913 Land Act was a major policy decision and from 1910 it was no longer a British colony that was being described but in 1917 Wallis only saw 'the native races' as 'the chief problem . . . great stretches of country have been set aside for their sole use'.[65] It was 1925 before a realistic view was offered:

> there is a distinct problem to be faced in the development of Africa. Its solution will depend upon an intelligent and sympathetic understanding of the native peoples by the whites and a gradual spread of education, so that the black man may learn how he may develop his lands for the lasting benefit of himself and the world in general.[66]

Such a view must have challenged a few orthodoxies of the time. Thurston also put a very pertinent question to his pupils:

> What are (a) the advantages, and (b) the disadvantages to Britain of her large possessions in Africa? To what extent is a white people justified in holding the lands of the blackman?[67]

This was questioning ahead of its time. Unfortunately no known pupils' responses survive. It was the 1930s before several authors joined in the debate. Ten of nineteen examined in that decade gave the issues fair mention, but often with vigorously opposed views. Farrar and Matheson, having described the unequal distribution of land perceptively commented:

> South Africa is the laboratory in which the problem is being worked out and upon the solution which is reached will depend the future peace of the world.[68]

In the same year, 1931, Laborde was unequivocal in his racism:

> The blacks thrive under European rule, but they have not yet taken in civilisation. This is partly because they have not enough intelligence . . .

But there is danger in allowing the black man to have power in a land of superior people.[69]

Western expressed the problem more calmly in 1933:

With increasing education and understanding of the situation the natives are not unnaturally demanding political rights.[70]

He asked his child readers to: 'Suggest ways in which the "Black problem" of the Union of South Africa might be solved'.[71]

Alnwick in 1936 took an uncompromising position with bold statements on attitudes and practice: 'The less intelligent the white man is the more stupid he thinks the black'; 'Blind unpreparedness and pathetic ignorance based on preconceived notions are only suicidal'.[72] His exceptionally vigorous language illustrates that the debate on racism was begun well before its post-war exposure and the 1948 National Government's policy. When Alnwick wrote it was a time of emerging Nazi racism which threw into sharper focus the promotion of ideas of racial supremacy. As one of a concerned group of people in the 1930s Alnwick was challenging the foundations upon which South African society was built and the assumptions of so many of his colleagues. Alnwick's text was still in use in schools in the 1950s.[73] His stance did not deter some post-war authors from returning to more conservative assessments of increasingly contentious developments in the Union of South Africa.

Against a background of formalization of racial policies, a retreat from Empire and large scale emigration from the Commonwealth to England the post-war authors had to convey 'apartheid' South Africa to British pupils. One response was to turn events upside down:

When the native peoples came to the conclusion that the whites had come to stay, several nations came into being and those called Zulus, Basutos . . . found their reservations in the better watered agricultural eastern parts.[74]

In this vein many superficial attempts were made to cope with a situation that was still being interpreted as a reasonable outcome of an historic situation. Explicit racism was rare in books published after 1945, but white domination was still accepted and as recently as 1967 the greater 'success' at development was claimed as sufficient justification.[75]

Some would have argued that it was not the geographers' role to deal with complex political and social situations. Many teachers in the classroom could not see it that way and had to work with books that ignored or trivialized the situation. For some it was clearly a concern because the consequences were of such serious human import – and geography espoused a concern with humanity. Further, the enormous impact of apartheid upon population distributions and economic relationships demanded the attention of a spatially oriented social science. All this would have to be argued forcibly by such as D.M. Smith in the 1970s, showing that some still needed convincing.[76]

In immediate post-war Britain the recurrent issue of sources for teacher and schoolbook writer remained problematic. Standard advanced texts on Africa like Fitzgerald's were revisions of pre-war publications, appearing as new books in the 1950s and reading like the old books they really were. The eighth edition in 1955 contained no reference to 'apartheid', still referred to 'cheap Kaffir labour' and dealt with segregation only as an economic problem.[77] More insidious was the abundant information supplied by the politically motivated South African sources needing to convince a hostile world of the merits of their policies. Propaganda was liable to be absorbed into the schoolbooks. A 1958 text, revised in 1966, assured its readers:

> Nearly half the negroes live in these kraals and the government spends millions on improving them . . . they are so vastly different in standards of civilisation that the needs of the African workers are far fewer than the needs of the European and the African people are able to live comfortably on much lower wages than the European.[78]

Children of the Cape in 1959, having enthused about coloured grape pickers reassured its readers: 'They all have their own native homelands covering vast expanses of land'.[79] These texts were still available on library shelves where they were located for this study in the 1980s.

More subtle examples of apartheid's conceptual base being incorporated into schoolbooks arises when 'temporary African workers in towns' are referred to; when 'self government' for the Transkei is claimed and when 'the shelter of Native Reserves' projects a comfortable image of segregated areas. Compliance with the terminology of apartheid remains a problem in British texts. The territorially segregated areas of South Africa, one of the great pillars of the racially divided society, continue to trap authors into collusion with their inventors via the much publicized titles. The 'Native Reserves' evolved into 'Bantustans', then 'Homelands' and more recently 'National States'. Acceptance of such titles may imply acceptance of the reasoning behind them and children could easily absorb the comfortable insinuation of a label such as 'Homelands'. The dilemma is apparent even in 1990 publications of merit in all their essentials regarding a balanced African geography.

A constituent part of any schoolbook has long been its pictures. Geography's emphasis on place lends itself to this medium of expression. They were used in the earliest of the books such as the Bankes volume, but early schoolbooks could not afford them. When they did come to be placed alongside the text they often did more harm than good as has been shown by Wright.[80] Given the strong visual imagery and its selective slant on a subject, the photographs used often reinforced undesirable aspects of their subject. At times they contradicted otherwise reasonable texts when we apply the racial litmus test. The many photographs of Zulu warriors accompanying the section on gold mining caught the childs' eye and probably stayed in the memory longer than facts about the tough life of a miner in the hottest of the world's mines. The temptation was always to illustrate the exotic. One example serves to reinforce the point. A successful author who had travelled in South Africa was Stembridge.[81] This enabled him to include his own photographs in his seventeen pages on the Union. Three of the eleven well-produced large pictures were his, the rest from South African Railways. People were prominent in four of the photographs of which three were quite acceptable images of Africans at work – grape-picking, gold mining and herding – a reasonable balance for the time. The fourth showed 'A Ricksha Runner in Durban' dressed in very fancy costume with a headress, no doubt a successful lure to his customers. It would also lure the eye of the readers. It is a good photograph which Stembridge was obviously proud of but however 'factual' it was it surely exaggerated the image of Zulu warrior Africa.

The books published since 1948 have given increasing attention to the issues of apartheid. Of the thirty-seven books examined with this research in mind four could be considered to have taken a pro-apartheid stance and six a firmly anti position. The majority endeavoured to adopt a degree of neutrality although it is often clear enough where the sympathies of the author lies. British authors and teachers mostly like to avoid bias as educators. This at times produces a studied neutrality which may be quite sterile in its impact. Jones, reflecting upon guidelines to teachers on the subject, asserts: 'no teacher can be neutral towards those values which underpin genuine liberal democracy'.[82] Perhaps too many have distorted the democratic ideal in their search for a neutral position on racism. When a teacher/author wrote in 1911 about the 'south African colonies . . . their attractiveness to English people is diminished by acute racial problems which have nothing to do with geography',[83] he denied an essential factor in explaining spatial patterns crucial to his subject. He also dismissed an opportunity to engage his pupils in thoughts critical to their development as citizens. Fifty years later there was not much to excite debate or thought in 'The government considers that different racial groups should be separated so that each group can follow its own way of life. This policy is called apartheid'.[84] The modern books like Hickman's[85] offer a wide range of points for discussion. They follow in a tradition that has its origins in the era of Empire. Searson and Evans were being as provocative as any modern liberal when they wrote in 1937:

> Perhaps the black people of South Africa will not always let the white people keep so large a share of the land. Perhaps they will not always agree to only do the unskilled work, to shop only in their own shops and to have a position that is poorer in every way than that of the white man.[86]

Such sentiments would have found little favour with their contemporaries, Bunting and Collen, whose view was of 'Zulus . . . under orderly rule of the British they prosper greatly'.[87] The minority who put the more challenging view must surely have edged us towards the more questioning attitudes of today.

South Africa may just be moving into a more hopeful phase in its race relationships. As the white government struggles to come to terms with the realities of admitting those other than themselves into a national political system it should make the textbook writers task easier. The responsibilities will still be there to represent fairly the complexities of a racially mixed society with many minority groups whose abuse because of some mythical racial traits is always to be guarded against.

The books reviewed here are mostly lost in the past, only dug into by the curious for purposes such as this one. However, many of those who were offered them to read when young are still alive in the present. Prejudices still held could have been gained or reinforced from some of the sources quoted. Greater awareness and care characterizes modern books on Africa. Their faults, when they occur, are less likely to be those of overt racism, more those of misjudgement of sensitivities. We surely owe it to the people of Africa, of all shades of skin colour, to ensure that the offensive comments of the past are never again repeated.

4 The Irish and others in Irish nineteenth-century textbooks

John Coolahan

With the Tudor conquest of the late sixteenth century Ireland became the nearest external English colony and, in ways characteristic of colonized countries, the customs, language, dress and general culture of the inhabitants appalled and, at times, fascinated the colonizers. Expanding, colonizing states usually adopted attitudes of conscious superiority towards other peoples in their path whom they aimed to conquer. Ireland fell into the general pattern of English colonial expansion. As D.B. Quinn remarked:

> The earliest stages of contact between Englishmen and non-English cultures were likely to be governed by the desire to define and limit their inferiority (or non-Englishness) and to find ways of forcing them into a new English pattern, reforming them or obliterating them.[1]

Of the Elizabethans, Quinn commented:

> Most of them wanted to know about Irishmen in order to learn how to turn them into Englishmen. Some of them recorded Irish culture traits in order to have a precise conception of what to destroy, others to have material for satire.[2]

He goes on to state, 'The use of the Irish as the standard of savage or outlandish reference was well established by 1560 ... It was to last until late in the seventeenth century'.[3]

Through various mechanisms, over the centuries, such as conquest of land, legislation, suppression of rights and evangelization, England endeavoured, unsuccessfully, to secure Ireland as a biddable, politically socialized colony on its Western periphery. Following the Act of Union of Great Britain and Ireland in 1800 efforts were made to foster and promote a cultural assimilation policy. Efforts were made to cultivate a sense of allegiance, a bond of solidarity between the allegedly fractious Irish and the imperial motherland. The use of a state-aided and organized national school system established in 1831 was to be a key agency in this policy.

Through a nominated Board of Commissioners the State exercised very significant powers in controlling this new primary school system. They set out the detailed rules and regulations which had to be fulfilled as a condition of state aid. Teacher training was under the Commissioners' control and the work of teachers was monitored closely by a highly structured school inspectorate. It was intended that one outcome of the new system would be to oust the indigenous 'hedge school' system in which it was alleged teachers and the books employed were sources of political subversion. Teachers of the new national school system were to be above suspicion in this regard. The school curriculum was a central area of concern and it was now firmly taken into the control of the State. One consequence of this was the exclusion of the Irish language and Irish history and tradition from the school programme.[4]

In the nineteenth century textbooks were the central mediators of the curriculum. The textbooks incorporated the curricular content. Pedagogical practice of the time greatly emphasized the centrality of the textbooks, with mastery of their content the key goal. Accordingly, the Board of Commissioners issued a range of textbooks very quickly after their establishment. These books were made available at subsidized prices to schools and the work of the schools was based predominately on them. A study of the content of the class reading books reveals a good deal about the values and attitudes which the State intended to promote among the teachers and pupils.

Textbooks emphasized clearly the close bonds which were held to exist between Britain and Ireland as the centre of the mighty British Empire. Short extracts such as the following convey the flavour of the content.[5] The *Third Reading Book* stated 'Great Britain and Ireland formed the most powerful kingdom in the world',[6] while the *Second Reading Book* stressed, 'On the East of Ireland is England, where the queen lives, many people who live in Ireland were born in England, and we speak the same language and are called one nation'.[7] There were two main corollaries to this emphasis on cultural affinity and unity of political, legal and administrative framework. One was the de-emphasis on separate linguistic, cultural and religious identity. For the first four decades of the national school system, 1831 to 1871, the school textbooks were largely devoid of material focusing on Ireland, its distinctive heritage, landscape and traditions.[8]

The planned omission of material relating to the Irish cultural heritage and environment may have been aimed at fostering a *déraciné* outlook among the pupils. On the one hand, it encouraged an attitude that the Irish experience or hinterland was not important and that it must have had little to distinguish it. Certainly, if the pupils were to have an informed awareness of their cultural roots it would not come from the school system. It is hard to calculate how potent this may have been in forming children's self-image. It may have tended to undermine the confidence which can come from being educated through curricular content which can be seen to be rooted in one's environment, experience and local tradition. However, the extra-mural dimension of a very vibrant folk culture in these decades is testified to in a wide range of contemporary literature. The lack of a school 'canonization' of such culture was an impediment, but not perhaps, a decisive factor in the children's sense of belonging and of being rooted in the rich folk culture of the non-school environment. The degree to which the schools succeeded in promoting a sense of 'Englishness' among school pupils may also have been less than impressive. The counter-thrust of popular public opinion in the homes, villages, work places and leisure activities outside of school was probably a more potent force. The feeling of disappointment at the effects of the Act of Union and the efforts to get it repealed formed strong currents of anti-English popular opinion in these decades. The miseries and tragedies of the great famine years of the 1840s tended to deepen the popular view that the English were uncaring at best, if not contributors to the ravages being suffered by the people.

Another outcome of the cultural assimilation policy was the exclusion of material which might depict the Irish in a racialist, stereotypic way. The Irish or their habits were not tarnished by the image of the savage, the outlandish, the crude or the backward in the textbooks. Obviously, if one was empha- sizing the closeness of the cultural ties and affinities with the imperial motherland this would be inappropriate, as it would reflect unfavourably also on the 'motherland'. This is not to say that the racial stereotype of the Irish was forgotten or dead. Rather it continued to appear in many popular newspapers, magazines, pamphlet literature and political cartoons. As Lebow's study, *White Britain and Black Ireland* states:

> Their [*The Times*' Correspondents] periodic reports portrayed the Irish peasant as ignorant, indolent, scheming and totally irrational and explained the poverty in terms of these characteristics.[9]

Similar views were contained in many other newspapers and magazines, *Punch* being particularly astringent. The following summarizes Lebow's analysis of the *Punch* approach:

> According to *Punch*, Irishmen were by their very nature the laziest and dirtiest people in all Europe, if not the entire world. Irishmen were 'the sons and daughters of generations of beggars. You can trace the descent in their blighted, stunted forms – in their brassy, cunning, brutalized features'. Their huts, 'Mr. Punch' insisted were 'monuments to national idleness', while the Irish themselves, he theorized, were 'the missing link between the gorilla and the negro'.[10]

Such assertions were part of the stock in trade of imperial establishments who denigrated colonized people so as to rationalize their treatment of them and to undermine the self-image and cultural identity of such peoples. These attitudes towards the Irish within the establishment in Britain were highly influential in the colonial policy of the nineteenth century. The magazines popularized the image. However, the school textbooks are devoid of this type of racial denigration and stereotyping. Thus, in the early period of the textbook publications of the Commissioners of National Education, the textbooks reflect nothing of the spirit of the contemporary articles and cartoons which depicted, for example, the Irish leader Daniel O'Connell as a monster, a beggarman, a loud-mouthed buffoon at the head of a rabble of irrational rustics. The

fact that O'Connell was a highly skilled lawyer, an innovative parliament-
arian, and a pioneer in the deployment of democratic, peaceful mass movements
in seeking political goals did not fit easily with the stereotype for the
cartoonists' pen.[11] Lebow's study of this period concludes:

> British organs of public opinion, the broadside and pamphlet literature and
> the statements of leading political figures abounded in virulent invective
> directed against Daniel O'Connell. The fury of these attacks rose in
> proportion to the success of the Repeal Movement in Ireland.[12]

On the other hand, O'Connell's mass meetings and newspapers such as *The
Nation* articulated the great sense of grievance felt by the colonized Irish and
targeted British misrule as a key source of their misfortunes. The more sober
material in the school textbooks was unlikely to outweigh in influence the
general consensus of attitude encountered by the young at the firesides, on
the hillsides, or in the marketplace. A strongly held perception of injustice
and a rejection of the inferior badge of the colonial stereotype were key factors
in the on-going resentment of the Irish to British rule, which resentment, in
the long run was to triumph in overthrowing this rule and breaking the Act
of Union.

A racialist view of the Irish and their intractible failure to accept what
English rulers thought fit for them was never far below the surface in the
press and pamphlet media. It became particularly pronounced in the post-1870
period, linked to land agitation and Parnellism. Again, the fact that Parnell
used the British parliamentary system with such skill, and contributed so much
to its evolution[13] did not sit happily with traditional images which preferred
to view the Irish demands for land reform and Home Rule legislation as
fundamentally subversive and irrational, hatched in a climate of crime and
deceit. Of course, the Irish were by no means unique in attracting racialist
propaganda, it was a significant feature of nineteenth-century attitudes towards
subject peoples. However, the intensity could be quite severe as in the writings
of J.A. Froude and the sustained ape-like representations of the Irish in the
cartoons of *Punch* and other publications.[14]

Writing about the nineteenth-century European racialist attitudes, L.P. Curtis
remarked in *Apes and Angels*:

> Virtually every country in Europe had its equivalent of 'white negros' and
> simianized men, whether or not they happened to be stereotypes of criminals,
> assassins, political radicals, revolutionaries, Slavs, Jews, gypsies or
> peasants.

He went on to point out that in the case of Britain, the 'white negros' were
the Irish:

> The widespread belief in Victorian Britain that Englishmen and Irishmen
> were separated by clearcut ethnic or racial as well as religious and cultural
> barriers was reinforced continually by political events in both countries . . .

Nothing fed the Victorian stereotype of the wild, melancholic, violent and feckless Irish celt more dramatically than the economic stagnation and political and social unrest which English tourists and officials found in Ireland.[15]

The school textbooks, however, did not contain any of the overt racialist images of the Irish contained in the popular press, nor can they be accused of more subtle racialist reflections. It would be unlikely that the textbooks could have been so successful in their circulation and usage if they did. The compilers resisted any pressures or latent inclinations to portray the Irish in other than a positive or realistic light. For instance, the *Fourth Reading Book* (1861)[16] defined the People of Ireland as

a clever, lively people; formerly very much given to drink, and very ignorant: but now it is believed that they are one of the soberest nations of Europe: and it will be their own fault if they are not also one of the best educated.[17]

However, usually no reference is made to their qualities. Describing the island of Ireland, the writer stated: 'And a beautiful land it is: well watered with rivers and lakes – adorned with many lofty mountains, green pastures, and good land for corn'.[18] The problem lay in the paucity of material relating to Ireland, rather than prejudiced attitudes expressed towards it or the Irish.

However, such restraint was not as evident in the references to other countries and their inhabitants, towards which racialist stereotyping and imperialist attitudes could have more free rein. About the Laplanders, the pupils were informed:

[They] are extremely ignorant, as might be supposed, from their wandering mode of life. They have no schools, and very few churches. In disposition they are quiet and harmless, but cowardly, indolent and extremely dirty in their habits.[19]

The nomadic character of their life is equated with backwardness and regarded as inhibitory to the establishment of schools and churches, symbols of true civilization. Unsurprisingly, no empathic effort is made to understand their patterns of enculturation or the complex skills and traditions which the Laplanders needed to evolve so as to cope with life in their unpropitious surroundings. It is not clear if the author(s) had more direct knowledge of the Icelandic way of life but a much more favourable attitude is in evidence towards the Icelanders!

They are peaceable and regular in their habits, and in general very well educated. The instruction of his children is one of the chief employments of an Icelander. During the long winter evenings when all without is dark and cold, the father reads aloud to his family assembled around the coffee table.[20]

The image of the family gathered together indoors, with the long, dark, cold winter nights excluded has a touch of atmosphere attached to it, but the 'coffee table' image may not be the most apt.

In many of the lessons on other peoples the wandering, nomadic character of life is seen as a significant impediment to civilized living. Shifting from the Northern climes to South America, pupils read:

> The lower parts of South America are inhabited by different races, generally becoming more and more barbarian as we approach the highest latitudes. The Patagonians .. are a very tall and large-boned ... extremely ugly in person, and of a reddish copper-coloured complexion. They live partly by hunting and partly upon wild roots.[21]

The inhabitants of the southern extremities of South America were represented in the following extreme terms, 'a set of savages, hideous in person, and so degraded, that they are said to be even below the New Hollanders in their habits of life'.[22]

The American Indians were not denigrated, but it was remarked, 'the wandering, unsettled life of the greater number is a great hindrance to their civilisation'.[23]

The view of life in Australia was very revealing of attitudes in the mid-nineteenth century. The lives, habits and culture of the original inhabitants, unaffected by colonial settlement were depicted as rude, barbaric and backward. Life in the settled areas was seen in a different light whereby the benign influences of schools, churches and structured systems were extolled. The 'natives of Australia' were described as follows: '[They] are either black or copper-coloured, very thin, with long straight hair and extremely ugly features. They are among the lowest and most ignorant savages in the world'. Their form of clothing and wandering way of life merited special notice

> They wear no clothes, except a cloak of the skin of the possum, which they throw over their shoulders in cold or wet weather, and tie around the neck ... They sleep in rude huts formed of the bark of trees, never remaining in one place but wandering about together in companies, resting whenever they can find food.

As was typical of such nineteenth-century portrayals, the religious practices of such people were denigrated: 'They have the same sort of gross and absurd superstitions as are common to other savage nations; and many, if not most of the tribes, are cannibals, or eaters of human flesh'. They are described as 'more like brutes than men'. The question was then posed, 'What makes the diffference between any of us Europeans and those poor savages?' The self-righteous conclusion is reached: 'Evidently it is education'.[24] No trace of the Rousseauistic notion of the 'noble savage' or the corruptions of 'civilized' society *vis-à-vis* the so-called more natural life style of man in a state of nature appears in these pages to temper the sense of superiority of European civilization and colonizing life.

In contrast to life among the original inhabitants of Australia the textbooks extol the benefits of life in colonized New South Wales. Again, schooling and formal education are seen as the key with the added and interesting feature that the very same books were in use in the schools there as in Ireland. At a time when the advantages of emigration were being promoted, pupils were advised:

> If you want to emigrate with your parents to any of these settlements, you would find schools there quite as good as our own; and, in fact, the very same books are used in them that you are now reading, for large supplies of the Irish National School Books are constantly sent for by the colonial authorities, and by the clergy of all denominations who are co-operating with them in promoting popular education.[25]

The process of colonization and spreading civilization was now regarded as well afoot in Australia with schools and Christianity the bulwarks of the campaign:

> And in Sydney, Melbourne, Adelaide, and other large towns, there are excellent academies and collegiate institutions for the education of the children of the higher classes of settlers. We may therefore hope, that at no very distant day, civilization and Christianity will be extended, not only round the coast, but also into the very heart of this immense country.[26]

The people of New Zealand were also represented as having benefited greatly from being 'discovered', colonized and civilized. Their earlier state is contrasted to their later much more favourable status: 'When first discovered, they were savage, and reputed to be cannibals, but have utterly proved more capable of adopting civilized habits than any other people of Australia.'[27]

The theme of geographical exploration and 'discovery' also featured in lessons on Africa, although we are reminded of how limited the exploration was by the 1830s and 1840s. The strong trumpet of imperial exploration and exploitation sounds in the following extract from an 1834 textbook:

> From the foot of the Pillars of Hercules, it [British Empire] carries dread into the remotest provinces of Morocco . . . from this new focus of action and of conquest; it casts its eyes towards India: it discovers, it seizes the stations of most importance to its commercial progress. Finally . . . the British Empire, possessor of the finest countries, the earth, beholds its factors reign over eighty millions of subjects.[28]

A textbook of the early 1840s reminds us of how little Africa had been explored: 'Africa is the barren region of the earth both as respects the nature of the soil, and the moral condition of its inhabitants'.[29] However, the developing exploration of Africa, it was confidently asserted, would allow scope for twin goals of imperialism – commerical exploitation and

'christianizing'. . . . 'it [Africa] will present new scenes and objects of commercial enterprise, and it is certain that it will open an almost unbounded
field for Christian philanthropy and missionary zeal.'[30] Christianity was
regarded as a great civilizing force as, for instance, in Tahiti, 'Tahiti, the
largest of the Society Isles, is now a Christian country, and there are many
others from which idolatory has been almost entirely banished'.[31]

Little emphasis was placed on the colour of the skin of native Africans,
although the Hottentots attracted racialist epithets, 'They are short, stunted,
ugly, with yellow skins and wooly hair'.[32] The Papuan people of New
Guinea and the Fiji Islands also attracted such epithets:

> They are men of immense stature, with wooly or cropped hair, black
> complexion, and those peculiar features which belong to the negro race.
> But they are far from possessing the gentleness for which many tribes of
> African negros are remarkable; their ferocity and dislike to strangers are
> so great that many Europeans who have landed on their coasts have been
> cruelly murdered.[33]

The texts do not carry the treatment of physiognomical features at all as far
as many of the nineteenth-century theoreticians in this field who laid great
emphasis on the relationship between types of physiognomy and racial forms
of behaviour and temperament and character.

A major Commission of Inquiry into primary education (Powis Commission) was intitiated in 1868 and reported in 1870. The textbooks in use came
under criticism for their non-national content, and for their difficulty in
vocabulary, but not for any racialist content. The introduction of a payment
by results policy for primary schools in 1872 also contributed to the need
for a general revision of the textbooks. The outcome was a more satisfactory
sequential grading of the books as regards vocabulary, less overt utilitarian
material and an increased amount of material focused on topics of a specifically
Irish interest. This was a significant change and would tend to project a more
positive image of Ireland and its culture than formerly. It also coincided with
the beginnings of a cultural nationalist movement. A striking change in textbook
content was the dropping of material relating to countries other than England
or Ireland. This was also significant and it is not clear why the shift of policy
was so comprehensive. Allowing for the shortening, simplification and
'nationalizing' of the textbook content it would seem a bit extreme to drop
all material relating to other countries and peoples.

The reading books in the last three decades of the nineteenth century were,
thus, very different from those of the decades prior to 1870. The absence
of material on other countries, peoples and cultures had the advantage that
the strongly stereotypical, racialist, social Darwinist emphases so evident in
the late nineteenth century did not penetrate the content of textbooks during
these decades. A disadvantage was that the absence of geographical data on
other countries, if it could have been fairly objectively presented, meant that
many young Irish people whose futures lay in emigration were denied

potentially useful knowledge of countries such as the United States, South America, Canada, Australia and New Zealand where many of them would earn a livelihood and set up a home.

It was also in these decades that the large-scale missionary movement from Ireland to Africa and other continents was gathering momentum.[34] However, there was nothing in their schoolbooks to give young Irish people an advanced orientation towards their fields of future activity. On the other hand, they may have benefited from avoiding material that was likely to be colonial, racialist and dismissive of local cultures and traditions. Perhaps, their 'white man's burden' may have been somewhat lightened by less encumberment than they might otherwise have had from textbooks emanating from a mind-set which saw European civilization and religion as pre-eminent, and which displayed no empathic feel for or understanding of cultures or different religious practices. It was not likely that textbook material if it had been included, would have shown much social anthropological insight.

During the period 1831 to 1871 when the textbooks had included material on foreign countries, aspects of racialism can be detected. However, except in the case of the Aborigines and the South Americans it was not of a rabid, racialist character. Little emphasis was placed on skin colour as a determinant of civilized status. Certainly, the denigration of 'Negroes' did not occur as intensely as in textbooks in some other countries. It is also the case that while the term 'ugly' is used frequently in relation to the features of various peoples, little emphasis is placed on the size of their craniums or other physical features which are sometimes found in more stridently racialist descriptions. It is mainly the strangeness of remote peoples such as the Laplanders, the Patagonians and the Aborigines that receive attention. Their wandering life styles are seen as particularly unsatisfactory to a set view of civilized living. The customs, clothes, and habits of such peoples are regarded as very 'non-standard'. When presumptions about cannibalism are made, then man is regarded as close to the state of the beast.

Such peoples, however, are capable of being retrieved. Through the good offices of the colonial administrations they, too, can become 'somewhat like us'. The bringing of schools and Christianity to such regions was regarded as an unquestionable boon and as an automatic duty. The fact that these regions could 'present new scenes and objects for commercial enterprise' was regarded as a legitimate quid pro quo for the European's efforts on behalf of the uncivilized.

The values and attitudes of the material in the Irish school texts of the mid-nineteenth century were reflective of a broadly accepted European view of the world which was being further explored and 'discovered'. The Eurocentric cultural assumptions were deeply ingrained in the *Weltanschauung* of the heyday of European imperialism. As an 1843 *Reading Book* put it:

So far as we can read the future designs of providence for the present aspects of affairs, it is from the nations of Europe, that all great efforts to enlighten the nations which still dwell in darkness, and in the region of the shadow of death, must proceed.[35]

However, the emphasis in the textbooks is more of the wonder about and misunderstanding of far-off, exotic cultures than it is of zenophobic and intolerant racialism. Furthermore, the emphasis was on the remediation of allegedly culturally impoverished people rather than the more truly racialist sterotype of races having inherently different degrees of genius 'which are seldom known to change'. It was this more idealistic view which was to inspire the Irish missionary movement later to bring Christianity and formal education to many countries far afield without an accompanying commercial exploitation. Perhaps Ireland's 'spiritual empire' became more enlightened over time due to its own colonial experience and from its long experience of being on the receiving end of aspects of colonial racialism.

5 Race, empire and the Maori in the New Zealand primary school curriculum 1880–1940

Colin McGeorge

From the 1890s until the syllabus was extensively revised in the 1940s, New Zealand primary school texts employed the concept of race to explain the growth and glories of the British Empire and New Zealand's unique place in that empire. By the 1940s, however, the imperial ideology had been tempered in the textbooks and had disappeared altogether from the *School Journal*; and the patriotic observances of the 1920s had withered away in many schools and become perfunctory in others. With the merging of history and geography into social studies in the late 1940s, the history texts in use since 1929 were dropped and along with them the exemplary deaths of Nelson and Wolfe and a long list of 'fights for the flag.

The syllabus revision of the 1940s was not, however, a complete break with the past; the treatment of the Maori and the New Zealand wars in subsequent social studies syllabuses, for example, simply repeated themes developed in Edwardian texts to incorporate New Zealand's history into a seamless account of the cultural and military superiority of the 'British race'.

New Zealand's first national primary school curriculum, gazetted in 1878, drew heavily on British codes of instruction and the list of approved texts consisted almost entirely of standard British works such as Colenso's and Barnard Smith's arithmetics, Cornwell's geographies, and Nelson's *Royal Readers*. Texts used in the 1870s and 1880s did not make much of Empire: Collier's widely used *History of the British Empire*, for example, was a standard history of Britain with the colonies and dependencies relegated to a five page appendix.[1]

MacKenzie describes a marked change in the method and tone of British history texts in Britain in the 1890s, attributable very largely to J.R. Seeley's conception of the moral and didactic purposes of history.[2] In New Zealand the newer approach to history was manifest in locally produced texts as well as in British works.

Only a few local texts were produced in the 1870s and 1880s, mostly 'capes and bays' geographies and outline histories in response to the slight and often inaccurate treatment of New Zealand in British works. In the 1890s, however, New Zealand publishers, most notably the Christchurch firm of Whitcombe and Tombs, began producing a wide range of texts tailored to revised local syllabuses and often splashed with legends like 'Specially prepared for the New Zealand code' or 'Approved by the Minister of Education for use in New Zealand schools'. By 1905, although many schools still used British texts for some subjects, it was possible to cover the entire curriculum with local works.

As Sinclair points out, when there was a revival of imperialism in Britain in the nineteenth century, some New Zealanders took up the imperial chorus with practised voices, having long hankered for an empire in the Pacific while fretting over the defence of their lonely islands and dreaming of imperial federation to ensure trade, security and a suitable measure of colonial autonomy.[3] Textbook writers took up that chorus with clear, confident voices and so, in due course, did the compilers of the monthly New Zealand *School Journal*, established in 1907.

Much of what texts and the *School Journal* had to say was, no doubt, standard fare in other white dominions. The Empire itself was a 'Good Thing': 'It is no ideal boast to say that British rule has made the world a better place to live in'.[4] British history was the story of long struggle to preserve ancient freedoms and of the clearer and clearer manifestation of the British passion for liberty and justice. With the growth of the Empire, these principles had been exported to the world's great advantage. 'We call the Union Jack "the flag of the brave and free" because we are always ready to defend the weak and all are free in the lands over which we rule.'[5] Weaker races could count themselves lucky to be under British rule.

> But perhaps the strongest reason for the maintenance of the Empire is the influence for good that it may exercise over the whole world. Britain is at the head of the most progressive and most just of modern nations. It is, therefore, fitting that she should guide and control the destiny of new and infant countries; to her and to no other should be committed the fate of the lower races of mankind, who are, many of them, engaged in an unequal struggle for very life with powers whose rule is not so merciful.[6]

The Empire had been established by stern struggle and school books dealt with a long list of battles and individual acts of British heroism. A New Zealand MP, at school at the turn of the century, recalled that:

> We once believed the fighting British soldier and the ships of the British navy to be able to face odds of any size. Our school books were full of the exploits of Drake and Collingwood and Nelson. We were mentally nourished on deeds that won the Empire, we read of the thin Red Line in the Crimea, of Wellington in Spain and at the Battle of Waterloo. Our history was of Kings and Captains and Conquests.[7]

While the Empire had been established by British military prowess, it was maintained by the inherent sterling character of the British race. The Dutch, Spanish and Portuguese empires had been opportunist and cruel to their subject populations, but:

We can say of the Englishman that he has a special talent for governing. . . . This talent includes an unrivalled ability to govern subject races, by which is meant the millions of coloured people of various nationalities who live within the Empire but have not a full share or any share at all in government . . . . Certain native races who would probably attack their British masters if they could do so with good hope of success, respect British honour and justice.[8]

Maintaining the Empire was not just the work of Sanders of the River. On one account the British had gained an Empire by going out and getting it, but alongside that was the suggestion that the Empire was a reward for the aggregate morality of the British race and that even childish naughtiness in the Pacific detracted from the total amount in credit. As a Navy League lecturer explained in the *School Journal*, 'every man and woman, every boy and girl, who does his or her duty in the peaceful walks of life is helping to build up the Empire'.[9]

Boys in primary school learnt that they might be called upon to fight in the Empire's wars but, in the meantime, Lord Meath told the children of New Zealand in an Empire Day message that both boys and girls should display faith, courage, self-discipline and a sense of duty 'to aid in elevating the British character, strengthening the British Empire and consolidating the British race'.[10]

God had cast down great empires in the past and, 'If the British in their turn become unworthy of Empire, their power also will be taken from them and better men will rule in their stead.'[11] While the Empire endured, however, it seemed that God was with us: early in the Great War the *School Journal* smugly concluded that 'Providence does seem to be on the side of the race that "plays the game" and plays it fairly and squarely in the interests of humanity.'[12]

Sinclair argues that New Zealand imperialism was an expression of an emergent nationalism and not, as some have supposed, evidence of a general absence of national feeling.[13] A similar claim can be made regarding local texts. Seddon's imperialism encompassed fervent protestations of love for the 'dear old country', criticism of British trade and foreign policy when he saw fit, and a wish to extend the bounds of empire by annexing a number of South Pacific islands to New Zealand. Similarly, textbook writers before the Great War made praise of the Empire a means of asserting New Zealand's special character, bright future and, by implication, its claim to a voice in the counsels of Empire by virtue of its special resemblance and loyalty to the Mother country.

The key concept was race. Texts in use in the 1870s and 1880s were clear and consistent in presenting a standard hierarchy of races.

Whites form by far the most important race, for they have the best laws, the greatest amount of learning, and the most excellent knowledge of farming and trade. There are five great races of men and of these the white race is highest.[14]

Here is a white man. This race is at present the most powerful. White men are the best scholars and the best workers. In their lands the people have more peace, more comfort and more freedom than the inhabitants of other lands enjoy.[15]

At the other end of the scale some groups failed on all counts. The sixth *Royal Reader*, for example, noted that the Australian aboriginal 'occupies one of the lowest grades in the scale of humanity'.[16] Tasmanians, Melanesians and Tierra del Fuegans were also on the bottom rung and to one author of a school geography the very humanity of Papuans seemed doubtful: 'Opposite is a picture of an Oriental Negro who is the lowest of all savages, living in trees and more like an animal than a man.'[17]

By the early twentieth century, British geographies used in New Zealand had dropped the 'capes and bays' approach, and in seeking to explain rather than simply catalogue they made much more use of the concepts of race and blood than earlier works. L.W. Lyde, for example, professor of Economic Geography at University College, London, and a busy writer of school texts, noted that the Mongols were generally 'fatalistic, apathetic, sullen and reserved', but he explained the high civilization of ancient Korea and Japanese industrialization by crediting these groups with a strong dash of redeeming Caucasian blood. Portuguese ugliness and intellectual laziness were the result of an infusion of Negro blood; and Papuans 'being essentially Negroes, not Mongols, are naturally on a lower scale than the Malays'.[18]

The stock explanation of racial differences and national character was geographical and climatic. The tropics bred feckless indolence and the frigid zones made life a grim struggle for mere survival, but temperate climates bred vigour, enterprise and forethought. And the location and relief of particular temperate regions or countries produced sub-races; another useful way of distributing praise selectively. Thus Lyde could attribute the virtues of northern Italians, their business habits, literacy and self-control to their Teutonic blood.[19] Naturally, island Britain was ideally suited to produce the highest type of the highest race.

British history was, for New Zealand textbook writers, the history of the development of the British race, shaped and strengthened by geography and history so that an island home, a temperate climate, Magna Carta and the Civil War had all, somehow, left a permanent deposit in the blood and bones as much as in culture and institutions.

On this account, the colony of New Zealand had a short history, but its European settlers had a long one because they were part of the British race. New Zealanders were naturally superior to Asians and Africans because they were white, superior to other Europeans because they were racially British, and because the early settlers had been specially chosen, New Zealanders were 'not only British, but the "best British"'.[20]

No colony was ever so carefully and wisely colonised as New Zealand. To begin with, only men and women of unusual courage and enterprise were willing to cross the world in sailing ships and seek their fortune in so distant a land. For settlements such as those of Canterbury and Otago, colonists were specially selected, and those pioneers, many of whom were well-educated men of unusual ability, left a deep and lasting influence on the history of a young nation.[21]

Furthermore, 'there was never in New Zealand that convict system which brought so much trouble to Australia'.[22]

New Zealand was uniquely beautiful with great natural resources and a magnificent climate.

The scenery of New Zealand too is famous the world over .... A land to be proud of, this Queen of the South in which we live.[23]

Have you ever thought that there are hundreds of thousands of children in the crowded cities of Europe who never see much of the sun, even in summer? These poor creatures live in cellars, or in dark, dirty rooms, among the lanes and narrowest streets of the great cities. One of these children suddenly placed under a New Zealand sky would be filled with amazement. Let us never forget that this glorious sky of ours and the warm life-giving sunshine that scarcely ever fails us are blessings for which we can never be too thankful.[24]

In this favoured land, further virtues had developed in the specially selected pioneer stock so that New Zealanders could take pride in being racially British and also stalwart colonials – resourceful, healthy, independent and egalitarian. After the South African War they could see themselves in 'the men who could ride and shoot' of Kipling's poem 'The Islanders'. New Zealand was British and even the New Zealand-born routinely referred to Britain as 'Home', but New Zealand itself was, in King Dick Seddon's phrase, 'God's Own Country'.

Pride of race and place were neatly combined in the notion that in New Zealand the general merits of the British race and the special virtues of the sons and daughters of pioneers were acting to create a new, better Britain.

This was not a new notion and not confined to New Zealand texts. Cornwell had dubbed New Zealand 'the Britain of the South' in one of his school geographies as early as 1858.[25] Parkin spent two pages of his *Round the Empire* likening New Zealand to Britain; and he concluded, 'As we sail away westward and look back upon New Zealand we feel that this Britain of the South is one of the most beautiful homes that our race has found anywhere in the world.'[26]

Histories and geographies routinely distinguished between the inner circle of white dominions and the rest of the Empire. The family was a convenient metaphor for the special relationship between the self-governing dominions and the Motherland.

The little Mother and her big children we call the Empire, and we keep up Empire Day just as we might keep up mother's birthday in the family, to show that we are still her loving children.[27]

And New Zealand had a special place among that family group for it was the most loyal and most like Britain, racially and geographically. As a local versifier put it, New Zealand on the proclamation of dominion status in 1907 was:

The nearest, because the dearest, with face most like her own of all the Children of Empire, that gather round her throne.[28]

When these temperate islands so much resembled the Mother Country it was easy to conclude that they were 'the appointed home of a white race'.[29] Unfortunately, 'Promised Lands' tend to be inhabited when 'Chosen Peoples' arrive, and the Maori inhabitants of New Zealand had to be fitted into the textbook account of God's Own Country and the glories of the British race.

First, where did Maoris come in the hierarchy of races? This, for writers of nineteenth and early twentieth century texts, was an important question, but not one to which they could give a consistent answer.

According to Patterson, Maoris were 'a Polynesian family of the Malay race'.[30] Mackay listed them as one of seven separate races.[31] Gregory held them to be of Caucasian stock, along with Somalis and aboriginals, but with an infusion of Mongol and Negro blood.[32] One of *Longmans' New Zealand Readers* simply described them as East Polynesians but was careful to distinguish them from 'the darker and inferior Melanesians of the West'.[33] Anderson's geography had them Melanesian along with the original inhabitants of Australia and New Guinea.[34] Thornton listed Maoris under 'yellow' along with Japanese and Lapps in a table setting out the races and sub-races, but in a subsequent footnote he described them as 'probably an Oceanic division of the Caucasic stock.'[35]

But while there was no general agreement on the Maori's place on the racial ladder, there was universal agreement that he was a very superior savage. Maoris were 'the most intelligent of all natives whom the Europeans met with on the Australasian colonies'.[36] They, like other Polynesians, showed 'a greater aptitude for civilization than any other barbarous race'.[37] They were 'savages, it is true, but noble savages'.[38]

Textbooks made an implicit distinction between the 'real Maori' and the brown-skinned citizens of contemporary New Zealand. The former were romantic, cloaked, tattooed warriors, poets and hunters whose carving, agriculture, weaving and poetry set them far above, for example, Australian aboriginals. All in all, Maoris had done so well for savages that their achievements could be compared with those of the British in the remote past. Miss Bourke's *Little History of New Zealand*, published in the 1880s, was the first local text to make this comparison, repeated in a number of later works, and in 1929 it became a required sub-topic in the history syllabus.[39]

Our Nation's Story followed the new syllabus faithfully and devoted a full chapter to the parallels between woad and tattoo, coracles and canoes, druids and tohungas, and the Maori pa and the British hill fort.[40]

The real Maori's part in New Zealand history ended with the last shot of the New Zealand wars and he receded into the past to join the Romans, King Alfred and the Vikings. Contemporary Maoris, to whom much less space was given, were praised for their rapid progress in meeting the new, higher standards of European civilization, for their ready adoption of European dress, religion and commerce.

> We are accustomed to see Maoris sitting at tables with Europeans, talking to them in the street and competing on equal terms in various sports and occupations. The good Maori stands as high as the good pakeha and the bad pakeha sinks as low as the bad Maori.[41]

As European culture was superior in every respect, Maoris could only be grateful for the white settlement of New Zealand. In the second *Imperial Reader* a Maori boy explains that:

> The men of our race sometimes complain because the white people have taken away so much of their land; but I am sure that our teacher is right when he tells us that we have more land left than we can use. He says, too, that the white men have given us peace and order, and a thousand blessings that we could never have enjoyed but for their coming to settle among us.[42]

Given their writers' assumptions, it is hardly surprising that New Zealand textbooks offered a romanticized and misleading account of the New Zealand wars; and Belich's recent study of the wars shows just how misleading and why. Maori military successes simply did not accord with the assumption that British soldiers would automatically triumph over 'savages'. The result, Belich concludes, has been a received history of these wars which is a travesty of Maori military ability. British victories have been exaggerated – created where necessary – and Maori successes have been played down as incidents on the way to European victory.[43] Maori victories have been explained away either by seeking scapegoats among European leaders or by concentrating on the qualities one might expect savages to possess, courage and bushcraft, for example, rather than the discipline, innovative field engineering and tactical flair which, Belich demonstrates, made the modern pa such a tough nut to crack and made so many 'successful' assaults costly or hollow victories.

School histories, selective and simplifying in any case, gave a predictably distorted picture of the wars. The two events most likely to be described in any detail were the battle of Orakau and the pursuit of Te Kooti in the Uraweras and the King Country. James Hight's *Public School Historical Reader for Standard VI*, for example, has one sentence on Rangiriri, where the British suffered heavy losses, but it devotes nearly a page each to Orakau and Te Kooti, nearly one-quarter of his chapter on the wars of the 1860s.[44]

Both Orakau and the scramble through difficult country after Te Kooti, of course, fit the received account of the wars nicely. Orakau pa was ill-sited, without means of supply or tactical withdrawal; the defenders were doomed to defeat by superior numbers and firepower and their quotable defiance and desperate and costly sally were taken to illustrate reckless Maori courage in a hopeless situation. And Te Kooti's ability to give troops the slip in rough country chimed with an emphasis on Maori bushcraft and local knowledge rather than their use of trenches and bunkers in modern pa.

On the received view, the wars had, in fact, done race relations in New Zealand a power of good by leaving each side with a deep respect for the other. The preface to *Our Nation's Story* explicitly linked the wars and good subsequent race relations:

> You will also, if you hear the story aright, feel a warm admiration for the courage and determination of the Maoris against whom we fought in some of the Maori wars. It is because of our great respect for the Maoris that white man and brown man now live side by side as friends and fellow citizens of New Zealand.[45]

To praise Maoris was, of course, to praise white New Zealanders indirectly. While the British Empire treated its subject peoples better than any other colonial power, race relations in New Zealand were a shining example to the rest of the Empire; and white New Zealanders in their dealings with Maoris once again displayed the purity of their heritage, their sense of justice and their characteristically British appreciation of courage and chivalrous conduct in war.

The Victorian interpretation of the New Zealand wars, Belich says, was not the result of a conscious effort to deceive; and the authors of Edwardian school texts, given their assumptions, had to make no special effort to tuck this loose end in neatly.[46] And even if the New Zealand wars had cast lingering doubts on pakeha New Zealanders' natural military prowess, these would have been whirled away in the great wave of bellicose patriotism which swept over the colony during the South African war.

Children were given time off school to cheer departing contingents of troopers and, in due course, to celebrate British victories. When New Zealand adopted the familiar blue ensign as its national flag, Parliament voted £1,500 for flags for schools and flag-saluting became a common part of patriotic ritual in schools. The war gave the primary school cadet movement, which had been languishing, a tremendous fillip. The movement's organization was clarified and strengthened, the government supplied or subsidized uniforms, arms and ammunition and the number of school corps grew rapidly. Cadets shouldering dummy rifles were regularly paraded on patriotic occasions. Thousands of cadets, for example, travelled by train or coastal steamer to Christchurch to take part in a grand military review in 1901 with the Duke of York taking the salute.

After the war, the cadet movement continued to grow under a Comman-
dant of Public School Cadets, appointed to the Department of Education. In
their weekly training sessions and at annual camps, cadets practised marching,
skirmishing and shooting and they heard lectures on military and patriotic
matters.[47]

Perhaps the most widely disseminated instrument of imperialist propaganda,
however, was the *School Journal*, founded in 1907 to provide cheap, uniform
school reading material. It has been estimated that from its first appearance
until the early 1930s, about one third of *Journal* space was devoted to imperial,
military and patriotic matters – inspiring messages from Lord Meath, cabinet
ministers, and visiting British naval officers, biographical pieces on members
of the royal family, articles on the symbolism of the Union Jack and the New
Zealand flag, accounts of battles and British military heroes, especially Nelson,
and poems by Kipling, Newbolt and lesser poets singing the imperial song.[48]

Patriotic organizations, seeing school pupils as important, impressionable
audiences for their particular messages, added their voices to the imperial
chorus in schools. In 1903, for example, in response to Lord Meath's work
on behalf of the League of Empire and at the cabinet's direction, the Inspector-
General issued a circular to schools.

> I have accordingly to suggest that at every school the children shall be
> assembled on the morning of Empire Day, and that they should salute the
> flag. The ceremony may be followed by a short address to the children
> reminding them of the privileges and duties of a citizen of the Empire.
> The remainder of the day should be observed as a holiday. It is possible
> that in some cases the school authorities may see their way, by means of
> lectures, magic lantern representations, music and song to draw the attention
> of the scholars attending their schools to matters of an Imperial and patriotic
> character.[49]

The Navy League was granted ready access to schoolchildren and worked
hard to organize patriotic rituals in schools on Trafalgar Day, to arrange school
visits to British warships in New Zealand ports, and to distribute its special
map of the Empire.

A number of patriotic organizations also offered essay prizes and some
New Zealand writers gained their first guineas thereby. In 1913, for example,
Ngaio Marsh, later well known for her detective novels, won a Victoria League
essay prize for her account of a conversation between Queen Elizabeth and
Queen Victoria in the Elysian Fields.[50]

Openshaw suggests that in comparison to the compulsory patriotism of
the 1920s, school patriotism before the Great War was 'limited in impact
and romantic in tone'; and he notes that the cadet movement was dismantled
in 1912–13, at which time the tone of the *School Journal* grew rather
milder.[51] School patriotism in Edwardian New Zealand was certainly
romantic; it celebrated an empire on which the sun never set and the noble
and adventurous life of the soldier and Empire-builder. That it was limited

in impact compared to the 1920s is much more doubtful. There were, for example, plenty of elaborate patriotic festivals before the Great War to match the elaborate occasions Openshaw notes in the 1920s; and the cadet movement was not dismantled for lack of enthusiasm for such matters but because the military authorities saw it as an impediment to a scheme of universal military training for older boys and young men.

The significant difference between the two periods lies, however, not in the amount of singing, marching and flag-saluting each saw but in the extent to which the authorities felt obliged to require such things by regulation as a bulwark against dissent and subversion.

During the Great War the *School Journal* became, predictably enough, more and more strident in condemning a barbarous and treacherous Germany and in celebrating the strength and virtues of the Empire, but there was no diminution of imperialist propaganda in the *Journal* with the Armistice, and the patriotic rituals which had been taken as a matter of course before the war were required in the 1920s. Malone provides a good summary of the anxieties underlying efforts to foster patriotism in the 1920s.

> To the anti-German sentiment which arose during the war was added the strain of casualties; the depredations of the influenza epidemic in 1918; the sectarian passions aroused by the activities of the Protestant Political League and echoes of the Irish troubles; the impact of the Russian Revolution, the difficulties experienced by thousands of men in adjusting themselves to civilian life, political instability and a short but sharp depression. There were many who felt that traditional concepts of life were in danger and that, in particular, the Empire itself was threatened by Bolshevik and other disloyalties.[52]

James Parr, Minister of Education from 1920 until 1926, saw enemies immediately to hand; he and the Prime Minister were both deeply suspicious of those who did not display suitable patriotic fervour. In 1921, an Auckland school committee which refused permission for a Navy League speaker to address the pupils yielded to pressure from the local education board and from William Massey himself. In the same year Parr told Parliament that a school committee was, apparently, within its powers to refuse admission to children who declined to salute the flag.[53]

In 1917 the National Efficiency Board had suggested weekly flag-saluting as a way to promote solidarity; in 1921 Parr required it and the history syllabus for primary schools was revised to include the requirement that:

> The instruction in History and Civics shall aim at instilling in boys and girls love for their country and pride in the achievements of the race throughout the Empire. Loyalty shall be the dominant note, and the lessons shall be selected and presented in such a way as to lay stress on the need for sympathetic cooperation not only on the part of the various dominions within the Empire, but on the part of every section of the community within which we live.[54]

Teachers who openly questioned popular patriotism had always risked their positions if they ran foul of zealous local authorities, but in the 1920s teachers who failed to display sufficient 'sympathetic cooperation' had the Minister of Education to contend with. In 1921 a teachers' college student was fined and dismissed from her college for selling a communist pamphlet. When Parr heard that other students had clubbed together to pay her fine, he demanded an enquiry into the activities and opinions of training college and university students in Wellington. The Education Act was amended in 1921 to require all teachers to take an oath of allegiance to the Crown and when a Wellington teacher wrote to a teachers' magazine criticizing Parr's heavy-handedness he threatened to revoke her teacher's certificate. She won a long battle in the courts, but in 1922 three teachers, one of them a decorated ex-soldier, lost their jobs because they refused to sign the new oath on religious grounds.[55]

The early 1920s saw the zenith of compulsory school patriotism. Parr's excesses may, indeed, have contributed in part to a diminished enthusiasm for the imperial ideology in some teachers. More important factors, however, were a more sober estimation of German responsibility for the Great War, the publication of popular anti-war novels following Remarque's *All Quiet on the Western Front*, and economic uncertainty.[56] Fluctuating and falling overseas prices for New Zealand left many ex-soldiers struggling or doomed on overpriced farms bought immediately after the war, and their plight could only add to the uneasy feeling that the war had failed to benefit anyone in the longer term.

The *School Journal* reflected the increasing strength of anti-war and internationalist sentiments. By the mid-1920s it included the occasional article on the League of Nations as well as material openly stating that the Great War had been a waste of lives and money and in the end brought happiness to no one.[57] In 1931, the editor was appointed an inspector of schools and was replaced by the woman who had been his assistant from 1923. By 1932 the change was complete and nothing of the old imperial ideology appeared in the *School Journal*.

It is easy to exaggerate the pace and completeness of the change. Taken as a whole, school work in the 1920s and 1930s embodied a variety of attitudes, with older and newer material often existing together uneasily. There was certainly a great difference between the *School Journal* immediately after the Great War and in the later 1930s; but many issues in between displayed a more complex skein of attitudes and concerns, including rather different accounts of the Empire itself. The Empire Day issue of 1923, for example, incuded two articles on the Empire. The first was concerned with the British Empire Exhibition to be held at Wembley and it fretted over lagging British technology and foreign competition and the under-population of New Zealand and Australia compared to the teeming millions of China and Japan. 'The closer settlement of our own lands is the surest guarantee against any possible risk of aggression from the coloured races'; and the British Empire could be self-supporting if only the Motherland would realise that its dominions were better customers than foreign nations and better homes for British capital.[58]

The second piece was in the old, familiar triumphalist mode and dealt with Raleigh, Wolfe, and Clive as heroes of the burgeoning Empire and moral examples.[59] The first piece sometimes referred to the Commonwealth; in the second it was always the Empire.

The revised history syllabus of 1928, part of a general overhaul of the primary school curriculum, also tempered its hymn to Empire with attitudes already manifest in the *School Journal*.

> The narrowly nationalistic interpretation of history should be avoided, international jealousy should not be aroused – a fatally easy course; but there should be sedulously cultivated a strong faith in a more peaceful, prosperous and harmonious world. Frequent reference should be made in the higher classes to the constitution and activities of the League of Nations and to some at least of the disputes it has settled. One of the teacher's main aims should be to implant in the minds of his pupils a detestation of war as a means of settling international differences.[60]

Such sentiments must, however, be seen in perspective. The syllabus went on:

> On no account should too great an emphasis be laid on achievements in war. At the same time these should not be ignored, nor should there be anything but the highest praise for who who sacrificed their lives for their country's freedom.

In the texts to accompany the new syllabus the standard triumphalist account of British history and the growth of the Empire got much more space than references to the League of Nations and the Kellogg Pact. A note in each volume of the series promised less emphasis on 'the lives of kings and queens and battles long ago' but Standard III pupils, for example, still read about Caesar's invasion of Britain, Alfred's wars with the Danes, Bannockburn, the Armada, Trafalgar, the Crimea, the American War of Independence and the landings at Gallipoli.[61]

By the late 1930s, some of the contrasts between the official syllabus and texts and other material were striking. School radio broadcasts, which began on an experimental basis in 1928 and were put on a regular basis in 1934, have yet to be examined by historians of the curriculum – if indeed, the necessary material still exists – but the surviving programme booklets for pupils indicate that the content and tone of these talks were much more in accord with the *School Journal* than with the older material fossilized in texts. *Our Nation's Story*, for example, has power in Russia falling to the hands of 'fanatical and blood-thirsty people called Bolsheviks', but a 1938 series of radio broadcasts to schools on 'Some Great Men of Europe' included Lenin, and later that year a series on travel in Europe included one talk each on Holland, Germany, Finland and Switzerland and two on Russia. 'Visitors returning from abroad', the pupils' booklet proclaimed, 'say that it [Moscow] is the most lively and joyous capital they have seen – and the most cosmopolitan.' Questions for discussion included, 'Can you find the origin of May Day?' and 'Why is Lenin revered so much?'[62] Post-war texts continued to draw a very clear distinction between the white dominions and the rest of the Empire, assuming white superiority over other races and British superiority over other Europeans, but they were less concerned to assign particular groups to their precise place on the scale of humanity, concentrating much more often on the dangers of unrestricted immigration.

The 1921 census report noted smugly that:

> Racially the population of the Dominion is and always has been of a high standard of purity; indeed the maintenance of the pure European or 'white' standard of population had invariably been a consideration of immigration legislation.[63]

It certainly had. At that census, after forty years of poll taxes on Chinese entrants to New Zealand, as well as a Natal-type literacy test, 'race aliens' made up 0.45 per cent of the non-Maori population[64] But in the 1920s prejudice against Asians notwithstanding their small numbers, reached new heights, fuelled by anxiety about Japan's growing strength, sheer horror at the prospect of white New Zealand women marrying coloured men, and the certainty that Asians would undersell white labour and drive small New Zealand businesses under.

The census report set out popular prejudice in official prose.

> The importance of racial purity has long been recognized. History has shown that the coalescence of the white and the so-called coloured races is not conducive to improvement in racial types . . . The alien races are naturally accustomed to other conditions of living, to different standards of ethics, to strange customs, to a social fabric wholly foreign to that of the land within which they find themselves. Amongst the people of that country they are not yet of them – separated by a barrier of colour, of language, of thought. And, again, race aliens are rarely a community balanced in sexes, and this abnormality is fruitful of its own peculiar difficulties.[65]

School texts set out the same concerns in simpler language. A civics text for senior primary school pupils or junior forms at high school explained that New Zealand was 'an outpost of the white race'.

> We want immigrants, but we do not want everybody. We do not want the destitute, the criminal or people belonging to the coloured races . . . . It would take too long to tell you why we keep out people belonging to coloured races, save to say that it is a question of ways of living and ideals, besides, of course, the desire to keep the blood of our people pure.[66]

Coad's *Dominion Civics* spoke of the 'progressive white peoples and backward coloured peoples' in the Empire and of Asia's teeming millions eyeing empty space elsewhere, and she explained that:

In a white man's country, John Chinaman, as New Zealand can testify, is not too cordially received ... and his presence in large numbers threatens to lower the standard of living for the white man, and to destroy the purity of the race which it is considered desirable to maintain.[67]

In the 1920s, as before, notions of white superiority were supported by the treatment of Maoris and Maori culture in the syllabus and school texts. When texts assigned Maoris to a specific race – and few of them now did – they favoured the 'Aryan' or 'Caucasian' branch of humanity. Thus the *Pacific Geographies* had Maoris as a branch of the Caucasian race, which included Indians and Malays.[68]

Generally, however, readers and histories concentrated on Maori migration down the Pacific rather than speculating on their remote origins. S.P. Smith's account of the first settlement of New Zealand, with its succession of Polynesian explorers and then a great fleet of canoes from the legendary Hawaiki was generally accepted and schoolbooks interleaved his chronology with notable dates in British history.[69] The 'Great Fleet' story made Maoris' arrival in New Zealand further evidence of their fine qualities: they were not descended from stragglers but from the adventurous crews of a colonizing flotilla – the 'Vikings of the Sunrise' in Sir Peter Buck's fine phrase.

Schoolbooks of the 1920s also contained the myth, still dear to redneck pakehas spluttering over Maori land claims, that the Maoris themselves had been expropriators who had found New Zealand inhabited by a weaker, darker race whom they had conquered and whose scattered remnants had fled to the Chatham Islands off the East coast of the South Island.[70]

The culture and artefacts of the 'real Maori' provided convenient symbols for a country short of them, and Maori traditions were ransacked by colonial novelists and versifiers struggling to produce a national literature, but there was no suggestion that Maori culture and values had any current relevance or worth and school readers which included extracts from Maori traditions generally labelled them 'myths' or 'fairy tales'.

The 1929 syllabus made more reference to New Zealand than any previous syllabus, but there were still only two passing references to Maori culture outside the history syllabus: one of the music books listed a collection of Maori songs and the language syllabus had a brief section on the correct pronunciation of Maori words. For the the first time, senior primary school children might begin to learn a second language, but the options were French and Latin, not Maori; and the art and craft syllabus made no place for weaving, carving or the use of Maori designs.

Current proposals that the syllabus should incorporate *taha Maori* – the Maori side of things – have brought redneck reaction and some unease from liberals. Not that dealing with things Maori in schools is a novelty, *au contraire*; what is disconcerting and threatening is the suggestion that children might be presented with Maori culture and values as valid perspectives on the contemporary world rather than a cabinet of ethnographic curiosities. This is particularly unsettling for New Zealanders whose schooling has made it clear that Maoris have every reason to be grateful for the European settlement of the country with no claims to redress or special recognition and that Maori culture has a commendable past and no future.

It would be nonsense to conclude that all children learned and believed every detail of the imperial ideology in its various presentations. Parr's excesses were a response to dissenting voices and the suspicion that the imperial ideology was not having sufficient impact on children because teachers, particularly younger teachers, were becoming less and less reliable as its agents.

On occasion the schools reflected popular sentiment very clearly, when for example, New Zealand was gripped with Germanophobia during the Great War or when there was an outcry against Asian immigration in the 1920s, but Sinclair is correct to conclude that generally 'The Empire belonged to an official rhetoric, to newspaper editors, to school teachers, to politicians, to Governors and Governors-General.'[71] If the average New Zealander felt national pride it was more often because a New Zealand rugby team had once more beaten Englishmen at their own game than because New Zealand had maintained the traditions of Wolfe, Clive and Wellington.

Schoolbooks also presented a much more sympathetic view of Maoris than pupils could have gained from many of their elders or from popular fiction or newspaper cartoons portraying Maoris as childishly cunning, lazy, superstitious, unreliable and speaking a strange dialect. But the official account of the Maori, and cruder, more openly racist attitudes, were two sides of the same coin. To confine oneself to the pre-European Maori and stress his nobility as a savage was to point up his inadequacy in a European setting: the cartoonists and saloon-bar chauvinists could take it from there.

Similarly, the schoolbook's account of the Empire and popular attitudes towards Britain were complementary, not in conflict. There was some antagonism in the depressed 1920s and 1930s towards British immigrants who increased competition for jobs; and 'new chums' were mocked for their mistakes as they adapted to local ways, but the textbooks reflected the man in the street's general assumption that British was, when it came to the point, always best.

The syllabus and schoolbooks in use before 1940 may not have given little New Zealanders a lasting knowledge of the details of Magna Carta or the development of the British colonial empire, but they helped give generations of white New Zealanders a comfortable, coherent account of themselves, their place in the world and their Maori fellow-citizens.

6 Racial stereotypes in the Australian curriculum

The case-study of New South Wales

Stewart Firth and *Robert Darlington*

The six British settler colonies in Australia federated as the Commonwealth of Australia on the first day of 1901. Australia was the creation of an Act of the British Parliament in London, and did not exercise independence in its foreign policy until the Second World War. Whereas today many Australians trace their origins to Italy, Greece, eastern Europe and increasingly South-East Asia, the Australia of the first few decades of the twentieth century was stolidly British, and Australian schools inculcated British values about race as about everything else.

Yet Australia was not simply Britain transferred to the other side of the world. For one thing, a quarter of the population was of Irish Catholic descent, and, with great sacrifices, had built a separate Catholic school system in all Australian states. Most Catholic children went to Catholic schools, where Irish brothers and nuns taught them a version of history and politics that did not see much to admire in England and the Empire. In the second place, the new white nation found a symbol of specifically Australian nationalism in the exploits of its soldiers during the First World War, above all in their defeat by the Turks at Gallipoli in the Dardenelles in 1915. The landing of the Australians at Gallipoli on 25 April 1915, together with troops from New Zealand in the ANZAC (Australian New Zealand Army Corps) force, made that day sacred in the official and patriotic memory of the country. In the third place, Australia was possibly a more race-conscious society than Britain itself. On the frontiers of settlement in the north of the continent, white men were still engaged in occupying the land of the original inhabitants of Australia, the Aboriginal people, often by force. The first Act of the Australian Parliament in 1901 was the Immigration Restriction Act, forbidding people of colour from migrating to Australia and defining the new country under the Southern Cross as a nation of white-skinned people.

The study that follows is of education in one Australian state, New South Wales, during the first forty years of the twentieth century. Its population of 2,600,000 in 1933 represented 39 per cent of all white Australians, and the state's school population of 451,000 in 1934 was a similar proportion of children in all Australian schools.[1] While there were some cultural differences between the states – South Australia, because it never had convicts, was less Catholic and Irish than New South Wales or Victoria, for example – we have no reason to believe that our analysis of school reading material is not true of Australia as a whole at that time, especially on the issue of attitudes to race.

As elsewhere in Australia, education in New South Wales was a state responsibility, financed and organized on a state-wide rather than local or regional basis. Our analysis focuses upon texts and monthly school magazines, distinguishing between those used in state schools and those used in Catholic schools. The magazine for children in New South Wales government schools between 1904 and 1916 was the *Commonwealth School Paper*. Every issue of the *Paper* was checked by the Chief Inspector of Schools before publication, and the editors were teachers or school inspectors: it thus bore the imprimatur of the New South Wales Department of Public Instruction, and reflected faithfully what the Department thought children should learn. From 1916 it was replaced by the New South Wales *School Magazine*, which went free to all primary schoolchildren in state schools. From 1923 Catholic schools had their own school magazine, which appeared between the wars under a variety of titles: *Our Own Paper, Our School Paper* and *The Catholic School Paper*.

Fundamental to the thinking of those who wrote for schoolchildren was the idea that humanity was divided into races, and that only some of those races were 'civilized'. The others stood in need of being civilized, a task best accomplished for them by being brought under the beneficent domination of the one truly civilized race, the British.

The introduction to *English History Stories for Third Class*, first published about 1899, was called 'Why you learn English history'. Children were told that they were learning English history so that they would know 'how the English-speaking races have gradually come to hold such an important position in the world'. People such as the English in Australia, the schoolbook said, 'are called civilized', unlike the 'tribes of blacks' who were there when they arrived, living a 'very wretched kind of life' without any knowledge of agriculture or money. People like this 'are called uncivilized'. 'What a difference there is', the book said, 'between them and the race to which Australian boys and girls belong!'. These progressive people were continually 'improving their condition, and making their new country richer.'[2]

Pride of race, and the military victories of the British over other races, were important themes in the pages of the state schools' *Commonwealth School Paper*. The minor wars of British imperial expansion were invested with an aura of chivalric romance, in which the thin red line of British troops triumphed over inferior, yet admirably plucky colonial peoples in thrilling clashes of arms. The Zulus of the war of 1879 were 'fanatical' and 'bloodthirsty'; the Sudanese of the war of 1884 'brave as ever men were' – even though it was the 'cruel, bloodthirsty bravery' born of 'the fatalism of their race'; and the Tibetans who attacked a British expedition in 1904 were possessed of a 'savage lust for blood'.[3] The same Zulus were elsewhere described as 'having 'marvellous skill and bravery' and even the Boers' 'unparalleled obstinacy' may have been seen as a point in their favour.[4]

In the *New Australian School Series Fourth Reader*, probably first published about 1908, children could read about the Matabele War of 1893 in a story called 'Men whose fathers were men'. It described the defeat of courageous British soldiers, led by a Major Wilson, at the hands of 'thousands of well-armed savages':

> No white man lived to tell the story of that fight – a fight which every man in the gallant band knew could have but one ending. The tale of how they died comes from the lips of the Matabele, who have never forgotten the heroism of Wilson's last stand. Thirty-four men, poorly supplied with ammunition, stood grimly at bay, resolutely facing thousands upon thousands, and picking off from behind trees or dead horses every black head that chanced to show itself. Their firing must have been deadly. The killed among the Matabele had nearly all been shot through the brain, and for every Englishman at least ten of the natives fell.
>
> The fight continued for something like two hours. The ranks of the small band grew thinner, but even the wounded did what they could, loading the rifles which they were no longer able to fire. At one time, says the Matabele account, they began to 'sing'. What this means we shall never know. Perhaps a cheer or some song dear to Englishmen, which recalled to them about to die the sweetness of their island home ...
>
> As they gazed upon the dead heroes, a kind of awe seems to have fallen upon the savage warriors. It was their habit to mutilate the corpses of their foes, but when their general had surveyed the field, he issued this never-to-be-forgotten order –
>
> 'Let them be; they were men who died like men, men whose fathers were men'.[5]

In the pages of the school paper, pride of race meant pride in being British. Its justification in history went back as far as Beric the Briton and Wulf, the Saxon boy who helped to make England. Wulf was their ancestor, children read, and it was he and the other 'Angles, Engle-men, or Englishmen' who had made Britain become England. These man had had many manly virtues which had been handed down to their present-day descendants, and for which the children could feel justly grateful.[6] Beric was a 'brave British lad' who saved a faithful Christian girl from death in the arena by overpowering a lion bare-handed, the hero of a story which was adapted from G.A. Henty *Beric the Briton: A Story of the Roman Invasion*.[7]

The British race, children learnt, was the one that had taken the inestimable blessings of civilization to a benighted, native world. The Australian Arthur Jose explained that the story of the British Empire was of 'how Britain, having set her own house in order, sought and found a great work ready to her hand which she alone could accomplish'.[8] In India the great work for civilization was establishing what the late Victorian historian W.E.H. Lecky called 'the greatest and most beneficent despotism in the world', which made the 'Hindu farmer or tradesman ... free to live his simple life of toil and contentment under the shadow of a great security'.[9] Englishmen should show pride in their 'great Indian Empire', children read in February 1908. 'Pride of race', they learnt, 'is a good thing for a nation.' It did not mean that they should 'shriek and gesticulate. That would be un-English'.[10] But they should be interested in their imperial possessions. As for Egypt, the development of the Land of the Nile was 'all the more glorious because the work was done on behalf not of British subjects' but of the Egyptians themselves. All the money spent under Lord Cromer's administration, 'every penny of it', had been used for the benefit of the Egyptians. The happy effects of British civilization and government had 'borne testimony to the truth that "righteousness exalteth a nation"'.[11]

Australian children were taught that the British race stood for honour and the word of a gentleman. This was shown by 'An incident in the life of Li Hung Chang', the Chinese generalissimo charged with suppressing the Taiping rebellion of the 1860s, whose 'first real lesson of the difference between a foreign gentleman and a Chinese nearly cost him his life'. The gentleman was Major Gordon, later to die at Khartoum and to be buried in circumstances also celebrated by the state schools of New South Wales. Gordon promised the Taiping leaders on Li's behalf that they would be safe to surrender, but when they did so Li decapitated them, and 'nine headless bodies were seen floating down the river'. Gordon's sense of honour was so affronted that 'if he had found Li, he would have killed him on the spot', and he refused money as compensation.[12] The story of 'The funeral of Gordon, September 1898', explained that the 14-year delay in giving this 'Christian soldier' a 'Christian burial' had itself been a triumph for the British: 'We may be slow; but in that very slowness we show that we do not forget. Soon or late we give our own their due'. And Gordon's due was to be buried 'after the manner of his race' with Maxim-Nordenfeldt and Bible beside him, his bones, lying beneath the Union Jack, being nothing less than 'the bones of murdered civilization'.[13]

In 1901 the Chinese-born in Australia numbered 30,000 in a total population of 3,774,000 or fewer than 1 per cent. They had joined the rush for gold in the Australian colonies in the 1850s and 1860s, only to encounter deep hostility from the colonists of British descent. Suspicion of Chinese and other Asians was to linger in the Australian national consciousness through much of the twentieth century, and it was initially encouraged directly by the education system. The Aboriginal population of Australia, which at the time of white settlement in 1788 might have been 900,000 and was certainly not less than 300,000 had shrunk by 1901 to about 95,000 as a consequence of disease and loss of traditional lands.[14] In school texts, and in society at large at the turn of the century, Aborigines were seen as members of a race intellectually and socially far inferior to people of European descent: the only question was whether they were to be pitied or despised. At the ideological level, the effect of depicting Aborigines in this way was to justify the British occupation of the continent.

The state schools taught that, in different ways, both the Chinese and the Aborigines could not begin to match the intelligence and achievements of the white race that had colonized Australia. On the track to the goldfield, children learnt in one story in the *Commonwealth School Paper*,

> some Chinamen and their cart were hopelessly bogged. Somehow or other John is always helpless in an emergency ... but if energy in the shape of chattering uproar could avail them, they must have been very soon out of their difficulties.[15]

The Australian poet Brunton Stephens' poem 'My other Chinese cook' was illustrated by an ape-like caricature of the Chinese, and told the story of lazy, cheeky, dirty, sly 'Johnny' with a 'lemon-coloured face' who was revealed as having made 'rabbit pie' from dog's flesh.[16]

An Australian poem which appeared in successive editions of primary school readers reminded white Australian schoolchildren that

> We won our land from a nerveless race,
>   Too mean for their land to fight;
> If we mean to hold it we too must face
>   The adage that 'might is right'.[17]

Children were taught that, in the universal hierarchy of races, the Aborigines were inferior to their counterparts in New Zealand, the Maori. An article in the *Commonwealth School Paper* on Sir George Grey, 'a master-builder of Empire', described the Maori of New Zealand as 'a far superior race to the Australian blacks with whom he had hitherto been dealing'. It told how Grey had quickly discovered that the Maori were 'not mere "naked savages"', as people contemptuously called them, but a nation of men, whose intelligence and skill made them formidable foes'.[18]

Aboriginal people were depicted in the *Commonwealth School Paper* as conspiring to kill white people yet lacking the courage of the whites. A story published in 1909 told how an Aboriginal woman vowed revenge on a country sheep station when her husband was killed by the overseer. She threatened to murder Captain Leslie, 'the fine, burly, red-headed country gentleman' who owned the station, to burn down the whites' homestead, and to abduct Mrs Leslie's 'only child, a sweet girl of about five years of age' in order to bring her up 'as a savage'. All these plans failed because the hero of the story was able to exploit the weaknesses of the 'savages'. He 'knew them to be cruel and revengeful, but at the same time real cowards', so that when he confronted them boldly after playing dead,

> not a single one of them was man enough to hurl a spear or throw a boomerang or waddy. They turned tail and ran for the scrub ... The savages, brave enough now that they were hid behind the scrub again, hurled a shower of missiles.

Mrs Leslie had been kind to a few of them but then they had brought all their relatives and, when she stopped giving goods away, they began to steal them: 'To them stealing was no crime; perhaps, in their uncivilized code of morals, a positive virtue'. [19] The explorers Frank and Alex Jardine struck even worse trouble from the Aboriginal people in 1863 and 1864, according to an article published in 1910. The 'Cape York natives' had seemed to rejoice that they had another party of white men to dog to death. They showed 'unappeasable enmity ... equalled before only by the Darling natives' and they made 'numberless treacherous attacks' which were nevertheless repulsed in a 'prompt and plucky manner'. In the final battle of 14 January 1864 'the whites were not in patient humour' and it was therefore 'brief and severe'. [20] In *Stories from Australian History*, first published in 1908, children encountered another image of Aboriginal people, this time as simple but faithful servants of the whites, objects of condescension. The Aborigines who accompanied the white explorers of the Australian continent, children read, had been

> of the utmost service to their masters. Men like Warburton, Hume, Sturt, and the Forrests ... knew that Tommy and Jacky and Charley and the rest were after all only big children, and that by kindness alone could their fidelity and affection be retained. [21]

A more positive image of Aboriginal people was conveyed by Book 4 of the *Approved Readers for the Catholic Schools of Australasia*, which pointed to the Aborigines' 'fine sense of manliness' and fairness, their harmonious personal relationships, 'their respect for the aged, their ready care for the sick, and their warm affection for their children'. Before they were influenced by the 'vicious elements in our civilization', Catholic schoolchildren were taught, the Aborigines were honest and trustworthy. [22] Here there was an echo of that recurring theme in European thought which sees 'native' peoples as noble savages who are corrupted by contact with sinful, calculating outsiders. According to this depiction, the Aborigines had once been honest and trustworthy, but were no longer so.

In other countries, the children of New South Wales were informed, black people were used benevolently for the white man's benefit. The blacks in the Kimberley mines of South Africa were working there 'merely that in some far-away country the sunshine may flash forth from the jewel on my lady's finger'. It was explained that the only reason the 'hungry natives' did not seek to live in the mine compounds was that they had a 'natural aversion to anything in the line of exertion'. Those who did go in were to work for 'at least three months'. If they then wanted to leave, they were 'thoroughly searched'. Escapes or attempted escapes were rare because the compound was quite securely enclosed. [23] Like most of his contemporaries in Australia, the writer of this article saw nothing wrong with the conditions of indenture under which Africans laboured in the diamond mines. Indeed he thought the experience did them good, and that work of this kind was the only genuinely useful function that Africans could perform.

In Papua, by then an Australian territory and rapidly being developed for Australian plantation agriculture, native labour was 'plentiful and cheap', according to the *Commonwealth School Paper* in 1913. The Papuan received 'Just treatment, good food, and payment for his labour', which made him 'an excellent servant'. The 'savages' were 'protected at every turn' and it was only 'right that they should be so'. They were 'only children' and 'wanted taking care of', although they did not lack initiative; they kept 'a sort of black list' of bad employers and gave them a hard time. But if a man gave his 'boys' good conditions, he would always be able to get labour.[24] In school readers children were told that the people of New Guinea were savages and that

the Papuan, although he is straight and agile, is not attractive in appearance. His frizzled hair seems to grow in tufts, standing out above his head like a great mop, his lips are thick, and his nose flat and broad.[25]

School literature before the First World War was full of notions of civilization and savagery, of higher and lower races, of their greater and lesser intelligence, of the British race as the apex of human biological and intellectual development, and of white, British-descended Australians as the exemplars of this racial superiority in the Southern Continent, bringing civilization in its most perfect form to a race that was seen as lying at the bottom of the evolutionary ladder, the Aboriginal people. And much of this thinking was to survive in schools until well after the middle of the century.

The First World War, which broke out in August 1914, was to have an immediate and lasting effect on the teaching of political values in Australian schools. Nothing could ever be quite the same again after this terrible conflict. The clock could not be turned back; the war, in which millions died in senseless, suicidal campaigns, left its mark on society around the world, and there could be no complete restoration of the values of the pre-war era. Yet, despite the bitter divisions the war brought to Australian society, much remained relatively unchanged in the conservative world of the school.

From 1914 to 1918 Australian public schools seized upon the Great War to involve children in patriotic training which was unprecedented in its intensity. Patriotic festivals, holidays and rituals were frequent features of school life. As the Empire's survival was threatened, schooling became an integral part of the war effort through the work of teachers and pupils for patriotic funds and recruiting campaigns, and almost every aspect of school life focused on the war. Lessons, ritual and reading material were aimed at maintaining pupils' enthusiasm for the imperial and Allied cause. Pre-war racial ideas continued to be taught but one of the many unintended consequences of the war was the introduction of an element of confusion into racial assumptions.

Nineteenth-century Western ideas of a racial hierarchy, with whites at the top and specific hereditary traits attributed to each race, permeated the literature used in schools before and during the war. But the alliances produced by the war were also popularized in wartime propaganda which was incorporated into the schools' message. Japanese, French, Russians, Americans, Italians and the non-white subjects of the British and French empire fought with the British against white Germans and their allies. The past sins of Britain's allies and subjects were forgiven and their virtues stressed. This change distorted some of the old racial certainties and further confusion was added as the fathers of many pupils returned from the war. Their experience under British command in the Dardenelles had lowered the high esteem in which they had held their English cousins but had given them the highest regard for their Turkish enemies who had been portrayed in their childhood texts as 'a cruel and barbarous race'.[26] Yet, through their schools, children were not told of such changes to the old racial assumption.

In the inter-war years, 1919 to 1939, school reading material contained elements reflecting both continuity and change. Changed values due to the influence of the Great War can be found in the treatment accorded to the internationalist values of the League of Nations and in the propagation of a distinctively Australian national pride.

The focus of Australian national pride was summed up in the word 'Anzac', and each April the nation paused for a day to remember the fallen on the other side of the world. On 25 April 1915, the original Anzac day, Australian and New Zealand soldiers embarked on a military campaign which ended in defeat and withdrawal but was to become a symbol of Australian nationhood.

The intensity of the patriotic focus on Australia (rather than the Empire) was new. Indeed the official policy of the Department of Education was now to see that the deeds of Australian soldiers were brought prominently to the attention of pupils in schools. But school reading material also revealed a continuation of the views which prevailed before the war. The ideas of nationalism and imperialism, with implicit assumptions of British racial superiority, the glorification of military virtues, the notion of unquestioning loyalty to the flag, and the belief that progress resulted from the heroic efforts of individual 'great men' who had helped produce the greatness of British Civilization are readily discernable in reading material used extensively during the inter-war period. From such sources it appears that schools' ideas about race after the war were much the same as before 1914 despite some changes in official conceptions of the kinds of attitudes and values that should be taught.[27]

Typical of the texts which perpetuated the pre-war racial attitudes during the inter-war years were the history texts of P.R. Cole. Cole wrote extensively on methods of history teaching and on teaching procedures generally.[28] Along with Peter Board and Alexander Mackie, Cole was one of the main influences behind the new history methods including use of oral work, pictures, aids and excursions which followed from the 'New Education'.[29] When he wrote *Great Australians. A Reader for Schools* in 1923, Cole was vice-principal of Sydney Teachers' College and lecturer in education at the University of Sydney. He was in a position to influence the professional development of teachers, encouraging them to adopt effective methods; and in perpetuating older beliefs and attitudes through teachers and texts, he also left his mark on pupils. *Great Australians* was recommended for children's reading in the primary history syllabus throughout the inter-war period.

Cole's racial attitudes were identical to those expressed in pre-war texts. In *Great Australians* whites who shot Aborigines for stealing stock were excused as having shot them as robbers; but blacks who killed whites were described as the murderers of defenceless people.[30] The tens of thousands of years of Aboriginal history were dismissed by Cole as unworthy of attention with the simple, sweeping statement: 'From the 26th January, 1788, Australian History begins'.[31] Echoing the many textbook writers of the late nineteenth and early twentieth centuries, Cole drew a moral lesson from the Aborigines' loss of the continent:

> Now, if people do not turn the natural wealth of a country to good account, nor toil to produce food, they will lack the strength and courage to use their weapons, and will fail to keep their country for themselves. Woe unto such a nation, for it must fall that humanity may rise on its ruins. Sad has been the fate of the Australian blacks, and that of the 'red' men of America, but their fate would be ours did we not toil, and learn, and strive ever upwards and onwards.[32]

Thus the white conquest was justified on the grounds that it was essential for human progress and a warning was given against failure to work hard to keep the white nation strong.

While the decline of the blacks was seen as being in the interests of progress, whites were approved of if they were benevolent toward the blacks. The kindness of the first Governor, Arthur Phillip, was stressed even though the Aborigines 'gave him trouble'.[33] Cole noted that, as their numbers declined, 'some of the natives became useful servants' while others became 'slaves to drink' because that was easier, but the survivors were now 'better treated' and some had been taught 'to till the ground which has been given to them'.[34] The attitude conveyed was simply that it was the role of the blacks to die off while adopting the virtues of white civilization as best they could and it was the duty of whites, for their own moral betterment, to emulate great men such as Governor Phillip by treating these unfortunates humanely.

Cole's view of other races did not differ significantly from the stereotypes presented before the First World War. Spaniards were still portrayed as sinister and cruel. In writing about the disappearance of the explorer Bass and his failure to return from South America, Cole commented: 'Probably the Spaniards, who hated to see men of other nations in their waters, caught the young explorer, and forced him to work until death in their mines.'[35]

Italians fared little better and were subtly condemned as both lazy and inclined to cheat. In discussing the Australian fishing industry, Cole claimed:

> A few hundreds [of the population of Australia] earn their living as fishermen, but a large proportion of these are Italians, and while it is said that their earnings are not large, the supply of fish is neither plentiful nor cheap.[36]

Cole's attitude towards the Chinese was, however, considerably milder than the view most often expressed a few decades earlier. He approved of their exclusion under the White Australia policy but argued that J.D. Lang's proposal in 1843 to settle a thousand Chinese families at Port Macquarie should serve as a reminder that they were men 'and should be treated as men'.[37] With the Asian threat removed by immigration barriers the white Australian could afford to be patronizing.

A few texts tried to avoid such racial stereotyping. C.H. Currey's *European History Since 1870*, set for the Leaving Certificate in 1919, largely blamed the militarism of the German ruling class for the outbreak of the First World War. Currey reminded readers that the German people as a whole were not to blame as the Social Democrats who formed Germany's strongest party had consistently denounced the military and naval propaganda of the ruling classes. He concluded by absolving the proletariat and peasantry of Germany from responsibility for the war, laying the blame on 'their military masters'.[38]

Racial attitudes could often be reinforced by the use of patronizing or derogatory terms for people, for example, referring to Aborigines as 'blackboys' or 'native boys'.[39] But more often, as with Cole's texts, reasons were produced for the unfavourable judgements passed. Karl Cramp's widely used *A Story of the Australian People* also provides several examples of the latter type of racial stereotyping. In numerous examples, Aborigines were portrayed as ignorant, lazy and cowardly. The judgements were always from the standpoint of white society. Cramp described the blacks before the white settlement in Australia as not knowing 'how to make the best use of the land they inherited'.[40] He also described the Aborigines of Cape York Peninsula as having a reputation for relentless cruelty based on their attacks on explorers. Repeatedly Cramp depicted Aborigines as savage cowards in their encounters with these white explorers. He placed some of the blame for the extinction of the Tasmanian Aborigines on whites but did not express any concern about their destruction and qualified his view that 'they were at first of a mild and harmless nature' by also noting that 'the Tasmanian natives were really of a very low type'.[41]

Typically, Cramp took a more favourable view of the Aborigines when making abstract generalizations about them:

> On the whole, the black man was a simple fellow with a peaceful disposition: and if his hostility had not been aroused by the thoughtlessness and cruelty of many white men, there would probably have been little warfare between the two races.[42]

While such generalizations were contradictory to the impressions of Aborigines in other parts of the text, it is doubtful that they would have modified such impressions. The derogatory view of Aborigines was presented by Cramp in the context of stories about heroic explorers probably had a more lasting impact than abstract statements. Further, Cramp appended to his general statement the line: 'Yet in some districts the tribes have proved very treacherous'.

Like Cole, Cramp assumed and helped perpetuate the view that undesirable events in Australian history and society could be linked with the influence of other races. Thus Cramp saw the Eureka rebellion as having been 'instigated by foreigners'.[43] On the Victorian goldfields in the 1850s, a group of gold-diggers constructed a stockade and staged a brief rebellion against British authority in protest against the imposition of taxes, in an incident which has come to be known as the 'Eureka Stockade'.

Some texts during this period expressed more tolerant racial views. *Australia in the Making* by H.L. Harris, a senior lecturer at the Teacher's College, Sydney, refrained from any value judgement on conflicts between explorers and blacks while showing sympathy toward the Tasmanian Aborigines: yet only five pages of the book mentioned Aborigines at all and these only in connection with explorers and the settlement of Tasmania.[44] Ernest Scott's *A Short History of Australia* and Arthur Jose's *History of Australia*, which were recommended reading for intermediate history throughout the inter-war period, took a sympathetic and, for the time, understanding view of Aborigines but also treated them very briefly.[45]

Much school literature, and particularly school texts, continued to foster ideas of racial superiority as they attempted to inculcate loyalty to the British Empire. In this context, despite the growing support for anti-war ideas in the inter-war years, school reading material still tended to glorify war. A favourite theme was found in the battles which helped win the Empire, invariably clashes of arms with people who were portrayed as racial inferiors. The benefits of membership of the British Empire and its glorious traditions were kept constantly in the minds of primary school children through such publications as the *School Magazine*, various issues of which featured articles on the throne, the colonies, the Empire's heroes and extracts from imperial poems, plays and songs. But nowhere was the message of British radical superiority and the correctness of imperialism presented more consistently than in the widely used history text, *A Story of the English People* by Karl Cramp, W. Lennard and J.H. Smairl. It was written according to syllabus requirements and issued by the New South Wales Department of Education. Teachers were instructed to use it as the basis for treatment of 6th class English history topics and it was also used as the history text for the first year of high school. Over 200,000 copies were distributed between 1919 and 1936.[46]

In all accounts of imperial wars *A Story of the English People* found reason to forgive the faults of imperial heroes and to justify their suppression of colonized people, or else simply ignored details which may have shown the British as sometimes less than noble and just and their conquered subjects as having a right to resist and rebel. In every case England's right to dominate the world was taken for granted. Emotive language was used freely to colour the pupil's interpretation of events. In its account of the Indian Mutiny 'treacherous' and 'brutally massacred' were terms used to describe the character of the mutineers' leadership and their actions respectively, while the English leader, Sir Henry Lawrence, was of course 'brave'. No mention was made of English reprisals after the suppression of the mutiny.[47]

British conquest was presented as a right, a duty and, for the conquered, a benevolent act. In summing up the role of Britain in India, the authors concluded:

> British rule has been a blessing to India. The country had become united and enjoys the advantages of peace – *Pax Britannica*. The deserts have been changed to fertile irrigated areas; trade with all its blessings has been carried along the canals and railways that run in every direction; the terrible famines that at one time carried off millions of inhabitants have been largely overcome; the natives appreciate the just laws and just treatment received from their rulers; and are being gradually trained to rule themselves.[48]

The detrimental effects of imperialism were so completely ignored and the benefits so grossly exaggerated that students reading this text might have been amazed to hear of any continuing dissatisfaction with British rule in India had they been permitted to learn of such a thing.

British interest in Egypt was given similar treatment. Pupils were informed that Egypt had been brought under British protection to maintain order and good government; the Anglo-French occupation of Egypt was justified by an account of the Khedive's bankruptcy and the British were portrayed as far-sighted benefactors who came mainly to help their inferiors towards a better life. Pupils were told of reforms under Lord Cromer in irrigation and finance and that

> above all he lifted the native races from a miserable state of poverty and famine to a condition of prosperity and enlightenment. As in India, the subject race of Egypt has learned that British rule stands for justice, progress, education and good government.

In line with this view Kitchener's reoccupation of the Sudan in 1898 was not placed in the context of the imperial scramble of the late nineteenth century. The text implied that the British merely wished to act against famine and disease which has spread since the British and Egyptians were forced to abandon the Sudan after the fall of Khartoum.[49]

On occasions when the text vaguely alluded to some unsavoury action of Britain or one her empire-builders, if the end did not exactly justify the means then it was held to at least make the means more excusable or worthy of being brushed aside from discussion. On Cecil Rhodes the pupil was informed: 'We cannot praise all his political acts or the means he sometimes took to gain his end. But that end was a magnificent one from the point of view of Empire. He reminds us of the great men in Elizabeth's reign'.[50] England's interests and those of the Empire were apparently the yardsticks by which the justice of questionable political and military adventures could ultimately be determined. After a brief account of Cromwell's bloody reprisals against the Irish the authors concluded: 'Terrible was the bloodshed. Yet Cromwell believed, as many military men do now, that this severity saved life because the strife was soon over. Other rebellions have dragged on for years'.[51] Similarly, though Chapter 41, ('The Union Jack. What it stands for') showed understanding of the reasons for Irish discontent in the seventeenth and eighteenth centuries, it also claimed, incorrectly, that the British Parliament had taken immediate action to counter the Irish famine of 1845 and portrayed a relatively prosperous contemporary Irish peasantry. A contented Ireland was seen as a necessity for a stronger Empire but the possibility of an Irish right to independence was never considered.[52]

The text's stress on the glory of military ventures for the Empire was underlined in Chapter LII, 'Two Great Soldiers', which dealt with Lord Roberts and Lord Kitchener. Their respective sections of the chapter were introduced by their quoted words — Roberts's 'In some form of national service is the only salvation of this nation and this Empire' and Kitchener's 'Discipline, discipline, discipline – that is the one thing needful'.[53] In Roberts's story students were informed that the British fought the second Afghan war of 1878 because the Afghans refused to admit a British representative. The British had been insulted and were therefore entitled to make war. Roberts's support for compulsory military service was taken as an opportunity to emphasize that policy's correctness. Similarly the tales of Kitchener's exploits in the Sudan and the Boer War reinforced the view of wars as glorious skirmishes against racial inferiors exemplifying the tradition of heroic adventure in the cause of imperial destiny.

Another, more sceptical tradition of historiography was also reaching the schools in the interwar years. Texts such as *Modern British History* by Roberts and Currey refrained from glorifying imperial conquest and were even prepared to cast doubt on the idea that the British race had a monopoly of virtue.[54] Yet such texts were usually written for secondary schools and did not appear until the 1930s. Their circulation was not as wide as that of texts like *A Story of the English People* which, in attitudes to race and Empire, perpetuated the tradition of propaganda and stereotyping characteristic of Australian school texts before the First World War.

Traditional attitudes to race were also modified by the growing influence on school reading material of the League of Nations Union. In 1938 the cover of the New South Wales Education Department's *School Magazine* carried the League of Nations Union credo, verses of which stressed the rights of members of each race to happiness and a fair share of the earth's produce.[55] Such material became common in school literature in the 1930s. The values it embodied were equivocal: many texts avoided detailed treatment of the League of Nations while others placed the hope for a better world in the desire that the British Empire would last, if possible, for ever. Perhaps because Britain's imperial reach was then at its height, the authors of such texts saw no contradication in praising past British conquests while supporting a world body to curb others who might aim to achieve greatness by the same means. British conquest was seen by such writers as having brought peace, justice, liberty and prosperity to the lesser races. As these ideals were held to endear British rule to the colonized peoples, their endurance and the endurance of the Empire were claimed to reduce the risk of future wars.[56] By this rationale the internationalist ideals of the League movement could co-exist in school literature with the older racial and imperial outlook.

Little in the texts suggests that the interwar years produced a shift in the images of race being conveyed in the schoolrooms of New South Wales. On the contrary, education was stultified, and, with a few qualifications, the same ideas of what children should learn guided textbook writers and syllabus-makers from Federation in 1901 to the Second World War. Children were still learning that it was the God-given right of the British race to bring civilization to the lesser breeds of the world. British imperial expansion and British conquest were still justified as necessary parts of the epic of human progress. Traditional peoples were still depicted either as obstacles to such progress or as fortunate in being brought under a rule that would enable them, within the limits of their capacities, to share in the benefits of the superior British civilization. Belief in the British Empire was the linchpin of all the other political ideas that found expression in the state, though to a far lesser extent the Catholic, schools of New South Wales and of the other Australian states.

The men who determined what was to be taught in schools often warned against narrow jingoism and prejudice but the system they administered continued to promote an ethnocentric view of the world. Something of the illimitable racial confidence of the pre-war years had gone, but the notion of British racial superiority remained vigorous: and British-descended Australian schoolchildren were taught to be proud of it.

7 Resistance to an unremitting process

Racism, curriculum and education in Western Canada

Jo-ann Archibald

The Missionary finds among a people that are so constantly moving about that if he is to expect real, good work, it must be done by gathering a number of the children together in a Home or Boarding School or Industrial Institution where they can be kept constantly and regularly at school and away from the evil influences of the heathen life.[1]

(T. Crosby)

The happiest future for the Indian race is the absorption into the general population, and this is the object of the policy of our government. The great forces of intermarriage and education will finally overcome any lingering traces of native custom and tradition.[1]

(D. Campbell Scott)

INTRODUCTION

These two quotations exemplify the dominant goals of Christianization and assimilation which were imposed upon First Nations[2] peoples of Canada by its government's religious and educational policies between 1850 and 1950, because it was assumed that the values, morality and knowledge of the British imperial culture were superior. First Nations peoples have been under the jurisdiction of the Canadian federal government since confederation.[3] The British North America Act 1867 (now Constitution Act 1867) s.91(24) gave the federal government's Department of Indian Affairs responsibility 'for Indians and land reserved for Indians'. Today in British Columbia First Nations land claims are either being negotiated, litigated, or prepared because the Indians' position is that they have not ceded their territories, nor have they been conquered. However, the fact remains that even today their political, social, economic and educational endeavours must be approved and funded by the federal government. In this chapter, First Nations' reaction to colonial goals of Christianizing, 'civilizing', and assimilating children through formal educational institutions and curricula will be examined through a case study of the Sto:lo people and their educational history.

The Sto:lo Nation area extends from Vancouver to Yale, British Columbia. Sto:lo lifestyle has and continues to be greatly influenced by the

river systems, especially the lower Fraser River. The educational history of
the Sto:lo people who live in the areas between Langley and Yale, BC will
be highlighted in this chapter. Three distinct modern phases of education
experienced by the Sto:lo people are the influence of religions, influence of
government, and the influence of the national Indian Control of Indian
Education Policy.

INFLUENCE OF WESTERN RELIGION

The Christian period began in the Sto:lo area in 1841 with the visit of a Roman
Catholic Oblate missionary, Father Demerts. For the next one hundred years,
the Roman Catholic and Methodist denominations exerted a powerful influence
upon the education of Sto:lo children. Despite differences in doctrine,
organizational philosophy and practice, both shared the common goal of
'Christianizing and civilizing' the First Nations' children. A brief overview
of these respective education systems will illustrate the imperialistic racist
aims and attitudes inherent in both Catholic and Methodist curricula.

When the first missionaries arrived in 1841 there were only a few fur traders
in the Sto:lo area so there had been no significant change in the traditional
lifestyle of the Sto:lo for generations. Initially, the people were suspicious
of the new religious teachings, but their curiosity and the priests' masking
of Roman Catholicism in Sto:lo traditions allowed Catholicism to gain a
foothold. Daily instruction generally utilized traditional pageantry, dress, and
processions which emphasized respect, spiritual power, and custom.

Drastic cultural trauma was experienced when the gold rush hit the Fraser
Valley in 1858 and hordes of gold miners passed through Sto:lo territory.
The introduction of alcohol and 'white' diseases greatly affected the traditional
way of life. In the interest of survival many Sto:lo people now accepted the
priests' teachings and help because they rejected the use of alcohol and
advocated native isolation. In 1861, Saint Mary's Mission was started as a
'centre of adult or community evangelization and westernization'.[4] This
centre was based on a 'reduction' church village model[5] where the intention
was to 'teach the Christian religion and the diverse trades of civilized folk
to the permanent population'.[6] The priest decided to start a youth version
of the reduction model by establishing a school for boys. A recruitment trip
by Father Gendre resulted in the enrolment of forty-two boys. In 1863, these
Sto:lo children experienced their first institutionalized schooling.

Values of 'faith, time, work and order' predominated in the Catholic schools.
'The hold of the stubborn older Indian generation was to be broken and their
influence of the debauched camp life counteracted'.[7] All classes were
subjected to strict discipline. After a year of operation, a 'Missions' report
written by Father Gendre affirms its success Christianizing the young boys:

> Trying to change the old generation so superstitious, and so hard headed
> is something very difficult but not impossible, while it was perfectly easy

to implant in the hearts of the young natives the religious beliefs and to make them good Christians.[8]

Of matters pertaining to curriculum he wrote:

Here we spoke only of God and the Immaculate Mary; here was the place of good prayers and songs of joy ... Most of these children showed good character for reading and writing; they started to spell easily the first books of English lectures, a few were already able to write in a way that was very reasonable.[9]

In 1866, Father Foquet, principal of the school, summarized their educational approach in a letter to federal government official, Mr Arthur Birch:

In the begin(n)ing our endeavours have been more especially directed to develop the moral, intellectual and physical faculties of the boys and furnish them with ideas and notions absolutely required before they can read with interest and understand what they read. When they will be able to comprehend fully the meaning of what they read we hope that they will make the same progress in reading they have made in writing, arithmetic, and geography. The school boys are also taught how to cultivate the soil ... these boys do all that is to be done in the establishment, some are fishermen, some woodchoppers, some bakers, some cooks, etc.[10]

A school for girls was started in 1868 by the Sisters of Saint Ann. It was located in a separate building at St. Mary's. Besides receiving a primary education, they learned housework, sewing, and English.

Annual reports to federal governmental officials from Father Fouquet continually cited examples of the successful results of Christian education for Sto:lo children. He assumed that children were conforming to the church's acculturation methods because they obediently learned the curriculum's content and the priest's religion. Furthermore, the Order's farming skills and various trades were quickly mastered and used mainly for the school's maintenance. The children's families established new homes next to the mission. Because the Roman Catholics willingly assumed responsibility for the First Nations' education and reported positive results they were given federal government grants to assist with the school's operation. Neither the federal nor the provincial government were willing to, or capable of, educating First Nations' children when confederation occurred in 1867, so religious denominations continued to accept this responsibility.

The federal government continued their earlier practice of granting financial assistance to the churches to operate schools for First Nations' children in Western and Upper Canada. Justification for this support is contained in s.93 of the British North American Act which states: 'Nothing in any law shall prejudicially affect any right or privilege with respect to denominational schools which any class of persons have by law in the province at the time of union.[11]

A new Mission school was built in 1873 to house both boys and girls. Additional subjects of geography and history were included in a half-day programme. Academic subjects were taught for half the day and the remaining time was spent on learning the trades – a way of carrying out school maintenance.

One Roman Catholic ambition was for school 'graduates' to intermarry and live in a model village separated from the non-Native communities. They wanted the Sto:lo to be devout Catholics and hard working Westernized farmers and recognized that an insular community would be less likely to be contaminated by the vices of white society.

In 1898, a total of 88 students attended St. Mary's, from a Catholic Sto:lo population of approximately 2,000.[12] These figures reveal that not many of the children were attending school! What were the Sto:lo people doing with their children? Many were involved in seasonable employment at fish canneries, berry fields, and hop fields, and in traditional food gathering and cultural activities. They also worked on the railway, on steamships and in mills.[13] The continued strength of the traditional lifestyle was also in evidence. The children participated in seasonal cultural activities with their adult relatives. The British Columbia newspaper wrote:

> The Lucky Indians of the Fraser Valley, arriving in Victoria at the end of August rich from the Fraser fisheries, then leaving next morning for Pullyallup and White River (Washington) hop fields. The good wages from fishing and hop picking were even more profitable than Indian gold mining.[14]

Sporadic and low student attendance at First Nations' schools across Canada eventually resulted in federal government action because the schools were considered to be expensive. In 1894 an Order-In-Council introduced renewed strong educational policies. First Nations' children between the ages of 7 and 16 now had to attend school regularly. Parents disregarding this law were liable to fines and imprisonment. The government could also build or authorize existing schools within the framework of a newer 'Industrial' system. The purpose of the Industrial school was to 'civilize the savage nomad — to ready the younger generation for self-supporting lives as farmers or workers on the reserve on the model of white citizens'.[15] These schools were to be located at various centres throughout British Columbia. They differed from early missionary schools by 'teaching scientific agriculture and trades and the English language not just the gardening and roof repairs offered at the missionaries' industrial school'.[16] The government also wanted First Nations' students prepared for work in white towns. The focus of education and the curriculum began shifting from Christianization to assimilation.

St. Mary's immediately converted to the new industrial system by enlarging their facilities, increasing the industrial trade courses and following the curriculum prescribed by the federal Indian department. Government policy and competition with the Methodist church prompted rapid change in the Roman Catholic educational system.

In 1840, the Governor and committee of the Hudson Bay Company agreed to let the Wesleyan Methodist Society establish missions in the area between James Bay (now in Ontario and Quebec) and the Rocky Mountains (in British Columbia). The Methodists gained notoriety through their evangelic zeal, schooling and medical services that they provided. In BC, Thomas Crosby was the best known Methodist who worked only with native people along the province's coastline, from 1862–1914. (If reference is required: C. Anderson, T. Bose and J. Richardson, *Circle of Voices: A History of the Religious Communities of British Columbia* (Lantzville, BC, 1983, pp. 198–201).

During the 1860s, the Methodist missionaries entered Sto:lo territory and established their first educational institution, the Coqualeetza Mission Home two decades later. The Coqualeetza Home was destroyed by fire in 1891 and replaced by a much larger educational facility by 1894, which was renamed the Coqualeetza Industrial School. (If reference is required: H. Edmestan (ed.), *The Coqualeetza Story, 1886–1959*, Sardis, BC available at the Coqualeetza Education Centre.)

The new Coqualeetza Industrial School was officially opened in 1894. Financial assistance was obtained from the federal government and administration was the responsibility of the Methodist church. The half-day academic and manual training system was followed with a wider variety of trades offered. Boys learned farming, carpentry, shoemaking and blacksmithing. Girls learned cooking, homemaking, sewing, and knitting. Sto:lo children of any religious faith were admitted. Religious indoctrination was not as strongly emphasized as it was by their Catholic competitors. The local newspaper, the *Chilliwack Progress*, often reported the activities and opinions of school personnel. An edition on 30 January 1895 published the school's aim:

> to turn out young boys and girls established in the Christian character, with as much general information on subjects of interest, as will enable them to take their place among white people with the idea of ultimately establishing comfortable and happy homes of their own.[17]

Student enrolment increased from 62 in 1894 to 115 by 1901. The *Progress* which faithfully reflected the dominant society's patronizing attitude toward First Nations, reported Coqualeetza as thriving in a later report on 24 July 1901:

> Everything (90 acres) is kept in splendid order, thus the pupils have an object lesson every day in order, frugality, cleanliness and thrift. The money expended is a splendid investment. The boys and girls are trained to be good citizens, most of them becoming useful and intelligent servants.[18]

After reaching 17 years of age, students could leave the school wth a maximum grade six education. However despite the ostensible advantages of the school, the first 'leaving' classes of 1905–6 contained fewer than fifteen students each. The low numbers again indicate that most First Nations' children were being kept away from school for various reasons. As we shall see shortly, First Nations' resistance to assimilation appears to have been one of them.

During the early 1900s the industrial schools seemed to be operating adequately in British Columbia. However, throughout the prairies and eastern Canada a different situation existed, which eventually changed the education system again. Failure of First Nations' people to conform to the school's expectations, resulted in the federal government assuming direct responsibility for First Nations' education. Greater governmental control over educational aims and curricula was now implemented.

INFLUENCE OF GOVERNMENTS

By 1910, the Department of Indian Affairs reorganized its education branch to remedy the problems of poor support and attendance experienced with the industrial education systems across Canada. Policy revisions appeared necessary. A contract was drawn up to improve standards in the physical facilities, in the criteria for hiring teaching staff, in the curricula to be taught, and in maintenance/operation procedures. The contract of 1910 became the blueprint for all industrial and boarding schools until 1940. Joint control now was shared by the churches *and* federal government. Increased financial grants were allocated to those schools which met specific government requirements.

> Female pupils were to be instructed in cooking, laundry work, needlework, general housewifery and dairy work .... The management was required to teach all the pupils in the ordinary branches of an English education, calisthenics, physical drill, and fire drill. As well, the pupils were to be taught the effects of alcoholic drinks and narcotics to the human system. The more advanced pupils were to be instructed in the duties and privileges of British citizenship, and have explained to them government and law of Canada. Schoolroom exercises were to be given for five days each week. Industrial, agricultural, and domestic science instruction was to be given for six days each week. Vacations were not to exceed one month every year, and could be held between the 1st of July and the 1st of October of each year.[19]

By 1923 the schools for First Nations' children were officially called Residential schools. In the Sto:lo area, the new Coqualeetza Residential school was officially opened in 1924. Its pupil capacity rose to 200, making it the second largest residential school in Canada. First Nations' children from the Northwest coast of British Colombia also attended Coqualeetza. Manual training, agriculture, horticulture, boat building, and domestic science were offered. An ever greater emphasis on vocational training developed during the late 1930s. The federal education branch no longer prepared the students for assimilation into the white communities. Was training for assimilation a failure? Were jobs not available in white communities? The aim now was to help the First Nations' students make a living on their reserves. Until 1927 the maximum grade offered was grade six. High school grades from seven to nine were included after that date.

During the residential school era, the children's own culture and language were forbidden. There are numerous examples of beatings and strappings for speaking native languages. The children's lives were rigidly timetabled and filled with religious instruction, basic academic subjects and homework, and industrial trades and school maintenance work. They lived in a strict formal institutionalized manner for ten or more months every year from the ages of 7 to 16: a lifestyle antithetical to that of their cultural community.[20] First Nations' leaders throughout British Columbia voiced their concern about the negative effects of residential education upon their children, families and communities. Children were returning home as strangers to the cultural ways of their society, and had become critical of the traditional family and community way of life. One pupil condemned the residential schools for devastating the family unit and denigrating the students' culture:

> Our values were as confused and warped as our skills. The priests had taught us to respect them by whipping us until we did what we were told. Now we would not move unless we were threatened with a whip. We came home to relatives who had never struck a child in their lives. These people, our mothers and fathers, aunts and uncles and grandparents, failed to represent themselves as a threat, when that was the only thing we had been taught to understand. Worse than that, they spoke an uncivilized and savage language and were filled with superstitions. After a year spent learning to see and hear only what the priests and brothers wanted you to see and hear, even the people we loved came to look ugly.[21]

In the early 1900s, many Indian band members throughout British Columbia began voicing their concern regarding governmental services such as education. Many Sto:lo parents did not want their children to attend the residential schools. They asked the federal government to establish schools on the reserves where their children would attend school during the day. The children could then live at home with their families. The McKenna–McBride Commission, a joint federal and provincial committee, was established to consider these requests and to document the reserves' living conditions. They surveyed the Sto:lo area during 1915–16. At each reserve they met with the Chief and a few band members. Concerning education they asked three brief questions which did not address either the quality of education or the importance of an appropriate curriculum:

1. How many children of school age, attended school?
2. Which school did they attend? (St. Mary's Boarding School, Coqualeetza Instructional Institution or local public schools).
3. If they did not attend school, why not?

Chief William Sepass, a respected leader, expressed a common concern regarding the quality and purpose of the education being received by the children.

When the children are sent to school both to the Coqualeetza and also the St. Mary's Mission, they don't get a thorough education. They just get nicely started – they just get their eyes opened the same as young birds and then they are turned out to fly. They don't get enough education for a livelihood nor are they taught a trade of any kind. We have just been talking about a day school, and if it is done in the same manner it would not be up to much.[22]

Reserve-day schools were subsequently established on some reserves. The curriculum of these schools offered the basic subjects of reading, writing, arithmetic, and religion.

By 1917, a day school was operating on the Chehalis reserve, with one teacher, and thirty-four students. The first teacher's report was positive.

The attendance at the school continues to be most satisfactory. The children have progressed rapidly, and have shown great anxiety to second the efforts of their teacher in every way. I am pleased to report that the older children continue to show very good ability in grasping arithmetic, a good test indeed of their brain power. The parents are quite keen in most families about the progress of their children. [23]

However by 1932, according to federal government education inspectors, attendance was a major concern. The local Indian agent explained the lack of attendance in a letter to government officials:

I gather that Mr Barry was most indignant that only three children were present at the school. I consider it only fair to point out to the Department that the Indians have to earn their living, and that the entire Band are away, picking berries and taking part in the other seasonable work in the Fraser Valley.[24]

The school's teacher wrote a lengthy letter to further emphasize attendance problems:

Here the average Indian child attends school for about five months in the school year. It is not reasonable for Inspectors or for anyone else to expect that a child, even a white child can accomplish as much or absorb as much in five months as in ten months. We have on our Roll Book children who have only been to school four days in the Quarter, others ten days, twenty-five days and thirty-six days during the same period.[25]

Government officials and educationalists considered economic survival and illness to be the main causes of absenteeism. However, a letter written to the Indian Department in 1936 by the Chehalis band members offers a rather different analysis of the problem.

On March 5th last a general meeting of our Chehalis Band with their Reserve Council was held. It was unanimously agreed to apply to the Indian Department for a change of teacher for our Indian Day School for the following reasons:

The children attending school will do so only under compulsion (sic) as they claim that their teacher is not giving them proper attention during school hours. The parents are sure that these children should make more progress in the school than they have been making. The parents are also certain that their children are not taught as they should be covering the subject of each grade thoroughly, before promotion to a higher grade. As this teacher has been here for over ten years we do not think he can change his method to suit us.

The Indians of our band are quite willing and anxious to do their part in educating their children, but we are asking the Department to give us a capable Instructor who will take a deeper interest (sic) in the progress of our children and our own welfare.[26]

The teacher referred to was not trained as a teacher, but government officials felt he did a satisfactory job. An inspector wrote on the matter:

While he is not a trained teacher, and the children do not make the same progress as they might with a modern highly trained instructor, he is rendering good service to the Department in a variety of ways.[27]

First Nations' leaders began requesting integration from federal and provincial governments. Because non-natives were gradually becoming aware of historical inequalities through public media reporting, there was increasingly more support for integration among the non-native population.[28]

Both provincial and federal governments indicated their support for this move by altering legal legislation. In 1949 the Public School's Act, amended s.13 Chapter 57 to allow for negotiations with federal authorities via joint agreements.[29] Financial assistance through tuition fees was the focus of these agreements. By 1950 the federal government paid an annual tuition fee payment of $150 for each Indian child attending public school. A year later, the Federal Indian Act was revised. The education section now stated that education agreements could be made with provincial school boards, religious or charitable organizations. The responsibilities of national and provincial governments were clearly established in the joint agreements. In British Columbia the province was responsible for the administration and supervision of the education experienced by First Nations' students. The role of the federal government was to provide financial support. In 1958 the school population of Indian children enrolled in federally run reserve-day schools totalled 6,411.

This brief consideration of the Chehalis reserve-day school is of some interest. Not only does it reveal significantly differing views of the causes of absenteeism on the part of the Sto:lo and government officials it provides evidence of an enthusiasm for, and desire for high quality Western schooling on the part of the Sto:lo leadership and a less acute concern with the quality of this education on the part of officialdom.

The forces in favour of integration of First Nations' children to the British Columbia public school system gained momentum after the Second World

War. First Nations' participation in the war resulted in 'eye-opening' experiences. Among other things, First Nations' people saw the nature and quality of government service provided for others, especially in education. Parents began questioning the necessity of teaching religion and the quality of teachers and resources provided in the residential and reserve-day schools. They wanted educational parity by enrolling their children in provincial schools. First Nations' children enrolled in provincial and parochial schools totalled 2,335. This situation changed drastically in the 1960s as the federal government's support for integration increased. The number of residential and reserve-day schools diminished. Residential schools now functioned as hostels for First Nations' children with home problems. The students attended the local public schools during the day and the hostels were their substitute homes.

Department of Indian Affairs (DIA) administration policies now stated that their long-term objectives were to 'assist the Indians to participate *fully* [emphasis added] in the social and economic life of Canada'. Education was viewed as the primary means to these objectives. A report issued in 1961 by the Joint Committee of the Senate and the House of Commons on Indian Affairs stated:

> ... the key to full realization of self-determination and self-government and mutual self-respect for the heritage and culture of Indian and non-Indian will be found in the field of education ... Education is necessary if Indian people are to be able to fit properly and competently into our economic and social structure and effectively fill the role, which will be demanded of them in years to come, as spokesmen and leaders of their own people.[30]

The federal philosophy of school integration was further exemplified by such statements as 'We believe that by having Indian children and other Canadian children grow up and play together in the same school yard, they will work together better in later life'.[31]

Because integration was a radical change, various groups were established to monitor the results. One was an Indian integration committee, which examined reports from local parent–teacher associations and suggested various recommendations. These recommendations called for increased First Nations participation in school programmes and more curriculum content about Canadian Indians.[32] Theirs was the first of many studies on integration.

The results of integration were examined from both educational and social perspectives. Three major studies were completed between 1955 and 1965. Peterson and Parminter[33] examined the situation in British Columbia while Hawthorn's report [34] was national in scope. Lester Ray Peterson's study[35] reiterated many native Indian concerns about the failure of the integrated school system. A major reason being that, 'They have very little to say in the kind of school their children attend, and no voice whatever in the curriculum followed by it ... The lack of initiative or perseverance which characterizes many Indian children is attributed by teachers and principals to different Indian values or attitudes'.[36] However, stated Peterson, it was much more likely to be lack of motivation arising from lack of parental involvement in decision-making. The exclusion of parental participation in the formal education process was a major weakness of integrated schooling. Parminter's survey indicated that teachers, administrators, and Indian Affairs Branch personnel considered initial integration a success. It might be reasonably inferred that these stakeholders either could not admit failure or naively believed that assimilation through public school integration was still the best type of education for First Nations' children. Parminter's summary of teachers' and principals' responses to integration also showed that First Nations' children were coping only adequately at best, and that problems related to attendance and academic progress were increasing.

Another survey directed by H.B. Hawthorn through the mid-1960s focused on integration of First Nations' children across Canada. The original purpose of this study was for use within the Department of Indian Affairs. Because it was the only major Canadian research to assess First Nations education during this time, it quickly attracted attention. Its influence was evidenced in provincial First Nations education remedial programmes of the 1970s. Programmes such as learning assistance, nursery/kindergarten provision, alternate high school classes, and cultural activities were established.

Hawthorn's conclusions emphasized the dismal situation that First Nations' students had to cope with within the school system. Many of their difficulties were traced to differences between school and home cultural values, beliefs, experiences, and expectations. Irrelevant curricula, students' fear of ridicule, failure and punishment, inappropriate testing and language difficulties were widespread problems. Hawthorn's report succinctly stated the problem:

> It is difficult to imagine how an Indian child attending an ordinary public school could develop anything but a negative self-image. First, there is nothing from his culture represented in the school or valued by it. Second, the Indian child often gains the impression that nothing he or other Indians do is right when compared to what non-Indian children are doing. Third, in both segregated and integrated schools, one of the main aims of teachers expressed with reference to Indians is 'to help them improve their standard of living, or their general lot, or themselves', which is another way of saying that what they are or have now is not good enough; they must do and be other things.[37]

Hawthorn's recommendations stressed the importance of increasing integration with critical adjustments to the school curriculum so that the First Nations' child could at least have his cultural identity acknowledged. Inclusion of local cultural content in provincial curricula was urged to replace the stereotyped images of Indians. 'The Indian is always portrayed as a plains Indian with the ubiquitous feather band. Much of the material is as unrealistic to the Indian child in school as it is to the non-Indian'.[38] Other suggestions however, aimed to ameliorate cultural and social difference by providing help through remedial pro-grammes. The need for special classes and preparatory programmes which would develop English language and related skills essential for functioning in public schools was stressed. Overall, the methods for addressing cultural differences focused on getting the First Nations' student ready to fit the educational system rather than making any significant change to the educational system!

Hawthorn's report recognized and emphasized differences between the child's home and school cultures. The conditions of the former were viewed by many educators as a handicap to learning. Lack of verbal participation, tardiness, absenteeism, and English language differences were common problems cited by teachers. Therefore, the decade of the 1970s brought an increase in social services provision and remedial learning programmes to aid First Nations' students.

Until the mid-1970s, if the cultures of the First Nations were addressed at all in the school curriculum, it was mainly through history textbooks. Harro Van Brummelen's 1986 review of textbooks used in British Columbia's public schools between 1872 and 1925 states that the general portrayal of 'Indians was . . . as cruel and revengeful, spending their time gambling, smoking and feasting . . . pictures made native people look backward at best, brutal and savage at worst'.[39] Even though British Columbia's First Nations' people were generally described as 'friendly', their totem poles were described as 'rude, imperfect monuments'.[40]

McDiarmid and Pratt's examination of textbooks utilized in Ontario and Manitoba during the mid-1960s indicated that the image of First Nations was still negative:

> The main feature of the textbooks under review is their tendency to treat the Native as an impediment to be removed so that the goals of European progress can be realised. After dealing with this conflict, the authors ignore the later history of native people.[41]

Their analysis of terminology used in social studies texts revealed that terms such as 'savage and hostile' were used more frequently than 'friendly and happy' to describe First Nations' people. Europeans were usually described as 'great and good', and less frequently as 'bitter and angry'.

In 1974–5, Walter Werner with colleagues completed a national study, *Whose Culture? Whose Heritage?* which examined the multicultural content of social studies curricula prescribed for elementary and secondary schools. They found predictably perhaps, that the cultural biases, stereotypes and perspectives of the group who has the power to control programme development thereby become legitimized as the proper interpretive schemes for Canadian history and for contemporary issues.[42]

First Nations and the Inuit were the most noticeable in this context. They were represented from either a British or French perspective. These interpretations tended to romanticize and stereotype Indian cultures, especially at the elementary school level. The image of native people was not one of multiple linguistic groups, pluralistic cultures, and diverse lifestyles. Rather, they were lumped together and given homogeneous characteristics.[43] Further-more, information on their cultures was presented as bizarre, disjointed facts which, in effect, trivialized and dehumanized them as the following teachers' information taken from a grade three curriculum reveals:

- the Native Indian is not dirty, alcoholic, or lazy by nature
- they did not work for work's sake but did work hard and were capable of extreme endurance when there was work to be done
- they had a mental telepathy as a form of communication because it was possible in a culture unhindered by materialism
- many Indian children own very few manufactured toys, but find sticks, tin cans, stones and old tires which are of little value to them and are readily replaceable; as he tires of his toy such as an old tire, he will leave it along the road for someone else to play with, for there is little individual owner-ship of toys.[44]

At the secondary school level, students studied First Nations predominantly in an historical context or examined First Nations' problems of integrating into Canadian society. How were these students expected to gain a realistic understanding of First Nations' cultures?

Werner described the common approaches to teaching about First Nations' cultures as 'museum and heritage' at the elementary level, and 'discipline and issues' at the secondary level. The former approaches tended to reinforce stereo-types because of the emphasis on tribal differences and lack of depth. The latter approaches tended to be paternalistic and ethnocentric because of the Anglo-French domination when referring to ethnic relationships. Through the discip-lines approach First Nations' people became objects of study in an early anthro-pological style. Ultimately this style of learning about ethnic peoples:

Tends to place the students in a detached relationship to ethnicity. He is encouraged to objectify various groups under social labels (e.g. integrated, acculturated, assimilated, alienated, adapted), to look at groups as if they were objects in a laboratory and to obscure the life goals, attitudes, and interpretations which groups' members have of themselves.[45]

The public school era of integration reinforced the devaluation of the Indian students' cultural background brought about by the emphasis by the dominant society administrators and teachers of the public school system on the dis-advantages created by their culture. At this time very few changes were made to include the Indian child's cultural background. The First Nations' culture was not considered to have any great social or educational value, and was therefore considered of little importance for the school curriculum. When it was included, content and pedagogy was of a 'piecemeal' nature and tended to reinforce or establish misguided 'myths' about First Nations. Frequently teachers did not understand, or were not prepared to teach about First Nations. For their part First Nations' people did not have any major power to influence the cultural curriculum either. The main focus of the education experience of First Nations' children of the public integrated school system from 1950s to 1970s was still assimilation. Therefore this fact coupled with the high drop-out rate (96 per cent of First Nations' children never completed high school) reported by the 1971 Standing Committee on Indian Affairs, provided the impetus for yet a further re-examination of education of First Nations' people.

Other factors which helped to bring about educational change were the increase of political awareness and the concomitant determination of First Nations' peoples to confront their problems. Local and provincial First Nations' organizations began to voice their concerns through conference recommendations, surveys, reports, and confrontations with DIA staff. Through these actions, a new federal Indian education policy, *Indian Control of Indian Education*, was adopted in 1973 and has significantly influenced provincial education systems.

The Indian Control of Indian Education Policy was created by the National Indian Brotherhood, a political organization. Regarding cultural curriculum its policy recommended greater parental and community responsibility and administrative control; improved curricula with accurate and appropriate native content and pedagogy; increased numbers of properly prepared first Nations' teachers; and the offering of cultural awareness courses for non-native teachers at the pre- and in-service levels.[46]

The non-assimilationist stance of this policy is reflected in the following statements:

> We want education to provide the setting in which our children can develop the fundamental attitudes and values which have an honoured place in Indian tradition and culture. The values which we want to pass on to our children, values which make our people a great race, are ... found in our history, in our legends and in the culture. We believe that if an Indian child is fully aware of the important Indian values he will have reason to be proud of our race and of himself as an Indian.
>
> Our aim is to make education relevant to the philosophy and needs of Indian People. We want education to give our children a strong sense of identity with confidence in their personal worth and ability. We believe in education:
> - as a preparation for total living
> - as a means of free choice of where to live and work
> - as a means of enabling us to participate fully in our own social, economic, political and educational advancement.[47]

CONCLUSION

Religious educational aims to convert and 'civilize' First Nations' children were sanctioned by the Canadian federal government. The religious and governmental institutions conveyed the dominant society's ethnocentric view that the culture of the First Nations was 'primitive' in comparison with that of British or European cultures. The intent to assimilate First Nations children into the dominant society's world view was evident from the focus on basic educational and religious curricula and the denial of First Nations' culture and language in the missionary, industrial, and residential school systems.

The beginning of institutional schooling signalled the beginning of the decimation of many First Nations' societies. Children for over seven decades experienced alienation from their families; varying degrees of emotional, physical, and sexual abuse; and shame or denial regarding their cultural heritage. Problems of family breakdown, loss of cultural identity, confused self-concepts, unemployment and poor health were related to their school experiences. Separation and institutional living over the years hindered family closeness and roles. Rigid school routines conflicted with the seasonally based cultural lifestyle. At school, students were told what, when and how to do everything, and disciplinary consequences for infringements were harsh. Students would either rebel or became 'docile'. Both reactions conflicted with First Nations' cultural interactions.

Even though the children were provided with an education which ostensibly was to enable them to 'fit' in to mainstream society, the truth was that they did not. Many of the students did not become religious clones as the Roman Catholics envisioned, nor did they integrate into non-Native communities. Even if they chose to live off-reserve they were not given the same rights as other Canadian citizens. In British Columbia, First Nations' people were not allowed to vote federally until 1960. Many students did not achieve sufficient academic skills to compete for jobs. The 1913 *Canada Year Book* revealed that after two generations of schooling with the half-day programmes and sub-standard teaching resources and methods only one in three students could speak English fluently, and only one in seven could write it!

First Nations' students who experienced the early integration period of public schooling (1950s to 1960s) were still subjected to the assimilationist attitudes of teachers and curricula which either ignored or patronizingly portrayed First Nations' history and culture.[48]

First Nations' national, political and social responsibility and action to counteract the ethnocentric world view and approach of the provincial (public) and federal school systems eventually resulted in the 1970s in the establishment of the Indian Control of Indian Education Policy. It has taken over 125 years for the First Nations' peoples of Canada to regain responsibility for their culture so that they have a voice in the type of education and curricula received by their children and to walk away from the darkness of colonialism and to create new pathways to enable their children to walk forward with dignity.

8 Racism, the school and African education in colonial Kenya

Anthula Natsoulas and Theodore Natsoulas

Since the early twentieth century, when missionaries opened the first schools in Kenya, until the outbreak of the Second World War, the educational opportunities offered to Africans were sparse, substandard and designed to permanently relegate them to secondary citizenship. Such education rested on a racist foundation meant to meet the needs and desires of the three European interlopers – the colonial government, the missionaries and the settlers. It was through schooling that those in power during the colonial period sought to perpetuate the image of Africans as inferior and to maintain their subordinate position in Kenyan society. The process of traditional education which existed before the colonization of Kenya by the British was replaced by external agents with a system which reflected Western European norms and values. The African response was an attempt at both adaptation to and rejection of the image. In adapting to the image, Africans experienced a crisis of confidence, being made to feel inadequate in the face of the cultural hegemony and technological superiority of the Europeans. By rejecting the image, however, Africans expressed a reassertion of their own cultural identity. In looking at the dissemination and assimilation of the image of the African by the colonizer and colonized, the factors which defined the curriculum and moulded the process of schooling for the indigenous population as well as the response of the African Kenyan will be explored. The analysis will take place along a chronological development wherein reaction to the imposition of British authority in the educative process progressed from acceptance to resistance. The scope of the study will be until the outbreak of the Second World War during which the educational system remained static; after the war, efforts to change the system were made.

Education for the African in Kenya may be roughly divided into two periods: from 1900 to 1924 and from 1924 to 1940. Educational policy during the early period, dominated by mission societies with incidental government participation, was critical because it laid the basis for attitudes and expectations throughout the colonial experience. During this period it can be shown that two major conceptions were established: (1) the legitimacy of Western knowledge, and (2) the intellectual inferiority of the African. In the process of establishing these beliefs and as a consequence of their acceptance, education for the African focused on basic literacy and some vocational training. The focus was continued into the later period during which government became more directly involved in educational activities. Agricultural and vocational training was expanded and training for the semi-professional positions formalized. Such education was viewed by the British as the only type appropriate for the African. The African reaction to the education system imposed by the British was twofold and seemingly contradictory. One the one hand, the Kenyans appeared to internalize the values of their colonizers with respect to schooling and accepted that education in the European manner was desirable because it provided opportunities for financial and social advancement. On the other hand, the Africans rejected the limited education provided by the British who, they felt did not have the best interest of the African in mind.

Education, in its broadest sense, may be thought of as the preservation of a culture and preparation for the future. The formal institutions of schooling are only one aspect, although admittedly a major aspect, of the process of education in a society. Schooling cannot exist in isolation from the cultural matrix in which it is embedded and, in this context, is viewed as 'a matter of social practice . . . permeated with normative considerations and relations of power . . . a political process that simply cannot be seen as either neutral or objective.'[1] In colonial Kenya as elsewhere in the world, an important element of any system of institutionalized schooling is the curriculum. Such curriculums can be said to encompass more than simply syllabi and textbooks. In accordance with curriculum theory, three major categories of the planned curriculum may be extrapolated: (1) the official curriculum, (2) the taught curriculum and (3) the attained curriculum.[2] The official curriculum is that set of goals defined by government authorities whether national, regional or local. The taught curriculum is that which the teacher implements in the classroom. The attained curriculum may be thought of as that set of experiences which reside in the learner and include both the acquisition of skills and knowledge as measured by examinations and other means of evaluation and those aspects of the hidden curriculum which, at either a conscious or subconscious level, become part of the world view of the learner. Glatthorn[3] defines three constants of the hidden curriculum which contribute to the environment in which the official and taught curricula are developed: the ideology of the larger society, the definition of legitimate knowledge and the organization of the classroom environment. Among other things, the classroom environment includes the physical facility, programme and course options, selection of content, methods of learning. Thus, schools not only serve as transmittors of knowledge but also function to perpetuate the existing class and social structure of the society. In this context they have a dualistic function: firstly, confirming the culture of the ruling class while at the same time denying the legitimacy of the cultures of other groups in the society; and second, legimating the economic and political structure of the state.[4] It was under this dualistic function that schooling in Kenya operated during the colonial period up to the beginning of the Second World War.

The curriculum in Kenya, as it was developed by the colonial authorities and the missionaries, was meant to reproduce the power structure established by the British administration. Overt evidence for this will be found in the official and taught curricula including programmes and courses. The aspects of the hidden curriculum which support the view of the effect of schooling as reproducing the power structure will also be explored. This will include such items as language of instruction, British attitudes towards the beliefs of the Kenyans, financial expenditures, availability of educational opportunities, participation by the Kenyans in educational decisions. One of the racist suppositions on the part of the authorities was that most Africans would quickly accept their position. It will be shown that this was not so and that there was a movement among the more politically aware Kikuyu to modify or change the education system. In this context, then, the Africans and the curriculum are viewed in an interactive context and the schools are seen as performing a 'potentially transformative' function.

Much of the literature on British educational policy deals with general practice over a number of African colonies. Certainly, there were universals in the colonial African context. In many cases, and to varying degrees, there were the concurrent interests of three alien groups: the colonial authorities, the missionaries, and the white residents. In the case of Kenya, the latter saw themselves as permanent and influential settlers. The Advisory Committee on Native Education in Tropical British Africa was established in 1925 to oversee the schooling of the indigenous populations and this was a common element in all of African education. The major components of schooling for the Africans as articulated by the British were the same. Five curricular essentials were identified: (1) the three Rs, (2) scripture and moral instruction, (3) nature study, (4) literary studies and (5) arts and crafts and manual training.[5] Each colony, however, had its own unique configuration of social, cultural, political and economic factors.[6] Although some generalizations may be conceptualized in looking at the larger picture, it is only by looking at each country in depth that the effect of educational policy may best be analysed and understood. With respect to Kenya, most authorities take a similar view regarding the racist assumptions for African education. In reviewing the development of education during the early period from 1911 to 1924, Osogo concludes that the education provided to the Africans continued to be of a technical nature becuase the British 'did not envisage the Africans rising to a position of equality with the European community at any time'.[7] King studied the effort to impose on the Africans of East Africa the paternalistic and racist educational policy that was modelled after the African–American experience in the American South. The 'Tuskegee' model advocated a policy of separate education and cultural development of the African within the confines of a distinctly agricultural and vocational education. Sheffield argues that in the stratified society of Kenya, the settlers who had a dominant economic and political role helped shape a paternalistic educational policy which afforded to Africans a limited literacy and practical skills. Schilling focuses on British policy in the formulation of educational theory and practice for the Africans within the total Kenyan environment. Both theory and practice were moulded by the Europeans in order to perpetuate their dominance, but altered as time passed to meet the changing conditions and demands of Africans.[8]

A major source of information about the curriculum and attitudes and expectations of the British towards the African can be found in the records, correspondence and other papers found in the files of the Colonial Office. It is important that such documents be read critically; often, just as important as what is written is how something is written or what has been omitted. In the case of the *Department of Education Annual Reports*, especially during the early period, the curriculum was not always clearly laid out; nevertheless, inferences can be made. For example, in reporting on the progress of education in the Protectorate, Europeans are listed first, then Indians, then Arabs and then the 'Native' education. The fact that the educational activities of the Africans were listed last, that the Africans and the Arabs, until 1932, were grouped together and the use of the term 'native' suggesting no distinction among the different indigenous peoples indicates that the Colonial authorities regarded the educational needs of the African last and that not only did they not distinguish among African ethnic groups but also categorized Africans and Arabs as somewhat equivalent from the point of view of educational needs.

THE EARLY PERIOD

In the early part of the century, education for the indigenous population was primarily left to the various missions whose responsibility it was to provide for the African a vocational and basic literary education. A limited amount of education was provided to train teachers, clerks and evangelists. By 1907 there was a total of eleven missions of British, Scottish, French, Italian, German, American and Swedish nationalities with a total of 62 stations within what was then called the East Africa Protectorate. Among those for which records are available, there were 61 schools with a total enrolment of 2,230 pupils.[9] In these early years, the educational needs of the African were considered to be very fundamental. At the very beginning, instruction in whatever schools were available consisted primarily of vocational training, reading, writing and 'scriptual subjects' and some handicraft instruction. The literacy training which was provided was of the indigenous language in Roman letters with the English missions also teaching a limited amount of English.[10]

Basic literacy variously included the 'three Rs', the vernacular, KiSwahili, some English and the gospels.[11] Three components of the literacy education for the African during the early period may thus be identified: (1) scriptures, (2) language instruction and (3) numeracy. The way in which these three components became an implicit part of the Africans' curriculum suggests that very early in the colonial experience the legitimacy of Western knowledge and values was established. All three components continued to be an integral part of the curriculum during the later period.

It is significant to note that the missionaries considered teaching of the scriptures as basic literacy. The Education Department *Annual Report* of 1924 states that the missions agreed to 'exempt objectors from attendance at religious instruction'[12] suggesting that previous to this attendance had been mandatory. This underscores the importance placed on Christian teachings and suggests the European view of the African as 'amoral' and in need of being saved. The missionaries saw their goal to be the inculcation of Christian morality to replace pagan beliefs; the religious practices of the Africans, immoral in Western eyes, were not acknowledged. Such practices included polygamy, female circumcision, and what was seen as 'lewd' dancing during traditional ceremonies. The message transmitted to the African was that his culture and beliefs were not valid and that the Western way was better. This concern among the missionaries with instilling Christian values and the Colonial Office's tacit approval through financial support for the mission's educational efforts were to set the stage for the eventual rejection of the British education effort by the establishment of independent schools in the 1930s.

Language is a powerful factor both in ethnic identification and with respect to access to employment opportunities. It is necessary to make a distinction among teaching medium, teaching a second language which might be valuable in providing access to employment opportunities, and teaching about a language. The question of teaching medium is a complex one. On the one hand, if students are taught in their native tongue, they are in a better position to succeed in mastering the skills which the schools are trying to impart. On the other hand, by teaching only in the native tongue and not providing the opportunity to develop linguistic ability in the 'lingua franca', students are maintained in the position of secondary citizenship, not being able to enter into the world of the ruling class. In Kenya, teaching was done in the mother tongue and in some schools very rudimentary English skills were taught.[13] The reasons for such practices with respect to language can only be inferred. At best it may be concluded that the authorities felt that the Africans would have difficulty learning English. At worst, it may be summarized that a conscious attempt to maintain the subordinate position of the African was made and that the limited English which was taught was for communication with the Europeans. Separately from teaching in the vernacular, the missionaries also taught the vernacular. That is, they introduced rudimentary reading and writing skills of the vernacular languages to the Africans. In teaching reading and writing, the local language was written in Latin script – a European symbolic system.[14] Thus the value of the written word was emphasized by use of a script which was not indigenous to the environment. This leads one to question whether any consideration or acknowledgement was given to the African tradition of oral history as a means of preserving and passing down the traditions of a people. Just by teaching reading and writing, the European value of passing on the history of a people through written rather than oral means was instilled. It would be interesting to try to imagine the reaction of an African, unfamiliar with the written word, when he was shown a set of symbols which the white man said represented the language he spoke.

It is fairly easy to present arguments that the areas of gospel and language instruction were presented in the schools in such a way as to emphasize the British orientation resulting in the imposition of Western culture while rejecting Kenyan beliefs and traditions. Indigenous languages, written in Latin script, were maintained as the teaching medium with minimal instruction of English. Readers, by and large, it may be argued, reflected a European environment, unfamiliar to the African. Gospel lessons emphasized Christian ideals and morality, not taking into consideration the prevailing indigenous religions. Of the three components of basic literacy taught the African, numeracy might have been considered to be the most neutral or culture free. However, as Bishop suggests 'it is possible to put forward the thesis that all cultures have generated mathematical ideas, just as all cultures have generated language, religion, morals, customs and kinship systems'.[15] Compelling arguments may be made that even the basic numeracy taught to the Africans was largely Eurocentric and not reflective of the mathematical way of thinking of the indigenous peoples.[16]

Although conceptually, much of mathematics may be thought of as universal, the way in which the universals are actuated may be based within the cultural environment in which they are used. In this context, it is possible to identify six universal mathematics activities: counting, locating, measuring, designing, playing and explaining.[17] Included in practically all primary level mathematics curricula would be problem solving, number concepts, number words, counting, time and measurement. Of all these areas, problem solving might be most obviously susceptible to a British orientation. For example, a typical problem from a Tanzanian colonial textbook which had been approved for use in the schools by British colonial authorities and thus may be reasonably assumed to be similar to problems used in Kenya asks: 'The escalator at the Holborn tube station is 156 feet long and makes the ascent in 65 seconds. Find the speed in miles per hour.'[18] Such questions are clearly irrelevant to an African's daily life. In being presented with such a problem, a Kenyan student would have difficulty, not understanding the question because of the unfamiliarity of the setting as well as the units of measurement. It is not surprising, therefore, that we find in the annual reports of the Kenya Department of Education that 14 Kenyan students at Makerere University are found to be weak in mathematics, especially in problem solving. It is encouraging that the writer goes on to say that 'The existing method of teaching this subject may be at fault and the question is being investigated'.[19] Too often, however, the teacher may interpret the inability to understand and successfully complete such problems as an indication of the Kenyan students' lack of ability rather than the inappropriateness of the materials.

Less obvious is the cultural bias in the mathematical ideas of number concepts, number words, counting, time and measurement taught in the primary schools. There is no indication that the colonial government recognized the existence of mathematical thought that was uniquely Kenyan. Mention in the *Annual Reports* is made to the teaching of 'village crafts' suggesting that in those cases where the British taught the indigenous knowledge, they so specified.[20] Such references do not appear with respect to mathematics. A few examples will illustrate differences between British and African mathematical thought and how such differences might affect classroom performance.

Counting is a concept basic to primary arithmetic. The activity of counting is done by finger gestures among the Luo and Masai peoples.[21] The use of finger counting in doing school mathematics at best is discouraged, at worst is punished in Western classrooms. Among the Kikuyu and other ethnic groups of East Africa, there is a taboo on counting living things based on the belief that if an exact count is obtained, then the living things will be harmed.[22] Thus a European teacher who asks the students to count children or animals and receives a wrong answer may assume that her students cannot count whereas they are actually obeying their cultural norm of not providing an exact count of the living things. The amazing accuracy with which Kenyans are able to provide precise estimations of quantities belies comparable abilities among many Westerners where such skills are not adequately developed in schools.[23] A Kenyan child will thus estimate a quantity rather than take a precise count, estimation being the accepted way to perform counting operations. Another taboo centres on the use of the number seven. Among the Kikuyu the number seven is crucial in casting spells and is important to the magician; as a result it is considered to be an unlucky number. In being asked to do a problem where the result may be a seven, a child will not give seven as the answer because it is associated with death. Actually, among the Kikuyu there is not a number name for seven; there is only a non-number word (*mugwanja*).[24] Such beliefs and activities are part of the culture of the Kenyan peoples; they certainly are factors which should be considered in teaching mathematics to young children.

Another area in which concepts differ among the Kenyans is in the concept of time. Since sunrise occurs at the same time of day throughout the year, for the Kenyan, the time at which the sun rises is 1 a.m.; for the British, it is 7 a.m.[25] Children in school may be confused in being taught time concepts or being given instructions to do such and such a thing at a particular time. The units used in measurement are items which vary greatly from culture to culture; even in the contemporary world, there are two systems of measurement in official use. Among the Swahili, a unit of length called the 'shibiri', defined as the span from the tip of the thumb to the little finger, was in use. Furthermore, it is not clear that the concept of exact and/or uniform measure was routinely used. For example, you could buy *kibaba ch tele* or *kibaba cha mufuto* of grain, heaped up or levelled off pint measure. One could also buy a cubit of cloth *mkonomkamili* or *mkonomkonde* that is, full or short as measured by arms length.[26] The children who may have been instructed by their European teacher to measure a certain length or a given volume may easily have been confused by the nature of the exercise.

Among recreational mathematical activities, the game of mancala which is widely played throughout Africa, requires the use of complex problem solving and game strategies. This is an activity which has been an integral part of the cultural environment of the Kenyans and is an indication of the level of complexity of their mathematical thought especially when rule diversity is taken into consideration. It is generally played on boards containing rows of holes through which counters are moved in a anti-clockwise rotation. The boards generally contain two rows of six holes or 'houses' but there may be 5, 7, 8, 10 or 12 houses or 3 rows. The ultimate goal is to render an opponent incapable of play through the capture of houses. Although the game may superficially appear to be straightforward because of rule simplicity, its complexity becomes apparent to anyone who tries to understand it and strategies are developed by players over a lifetime of involvement with the game.[27]

In addition to basic literacy, the British authorities provided industrial and technical instruction for the African because, they stated, it is 'generally acknowledged that this is the first step in the regeneration of the savage'[28] and again, 'there is no doubt that this form of instruction is almost valuable discipline for the African native, whose intelligence is often sufficiently developed to appreciate fully the spiritual side of Christianity'.[29] The colonial authorities encouraged the missions to provide industrial and technical training by providing grants-in-aid to the missions for developing native technical education and through the establishment of the Ukamba Industrial School at Machako.[30] By the end of 1916, there were 38 pupils at the Ukamba Industrial School and the training in mission industrial schools produced 'several natives' who passed examinations as carpenters, masons and bricklayers.[31] The technical training which was provided consisted of the following areas: carpentry, masonry work, agriculture, saddlery, wagon and coach building, brick and tile works, general building, telegraphy, hospital dressers, tailoring, printing, gardening and road construction. In most cases the teachers were European.[32] It is reasonable to assume that the skills which were taught were imported from England. At best, it can be said that such techniques were adapted to the African environment. A reasonable question which might be asked is what were the Africans supposed to do with these skills once they were successful at mastering them? Either they were to build roads, houses, gardens, furniture, clothing and print books for themselves or for the Europeans. If it was for themselves, again the message that the British way is better is imparted; if it was for the Europeans, then they were being put in a position of subservience. It can be said that through vocational instruction, the British were assured of having the trained labour which would be needed to develop the colony according to the European vision.

Thus, by 1924 the foundations of the curriculum for the African had been established. In this early period, training for the African supported the ideological and practical concerns of the European community. Basic literacy imparted European-oriented knowledge. The teachers were to go out and teach the curriculum of the Europeans; the clerks were to work in the offices of the British; the evangelists were to teach the gospel of the Christian West. The vocational and technical skills were to be applied to both the indigenous and settler economies. The establishment of the legitimacy of Western knowledge had been accomplished in a covert manner and perhaps the missionaries and the colonial authorities themselves were not aware of the implicit assumptions upon which the schooling system which they established was based. The missions and the colonial government decided what was to be taught in the schools, in particular, reading, writing, numeracy, handicrafts, and technical skills; the missionaries introduced Christian teachings and established as their goal the inculcation of Christian morality to replace pagan beliefs. Thus, Western knowledge as imported into Kenya by the British, was legitimized in the schools and the value of African learning was denied.

In this context it is hardly surprising that the Africans were imbued with a lack of confidence in their own culture and traditions. In the presentation of the European religion and language, in the implicit and explicit rejection of African tradition, in technical schooling and even in a supposedly neutral discipline such as mathematics, the authorities sought to break down the Africans' sense of self-worth and to deny the validity of their own history. The colonial rulers delivered a shattering blow to the Africans' sense of confidence in themselves and in their traditional society. The British had been able to come in, take control and present an image of superior material well-being. Could this not be due, the African might have wondered, to the efficacy of the ways of the foreigners?

THE PHELPS–STOKES COMMISSION AND THE ADVISORY COMMITTEE

In the mid-1920s, an effort was made to create a system of agriculture and industrial schools, which would include some literary education, operated by mission societies and partially supported by government grants-in-aid.[33] The policy was one on which the colonial administration, missions, and settlers generally agreed; however, there were differences in their respective conceptions of what the ultimate function of education would be for Africans. The aim of the administration was twofold: (1) the development of 'the relations between the native and the European with all its social, political and economic repercussions' and (2) an apartheid-type situation in which most Africans lived in the reserves. The missionaries wanted to emphasize moral and religious development; the settlers wanted Africans to be provided with agricultural skills so that they could be useful on the European farms.[34] One of the most important points of agreement was that Africans should begin replacing Asians within the colonial economy. The Europeans had received a shock in the early 1920s when the Asian community challenged the settlers for supremacy in the colony. The resulting 1923 White Paper enunciated the principle of 'native paramountcy' which held that Kenya would be an African country, and that the Europeans would administer the colony until the time came that the Africans were able to take over themselves. The preparation of Africans for such an eventuality was perceived to take a long time, and therefore, European domination was to be indefinite.[35] A second point of agreement within the European community was too much of a literary education was not good for the Africans.[36] One fear may very well have been that there would be a repetition of the situation in India where the large numbers of the indigenous population who had received a literary education were unemployable and as a result were agitating for political rights.

In order to assist in the planning of the educational system for the African, two vehicles were used: the Phelps–Stokes Commission's recommendations and the Advisory Committee on Native Education in British Tropical Africa. In 1924 the Phelps–Stokes Commission was invited to summarize the current status of education in Kenya and make recommendations for its future direction. The leader of the Commission was Thomas Jesse Jones who supported a system of education based on the model of the black institutions in the American South. The Commission reported that the population of Kenya consisted of 2,500,000 Africans, 10,000 Europeans and 36,000 Indians. Of the £75,000 spent on education, £24,000 was for the Europeans, £12,000 for the Indians and £37,000 for the indigenous population; thus 49 per cent of the education budget was spent on the Africans who represented 98 per cent of the total population.[37] Government assistance was distributed among government institutions and the mission schools. In most cases, the teachers were European although there were attempts to train Africans. It appears that the general format was a mission station where the central school was located and a series of 'bush' or out-schools distributed around the countryside where the bulk of the population lived. The teachers at the central schools tended to be European; those at the out schools were African.

The recommendations set forth by the Phelps–Stokes Commission set the tone by which the future direction of education for the African should take. This group claimed to have the best interests of the African in mind and its paternalistic concern for the African was a reflection of the attitude expressed for the African American in the United States South. Two of the recommendations may be identified as laying the foundation for the nature of education for the Africans in Kenya. The first of these was the establishment in 1925 of the Central Advisory Committee on Native Education with representatives from the colonial authorities, missionaries and settlers.[38] It is significant that representatives from those for whom the education was intended, the African, were missing. The second recommendation of concern is the one which shaped the curriculum by defining the objectives of the schools to include: (a) the improvement of the health of the indigenous population, (b) the provision of skills in agriculture and industry, and (c) the inclusion of the education of women because such is seen to be 'essential both to the improvement of health and the morals of the people'.[39] These recommendations coincided with the objectives of the colonial authorities in that they were expected to be carried out within the confines of a separate cultural and social development of the Africans.

To achieve the stated objectives of schooling, the Commission made specific recommendations regarding language of instruction, and establishment of primary and advanced level schools. Regarding the use of languages, the Commission recommended the main languages, including Kikuyu, Luo and KiSwahili, serve as the first language of instruction, with English being taught to the more advanced pupils. To make schooling opportunities more accessible to the African population, it was recommended that schools be established on settlers' farms since such schools 'can be of great value in the increase of agricultural skill and in the maintenance and improvement of the morals and morale of the Natives who are employed in large numbers by the settlers'.[40] The Commission further recommended government support in the establishment of an institution which would provide advanced education to focus on the training of African teachers and medical assistants. The Commission supported the training of African teachers to attend to the many out-schools 'so that they may become centres of influence for the improve-ment of the masses of the Native people in the essentials of health, agriculture, industrial skill, village crafts, homes and character'.[41] The establishment of the Jeanes School for the training of the African teachers, which will be discussed below, was based on this recommendation.

The focus of educational efforts for the Africans continued to be from the point of view of the needs of the English colonial effort. Osogo, commenting on the Report, writes that the British 'did not envisage the Africans rising to a position of equality with the European community at any time'.[42] The objectives, as stated, highlight the secondary citizenship status in which the colonial government continued to hold the African population. Missionaries were to continue to co-ordinate much of the educational effort. Agricultural and vocational skills were to continue to be the emphasis of schooling, as was moral education. Teaching was to take place in the vernacular languages and the teaching of English language skills, a valuable commodity for advancement in an English-speaking environment, was to be limited to a small number of Africans. The establishment of schools on settler farms would make schooling easily accessible to those Africans who worked on the farms, a small and selective proportion of the indigenous population. The recommen-dations of the Phelps–Stokes report assured that the continuous thread of emphasis on vocational training and moral education was to be continued from the earlier into the later period.

The Advisory Committee on Native Education in British Tropical Africa was established in 1923 within the Colonial Office in order to oversee African education. It was very much under the influence of the philosophy and educa-tional principles espoused by the Phelps–Stokes Commission.[43] In its 1925 memorandum on African education it issued a series of recommendations that were to form the broad basis of British educational policy in the colonies. It recom-mended the fostering of education within the 'mentality, aptitudes, occupations and traditions' of the African people and to conserve as 'far as possible all *sound and healthy elements* [emphasis added] in the fabric of their social life'.[44]

The Africans, the memorandum continued, would be trained in agricultural, health, and industrial pursuits within their own cultural and social milieu thus leading to material improvement in their standard of living. The development of their moral character would be in the hands of the missions with whom education still predominantly remained. Specific recommendations included the recruitment of more European teachers, faster training of an African staff, teaching in the vernacular, and education for women.[45] In order to help support the missions, the Government provided a policy of grants-in-aid. Such payments helped to assure that the training provided by the missionaries was that which the authorities 'demanded.'[46] For the next fifteen years the colonial authorities were to struggle to create a system of African education more or less consistent with the Phelps–Stokes paternalistic spirit and the Advisory Committee recommendations.

THE LATER PERIOD

By the late 1920s, and despite the acceptance of the spirit and substance of the Commission, a clear definition of African educational policy still had not been articulated. In the annual report of 1929, H.S. Scott, Director of Education, outlined several factors that complicated education for the Kenyan: (1) more was needed to assist the African in his 'mental development' than the simple missionary objective of conversion to Christianity; (2) through contacts with the Europeans, Africans had come to believe that they wanted what the Europeans possessed; (3) along with the rising expectations of Africans came the realization that what the missionaries were offering was not sufficient; (4) the desired goal to create and develop an African artisan class to replace the Asians was intensified by the 1923 constitutional struggle between the European settlers and the Asians.[47]

The Government was committed to the notion that the missions would provide the basis of education in Kenya. A diagram of schooling opportunities for Africans, Asians and Europeans is shown in Figure 8.1. According to this schema, true primary schooling for the African did not begin until the fourth year; the first three years were devoted to elementary schools which must have provided training of the most rudimentary kind. Post-primary schooling for the African was available only through the tenth year or in the form of teacher and vocational training. A limited number of opportunities for advanced literary schooling was provided by the Alliance High School, a grant-aided secondary school established by several Protestant missions. At the apex of the vocational system was the Native Industrial Training Depot (NITD), a post primary school designed to provide additional instruction. Although the NITD, established in 1924, was considered adequate, primary education leading into admission was 'spasmodic and unorganized'.[48]The ultimate purpose of the training in which government and missions were to co-operate was to create the African artisan class.

The year 1929 was a watershed in African attitudes toward education. Africans were demanding educational facilities other than those provided by

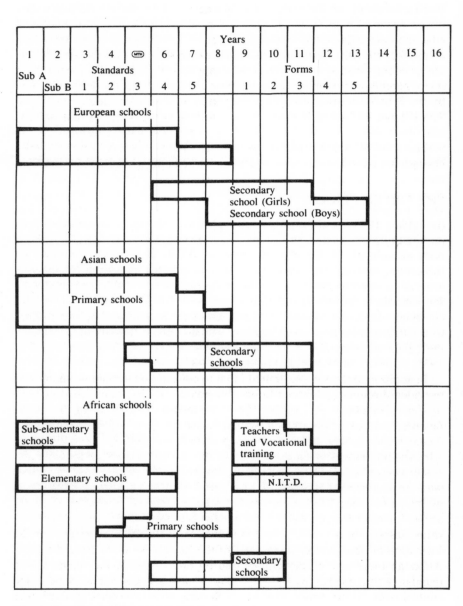

Figure 8.1 Classification used in Kenyan schools
Source: *Education Department, Annual Report, 1935.*

the missions. In Kikuyu and Kavirondo provinces, according to the Education Department, the Africans no longer agreed with the educational policy of the Advisory Committee. There was concern on the part of the colonial education authorities that unless a clear policy on indigenous education was delineated, the Africans themselves would expand their options by establishing independent schools. This had already happened in Kikuyu province where many parents had opted not to send their children to the schools controlled by the Protestant missions which supported a ban on female circumcision. The Kikuyu had asked the government to help them open the non-mission schools.[49]

The level of commitment of the Africans for the provision of expanded educational opportunities was evidenced by taxation which they imposed on themselves. The Local Native Councils (LNCs) for which Africans chose representatives and which raised money to help finance local improvement were formed in the reserves in 1924 to encourage participation in local initiatives. Through the years the Africans taxed themselves to improve both the quality of education and to expand opportunities. The disbursement of the thousands of pounds which had been raised by the LNCs, however, was subject to government approval. For example, in 1929 the LNCs were awaiting a decision as to whether or not the money they had raised would be used for schools to be erected in the reserves.[50] Furthermore, the *ex officio* chairmen of the LNCs were the District Commissioners thus imposing a limit to the degree of independent action that these bodies could take.[51] During the 1930s their contribution increased from £12,786 in 1932 to £14,711 in 1935, £16,387 in 1937 and £17,612 in 1939.[52]

In addition to the LNCs, limited input to educational decision-making was provided through the District Education Boards (DEBs) established in 1934 to supervise educational affairs. The composition of the DEBs, however, favoured control by government and the missions. Members included district medical and agricultural officers, representatives from the missions, and Africans nominated by the LNCs. As with the LNCs, the District Commissioner was *ex officio* chairman and the Inspector of Schools for each district was the secretary. Responsibilities of the DEBs included the allocation of grants from Central funds and from the LNCs, the establishment of salary scales for teachers and a fee structure for students, allocations of scholarships, inspection of schools, and approval or denial of applications for the formation of new schools. Decisions of the Boards were considered final.[53] Although there was an African or two on these Boards, the intent was to maintain a firm control over education by the authorities and missions through control over disbursement of funds including those collected by the LNCs and the granting of permission to open new schools. The latter was directed at the emerging independent schools which were not under control of either the missions or the government.

In attempting to extrapolate the attitudes and level of commitment of the colonial authorities for the educational needs of Africans during this later period, there are two major areas which can be examined. These areas are first, provision of financial support and opportunities and second, type of articulated curriculum. The first includes such items as expenditures, number of schools, number of students, preparation of teachers. The second includes such considerations as programmatic options, subjects taught, language of instruction. Both areas have implications for a hidden curriculum.

Data for government expenditures are provided in the annual reports of the Department of Education. A summary of such expenditures for African, Asian and European education as reported is shown in Table 8.1. Inconsistencies in the reported numbers may be due to inaccurate reporting. For all three groups the number of students increased as did government expenditures. Between 1928 and 1939 the number of African students increased by a factor or 1.5 while expenditures rose by a factor of 1.1. The number of Asian students increased by a factor of 3.9 while government expenditures doubled; the number of European students rose by a factor of 2.4 with an increase in expenditures of 1.2. For all three groups, the rate of increase in expenditures appears not to respond to the increase in numbers. Clearly, the financial support for African students did not keep up with increased enrolments even assuming that it was adequate in 1928. Support for Asian students came closest to keeping pace with increased enrolments; European parents can be assumed to have had other resources available to them to help assure the quality of their childrens' education. The year 1935 is one for which total population figures are also available. For this year, the report shows 3,024,975 Africans, 41,434 Asians and 17,997 Europeans residing in Kenya. A comparison of the number of students to the total population gives figures of 0.03, 0.16 and 0.06 for the proportion of African, Asian and European pupils in schools respectively. Clearly the proportion of Africans is lowest even assuming comparable proportions of adults and children in the total population for the three groups. It is also likely that European children were sent abroad for their education resulting in fewer numbers requiring schooling in the colony. Furthermore, not all of the African schools received government aid. For example, in 1937, of the 1,611 schools for Africans, 1,189 schools did not receive government financial support; in 1939 the comparable figure was 1,534 of the 2,096 schools for the indigenous population. The 1,534 schools that did receive government aid contained 71,285 of the students or 55 per cent of the African student population.[54]

In trying to determine the level of financial commitment on the part of the colonial government, it is useful to consider per-pupil expenditures for African, Asian and European students. This is done in Table 8.2 for selected years between 1929 and 1939. Per-pupil expenditure remained consistently higher for Asian and European students as compared to Africans. By 1939 per-pupil expenditure for Africans, Asians and Europeans had decreased by factors of 0.31, 0.15 and 0.39 respectively. In 1929 Asian students were apportioned six times more than Africans and Europeans were receiving forty-four times more; figures for 1939 show comparable factors of 7.4 and 38.5 for Asians and

Table 8.1 Educational statistics, 1925–39

	Africans[1]			Asians			Europeans		
	no. of schools	no. of students	Government exp. (£)	no. of schools	no. of students	Government exp. (£)	no. of schools	no. of students	Government exp. (£)
1925	2,536	8,634[2]	36,017	n.a.	1,644	11,943	n.a.	926	26,246
1928	2,536	85,556	72,003	44	2,554[3]	22,963	22	900[3]	42,492
1929	2,276	82,445	74,131	47	4,765	25,603	25	1,249	49,360
1932	n.a.	n.a.	76,472	51	4,856	32,371	n.a.	1,558	48,126
1935	1,467	96,523	74,097	75	7,431	34,060	32	1,790	44,041
1937	1,611	110,502	77,193	73	7,621	39,140	32	1,984	49,255
1939	2,096	131,125	81,869	85	10,004	45,602	35	2,171	51,881

Source: Figures compiled from Education Department, Annual Reports, 1925–1939.
Notes: 1 Until 1932 this group included Arabs; 2 This is the number of students in the government assisted schools: comparable figures for non-assisted schools are not available for 1925; 3 Does not include unaided schools.

Table 8.2: Government per-pupil expenditures and number of students per school, 1928–39

	Africans		Asians		Europeans	
	Per Pupil Expenditure	Students Per School	Per Pupil Expenditure	Students Per School	Per Pupil Expenditure	Students Per School
1928	0.84	33.7	9.0	58.0	47.2	41.0
1929	0.90	36.2	5.4	101.7	39.5	50.0
1935	0.77	65.8	4.6	99.1	24.6	56.0
1937	0.70	68.6	5.1	104.4	24.8	62.0
1939	0.62	62.3	4.6	117.7	23.9	62.0

Source: Figures compiled from Education Department, Annual Reports, 1928–1939

Europeans with respect to Africans. Although there was a decline in the proportional expenditures for Europeans and Asians versus Africans, the expenditures for the two non-African groups remained astronomically high. A careful appraisal shows that more money rather than less was being apportioned to Asian education – and at a time when the colonial government had articulated an interest in investing more money in African education so that the Asian artisan class could be replaced with trained Africans!

Thus, educational opportunities and government expenditures provided to the Africans continued to lag behind those of the Asians and Europeans. Furthermore, true primary schooling, as shown above, began later for the African student and did not last as long. Such pupils did not attain the levels deemed desirable by the Africans who felt that the missions did not provide adequately with respect to both sufficient number of schools as well as the kind of education. Proportionally, there were significantly fewer schools for the African than for either the Asian or the European. Furthermore, many of those schools were unaided bush or out-schools which had rudimentary facilities and improperly trained African teachers. African parents continued to seek not only better and more educational opportunities but also sought the teaching of English for more students and at an earlier level, since knowledge of English was seen as the path to economic advancement.

There is no doubt that the effectiveness of schooling depends upon the qualifications of the teachers. Another clear difference among African, Asian and European education may be found in the area of teacher preparation. Teachers in the European and Asian schools were required to have a higher degree of professional attainment than those in the African schools. In the European schools all teachers were white and had either to be university graduates and/or hold a 'recognized professional certificate' in order to teach in the primary schools. In the Asian schools as well, teachers had to be either university graduates or hold an approved teaching certificate. In contrast, in the African schools, only the European teachers were required to be either university graduates or hold a professional certificate or diploma 'approved' by the Director of Education. The African teachers who were in a supervisory capacity were required to hold a certificate from the Jeanes School and those who were technical instructors were required to hold their certificate from the NITD. Those teaching elementary school were required to have a Standard II certificate or 'endorsement' up to Standard III. Lower Primary school teachers were required to meet only a Standard IV requirement, and primary school teachers were required to have a minimum of a Standard VI certificate and a maximum of that certificate and 'endorsement' up to Form 2.[55] Thus, the African teachers in the elementary and primary schools, which most of the Africans who were in school attended, were significantly less prepared than their Asian and European counterparts.

Language, whether as a medium of instruction or as a school subject, is an important determinant of progress in learning as well as career options. The Africans' desire for a literary education to include the development of

English language skills was not met. In 1929, the Education Directors of the East African colonies met in Dar es Salaam and agreed that the colonies should have a standard policy toward language instruction. They recommended that in all the elementary schools the first medium of instruction was to be the vernacular language. This language was to 'give way' to the dominant indigenous language as soon as feasible. It would first be taught as a subject, then as the medium of instruction. The use of English would begin once students had mastered an 'approved standard' of the indigenous language and whenever there were qualified English-language teachers. The Kenya Legislative Council further refined these recommendations. The vernacular was the medium of instruction for the first four years; KiSwahili would be introduced as a subject during this period and then be the language of instruction in the fifth year. English was to be introduced at a time when there were sufficiently trained teachers. It was desired that English would be brought into the curriculum after six years of school. In those schools where English had been taught, it would become the medium of instruction.[56] In 1935, a revised syllabus provided for both English and KiSwahili as required subjects with the latter as the medium of instruction and for the examinations. Schools could petition the Director of Education to use English as the language of instruction. In 1934 there was one such application, and there was no increase between 1934 and 1938 of English medium schools.[57] The vernacular and KiSwahili remained the languages of instruction in all African schools except one in Kisii where English was used from 1939. The colonial authorities continued to discourage the widespread teaching of English. In conceding that some Africans ought to be trained for government work or teaching, the Director of Education in 1937 bemoaned the fact that 'it is to be regretted that the number of unemployed boys who can read and write and who have a fair knowledge of both English and KiSwahili is rapidly increasing'.[58]

Although there were some efforts to increase the literary content of education, the emphasis continued to be on vocational education. Crafts, including basket making, pottery, carpentry, and tailoring were taught. Students in the carpentry classes produced boxes, beds, tables, and repaired home furniture.[59] In 1937, the Director of Education commented that the importance of manual work must be emphasized by making handicrafts and agriculture compulsory in elementary and primary schools.[60] Until 1939 emphasis in the African schools was strongly on agriculture and vocational tasks for the male pupils and provided training in the 'domestic services' for the females.[61] The annual reports indicate that a form of tracking was present in the African schools. In the government school at Kakamega, all the boys took the same course until the end of Standard V, at which point they were divided into A and B groups. Pupils in the former track continued to take all courses which was considered the literary track; those in the latter dropped nature study and history and greater concentration was placed on vocations.[62]

In order to emphasize agricultural education, an agricultural scheme was made an integral part of the curriculum at the government schools. It was hoped that once students were taught proper agricultural methods, the use of the plough and draught animals they could introduce, in gradual stages, a mixed farm economy in the African reserves. Students first would be taught to grow cash crops, produce poultry, eggs and beeswax for sale in order to buy agricultural implements. They then would be taught to use draught animals, ploughs and to cultivate a small plot. Finally they would be given instruction in running a mixed farm of about nine acres. In the yearly reports on education there was constant reference to the progress in agricultural education made at various African communities. A description of further aspects of the curriculum reported that the pupils were instructed in terracing and methods of composting and in one school they were taught 'the value of penning cattle as a good and easy way of obtaining a regular supply of manure'.[63] Pupils and teachers contributed to the erection of buildings, the clearing of fields, and the planting of trees and shrubs. There even existed a type of outreach programme where local farmers were given demonstrations on proper methods of farming and forest conservation, and discussion of soil erosion. Products grown and raised on the school farms such as maize, seed potatoes and poultry were distributed to the local population.[64]

One of the stated objectives was to send the better pupils for post-primary training at the NIDT which, founded in 1924 and not fully operational until 1927, was to supplement vocational training provided by the missions. It was described as 'a crown to the mission technical school'. The authorities hoped that from the NITD the elite of the African artisan class would emerge.[65] Completion of Standard VI did not appear to be a necessary prerequisite and thus it was not a true secondary school since most students never completed primary school. In 1937, only one student out of 126 had passed the primary school examination; many of the boys had been in Standards IV and V, and none were accepted before the completion of Standard III. Although not a true secondary school, the Director of Education, however, considered that this indicated 'a certain amount of progress'. Between 1924 when it was first opened and 1937, 1,286 boys were given further training including 654 carpenters, 80 smiths, 22 tailors, 487 masons and bricklayers, and 43 painters and signwriters.[66]

Although the emphasis on education for the African was at the primary level, an effort was made to provide some post-primary opportunities. During the fifteen years between 1924 and 1939, several such schools were established. The three most important were the Native Industrial Training Depot (NITD), the Alliance High School, and the Jeanes School. The goal of the NITD, as discussed above, was vocational training and, as such, it was not a true secondary school.

The Alliance High School, created in 1926 by several Protestant mission societies and described as the academic counterpart of the NITD, was designed to provide the 'literary' side of African education. It was envisaged that the African professional class which would be engaged in commerce and teaching would emerge from this school. Although some science, history and maths were taught, especially in the first two years, emphasis was placed on agricultural education in the third year.[67] In 1929, of the twenty students that left the school, twelve became teachers, ten in non-government schools, one each in the Agricultural and Veterinary Departments, five others became clerks and another an 'agriculturist'.[68] By the outbreak of the Second World War the school had grown considerably, enrolling 119 students, but had not attained the hoped for position as a premier institution of learning. The curriculum still emphasized a vocational orientation including such subjects as typewriting, book-keeping, agriculture, carpentry and teacher training for primary school teachers. It was not until 1940 with the appointment of Carey Francis as its headmaster that the Alliance High School began to undergo a change and become a major force in Kenyan education.[69]

The Jeanes School was the third major post primary school in the 1920s and 1930s. It was established in 1924 based on recommendations by the Phelps–Stokes commission, modelled on black schools in the American South, and was designed to train a cadre of itinerant teachers who would supervise village schools and be closely associated with community improvements.[70] The Central Advisory Committee for African Education consisting of government officials, missionaries and settlers made the decision to open the school. Each of these groups appeared to have a different reason for supporting this venture. The colonial authorities believed that these teachers, coming from a government institution would extend government influence into the reserves at the expense of the missions. The missionaries believed that many of the Jeanes teachers would be former mission pupils already educated in Christian morals and ethics and thus become evangelists in the village schools. The settlers anticipated that thus there would be available a greater number of trained Africans for the schools on their farms leading to the improvement of the level of agricultural productivity.[71] The overall hope was that the Jeanes teacher would be trained to introduce into the African village school efficient and modern agricultural and animal husbandry techniques, health and hygiene education within the context of the indigenous cultural and social environment.[72] In this way not only would Africans benefit practically, but they would also be shielded from the deliterious effects of rapid Westernization. The underlying principle was the indefinite maintenance of white political and economic domination in Kenya with control over the rate at which Westernization would occur. Thus, the African would have to go through a considerable period of self-improvement under white supervision before being in a position to deal with political issues.

The mission schools, the Jeanes Schools, the NITD, all part of the colonial educational system, combined to instil in the Africans a doubt of their own ability to break through educational barriers which were designed to keep them in a subordinate socioeconomic status. The emphasis on a curriculum replete with vocational subjects, a minimum of literary subjects and English language instruction contributed to the frustration felt by the Kikuyu with the educational system provided for them by the British. There can thus be seen a tension within the African because of the two contradictory norms which the British had tried to establish: (1) the superiority of European learning and (2) the inferiority of the African as a learner. This resulted in a breaking apart and a regrouping in the self-worth system of the Africans. Accepting the value of European learning because it was seen as a vehicle for material advancement, they rejected the idea that they were unable to succeed in this arena resulting in demands for more European-style learning.

The lack of a literary education was a major factor in the resistance offered by the Africans towards colonial schooling, for the Africans had learned their lessons well. They had so well internalized the benefits afforded by Western-style education that at the same time that the African wanted to establish his own system of schooling, he wanted to emulate the British model of emphasis on literary training. The breaking point, however, as will be shown below, was the ban on female circumcision. Although the missionaries had tried to provide 'good moral training' for the African in the schools, it appeared that this aspect of the curriculum failed in achieving its goal of imparting the desired moral values and instead laid the foundation for resistance.

Amongst the Kenyan Africans, the Kikuyu had been most affected by European and mission education and, therefore, it was logical that it would be they who would lead the struggle to change the education system. They lived in reserves in central Kenya in the areas adjacent to Nairobi and the White Highlands. In fact most of the European settlements were on land that had been alienated from the Kikuyu who thus toiled on land that had traditionally belonged to them. It was also among the Kikuyu that missionaries made a concentrated effort of proselytization and education. Of all the Kenya Africans, the Kikuyu had the greatest contact with the European administrators, missionaries, and settlers.[73] They had two basic difficulties with the education provided by the misssions which, until the late 1920s, had held a virtual monopoly over African education. First, the Kikuyu believed that the missions did not provide sufficient educational opportunities to meet the needs of the population. In 1928, only 13,000 pupils were going to school out of a population of approximately 500,000 in Kikuyu Province in central Kenya.[74] The central and 'bush' schools provided by the missions were considered too few in number and inadequate in facilities. Secondly, the Kikuyu recognized that the agricultural and vocational training that was being provided was designed to maintain the economic and social status quo for them indefinitely. For those ambitious Kikuyu who considered a literary education as the only source for upward social and economic mobility the result was frustration.[75] Underlying these two concerns was a general loss of confidence in the missionary as an 'educationist'. The Director of Education, H.S. Scott, conceded that Africans wanted education as distinct from evangelization.[76]

Some private schools, with little success had been opened by the Africans during the 1920s, but the opportunity to launch a full-scale assault on the education system occurred in 1929. In their desire to rid the Kikuyu of 'barbarous' activities, three mission societies led by the Church of Scotland Mission (CSM), issued a ban on the practice of female circumcision. In October 1929, these missions announced that henceforth all of their African 'agents', primarily teachers, would be required to sign a declaration foreswearing female circumcision and including a clause which denounced the Kikuyu Central Association (KCA),[77] the premier African political organization, thus injecting a political element. This action by the missions was seen by the overwhelming portion of the Kikuyu population as a direct attack on their traditions and they, therefore, boycotted the affected missions' churches and schools. In many schools, especially those in the countryside, the boycott was 90 per cent effective. The boycott and subsequent demand for non-mission education was strongly supported by the KCA and education became an issue in its anti-colonial programme.[78] In order to restore to their schools and churches a degree of normalcy, the missions were forced to retreat. By 1931 they no longer required a signed declaration, and partially due to government pressure, they ceased to preach actively against the practice of female circumcision.[79] Consequently many students returned, but a considerable number remained outside the mission system.

The immediate problem faced by the dissenters was the education of their children. The two alternatives were the opening of more government schools or the establishment of African independent schools. In late 1929 the Director of Education was presented with a petition by the parents of boycotting pupils requesting that the government establish non-mission schools and offered to pay one-third of the teachers' salaries.[80] The CSM and other missions opposed this proposal arguing forceably that it was the policy of the Colonial Office to leave education in the hands of the missions.[81] The government response was in essence a support of the mission position. The authorities concluded that if they were to open government schools, the schism that existed between the missions and the populace would be further widened. Government policy had been and would continue to be one of support of mission education and government schools were not to be opened in areas where the missions provided education. In addition, the colonial authorities did not wish to incur the expense for the operation of a school system.[82] The KCA strongly suggested that despite the expense, the British should institute compulsory education 'as practised by all the civilized people of the world'.[83]

The government's position on the second alternative, the establishment of independent schools by the Africans, was not as clear cut, nor as easily taken. There was a fear that the KCA wanted to control an independent school system which would have a 'strong political bias' and would attract Kikuyu nationalists who would form a 'pan Kikuyu' movement.[84] The KCAs very strong support of these schools was viewed as one way in which the breach between the missions and the populace would be widened and the traditional leadership which was supported by the colonial authorities would be undermined.[85] The colonial authorities recognized the dilemma that they faced over the independent schools. The KCA could not be allowed to dominate the movement and yet if permission for new schools was denied, a growing portion of the population might be alienated and politicized. In several cases they were faced with a *fait accompli*. Some new schools had already been opened in defiance of the missions. In many instances in the 'bush' there was a struggle between the boycotters and the missions for physical control of the school sites.[86] The government continued to equivocate; a coherent and consistent policy was never clearly articulated during this period.

The independents were in the process of creating an infrastructure during the early 1930s, and although there were differences among them, they tended to consider themselves as part of a single movement. The schools were formed on a local level, with each dissenting community developing its own organization. The independent school impulse gave birth to two organizations – the Kikuyu Karing'a Education Association (KKEA) and the Kikuyu Independent School Association (KISA). The latter, by far the larger, located primarily in northern Kiambu and Maranga districts, had the reputation in government circles of being the more moderate body. The former, closer to European settlements, felt itself to be under more intense pressure from the European capital and saw their culture subject to a direct threat from Westernization. As a result they tended to be more jealous of their rights and customs as Kikuyu, even incorporating the Kikuyu word *karing'a* meaning pure or orthodox into their name. The KKEA tended to be more politically oriented and the KISA were more interested in purely educational matters. The independent schools eventually identified with one of the two organizations. Most of those in southern Kiambu eventually became part of the KKEA and those further away from Nairobi became part of the KISA.

One of the government's consistent criticisms of the independents was the failure to follow the Department of Education's prescribed syllabus.[87] The independents, however, claimed that there was very little difference between their course of study and that of the mission schools.[88] The differences appear to have been more of emphasis rather than of substance. The objectives of the KKEA were twofold: the first was to provide an education that would enable their students to compete for positions, albeit minor ones, in the civil service, business etc.; the second was to preserve Kikuyu identity and independence. For the former, a literary education with an emphasis on English was required. KiSwahili and subjects in the industrial and agricultural areas were de-emphasized, but not eliminated. For many dissidents learning KiSwahili was considered a waste of time for it was seen as a colonial tongue designed to keep the African subservient. The KKEA believed that if one learned to read and write English well, avenues that had been previously inaccessible would be opened. At the independent schools, English was introduced in Standard III, while at the mission schools it was introduced in Standard IV at the earliest.[89] A government official sarcastically commented that the 'chief bait' of these schools was the teaching of 'so-called English'.[90]

The second objective of the KKEA, that of making the pupils aware of their cultural heritage, was of concern for the colonial authorities. The underlying philosophy and practices of the KKEA schools made them suspect. Stress was placed on Kikuyu culture and pride in being a Kikuyu was emphasized; although customs such as female circumcision and polygamy were not encouraged, they were not overtly discouraged. Stories on land and culture were related, warnings were given to the children not to believe the missionaries who were accused of trying the confuse them, and not to trust the white man who was a threat to the survival of African heritage and traditions. These tales were meant to instil in the youth cultural, territorial and self-pride, cultural identity, and self-reliance. It was stressed that changes would occur, but within their own cultural environment.[91] A conscious affirmation of and expression of confidence in their heritage was thus explicitly made. The colonial authorities, on the other hand, found offensive the Kikuyu hymns and songs that were sung by the students after school and considered them as proof that the independent schools spread sedition and anti-mission sentiment. The following examples are illustrative of the songs:

Children of Mumbi, if they miss education, the
European never bothers.
The Indian has never missed sleep,
thinking what can help the Children of Mumbi.

Parents give us Pens. So that, if we are
attacked, we may be able to defend our black
warriors, when leadership grows old,
it needs to be renewed.

God renews Promises,
and they become whiter than the Sun,
and doesn't see any barrier,
which prevents Him from fulfilling them,
because God is omnipotent.[92]

Former KKEA students have insisted that there was no political content during the school day and that there was a separation of education and politics.[93] Since education, however, is one of the most effective means of socialization and the schoolroom is a place where attitudes are formed and an atmosphere for a particular ideology can be developed, the KKEA students and teachers were likely to have been more than sympathetic to Kikuyu political aspirations. To justify their claims of subversion, the colonial authorities did not need to see any overt anti-government instruction demonstrated.

CONCLUSION

During the years prior to the Second World War, the African Kenyans were forced into an educational system neither of their own making nor in their own interests. The colonial authorities, missionaries, and settlers engaged in both overt and subliminal collusion to introduce, foster, and maintain at best a paternalistic system, and at worst a racist system in which Africans were permanently relegated to a subordinate position. This European ruling class attempted to legitimize two aspects of its own culture in colonial Kenya. The first were the broad philosophical assumptions of a stratified British society as set forth by the Colonial Office. The second was reflected in the missionaries' desire to proselytize under the assumption of the superiority of Western religion. Supporting these two factors was the need to establish a power relationship between the British and the Africans with the former in a permanently dominant position. The economic needs of the colonial authorities were for low level clerical staff and that of the settlers were for African labour on their farms and other enterprises. A common concern of all three European interlopers was that the African should not become politically active. As a result, the goal of the schools was the preparation of Africans who would either continue in their traditional agricultural or pastoral occupations or work on the European settlers' farms and undertake menial tasks of the colonial administration.

To achieve these ends, the education which was provided for the Africans focused on 'industrial' training, and included hygiene, and some reading and writing. School subjects legitimated Western knowledge and the Western mode of learning. The stated intention was to turn them into 'useful citizens' who were to be taught the 'value of hard work'.[94] The missionaries, for their part, additionally sought to provide the Africans with a basis in Christian morality and theology which included elementary knowledge of Christian ritual, catechism and ethics. This aspect of the African's education was meant to lead to the elimination of 'native' practices that were considered unChristian such as polygamy and female circumcision.

The Africans both accepted and rejected colonial education. In this simultaneous acceptance and rejection can be seen the ambivalent feelings of the Africans of self-confidence. Feelings of self-confidence were eroded by the seeming superiority of European ways. The African affirmation of self-confidence was dualistic when it did come. First, they accepted the British style education because the European interlopers so entwined the Africans into the colonial economic fabric that this became the only avenue to material advancement. The Africans felt they had both the right and the ability to succeed in the European arena and should be provided with the appropriate opportunities through schooling. Second, Africans, as represented by the independent school movement, realized the value of their cultural heritage and consciously rejected a thoroughly European educational environment deplete of African ways.

In the last analysis during the period under consideration, neither the type of education nor its limited nature allowed the Africans any real socioeconomic mobility and certainly no political empowerment. Africans sought to go beyond the paternalistic and racist education provided primarily by the missions. In the 1930s, the militant minority which established the independent schools provided a breeding ground from which many of Kenya's future activists and leaders emerged.[95] The Africans' demands and pressure for greater educational opportunities were to lead to the reforms of the late 1940s. The colonial effort to perpetuate a stratified economic political and social system based on a racially divided society in the long run met with failure.

9 The creation of a dependent culture

The imperial school curriculum in Uganda

P.G. Okoth

INTRODUCTION

It is the aim of this chapter to argue that between 1894 (the year in which Uganda was colonized by the British) and 1939 (the year when the Second World War began), the foundations for the incorporation of Uganda into the world capitalist system had been established. This object was achieved through various policies adopted by the British. During this period, British colonialism deployed forms of cultural and ideological domination to destroy or paralyse the cultures of the Ugandan people. Western cultures and forms of ideology were introduced. In this exercise, Western education played a crucial role. Indeed, school curricula were designed to suit the needs of the colonizers rather than those of the colonized. In this way, Ugandans who passed through the colonial school system were 'brainwashed' to discard their own cultures and embrace Western cultures which were supposedly 'superior'.

Furthermore, the chapter contends that British imperialism during its colonial phase had a false start in Uganda, as in other colonies in Africa. Although there were other factors involved, the colonization of Uganda, as of Africa more generally, was done on the basis of racism. It was done to 'civilize' the so-called 'primitive' and 'backward' peoples of Africa.[1] This was done by superimposing on the colonized, an alien culture, education, political institutions and economy based on paternalistic and racist policies which created and fostered a culture of dependency, mental enslavement and inferiority complexes.[2]

IMPERIALISM AND THE COLONIZATION OF UGANDA

The architect of British colonialism in Uganda, Fredrick Lugard declared in 1893, 'We have a prescriptive right in East Africa and its lakes. They were all discovered by British explorers . . . Our Missionaries first penetrated to Uganda in the footsteps of our explorers.'[3] It is clear, therefore, that the colonization of Uganda was premised upon British arrogance, racism and imperialism. The process started in 1894 when the 'Protectorate over Uganda' was proclaimed. In 1895, the 'East Africa Protectorate' included Kenya and Uganda.[4] By 1896, Uganda's occupation was completed when the Protectorate was extended to most of the other regions which were then included within what became 'Uganda' and this term, adopted from the kingdom of Buganda, was thereafter applied to the whole territory.[5]

The colonization of Uganda followed the classic African pattern – the use of armed force, the use of missionaries as pawns in the imperialist game, the encouragement of commercial enterprise in the form of a chartered company, and the final assumption of full power by the state.[6] Created arbitrarily by the colonial regime to cater for its own interests, the state of Uganda was established with virtually no regard for the national, linguistic, economic or geographic features of the peoples deemed by colonial providence to become nationals of the new country as perceived and created through the lenses of colonial geo-political *force majeure*.[7] Nor was it created with the view of encouraging political participation and accountability. Instead, imperialism orchestrated nationality cleavages as part of its *divide et impera* policies in which it, rather than the Ugandan masses, benefited.[8] Imperialism sought to exploit whatever divisions existed among the people, building on these and multiplying them with a view to dividing that people further, and winning over a small minority as junior partners in sustaining the external domination of Uganda.[9]

However, it was prohibitively expensive and extremely difficult for the colonial state to control millions of the colonized. Thus 'indirect rule' bcame necessary. The British, therefore, used the people of Buganda – a class of collaborators for purposes of administration. This policy was embodied in the Buganda Agreement of 1900. By this Agreement, a class of notables, a 'landed gentry', was created with the express purpose of maintaining the colonial status quo.[10] D.A. Low has demonstrated how the establishment of colonial rule was immensely facilitated by the collaboration between the Baganda and the British, emphasizing that the Bagandans' 'readiness to co-operate was always coupled with an unremitting determination to see that the integrity and autonomy of their Kingdom was not impaired'.[11]

Another feature of the collaboration between the British and the Baganda was the application of the so-called 'Buganda model' of administration to parts of Eastern, Western (and to a lesser extent Northern) Uganda. This system of administration entailed the employment of Baganda 'agents of colonial rule' and the use of Luganda (language of Baganda) for official business.[12] This led the Baganda to develop 'a deep sense of their own importance to Uganda'.[13] Simultaneously, elsewhere in the colonial state, non-Baganda nationalities became resentful toward the Baganda. Thus, during the period under discussion, imperialism had managed to create these difficulties in Uganda: unity was fragile, non-Buganda nationalities became and remained suspicious and the economy became lop-sided.

In the eyes of the colonizers, although Uganda Africans had to bear the burden of colonial rule, the British brought them 'within the orbit of world civilization': a clearly racist view. The argument went further that because the British built the Uganda railway which connected Uganda to the port of Mombassa, thereby connecting this part of the 'Dark Continent' with world trade routes, this in itself was the more reason for their permanent stay in Uganda. Similarly, roads were built, other infrastructures built, and the people of Uganda were brought within the fold of a cash economy. All this was done, according to the British so as to 'develop' Uganda. But what is development and who sets the agenda? 'Development' throughout colonial rule was predominantly controlled by a class of colonial civil servants.[14] And for reasons of political control, the colonial regime was reluctant to foster the creation of associates beyond the immediate tutelage of the state.[15] Pre-colonial Ugandan societies were shaping their own path of progress, which progress could have been attained by the people of Uganda in their normal course of development if they had not been 'raped' by the British invaders. They need not have lost their sovereignty and independence.[16]

The true character of the colonial economy was that British imperialism, rather than the masses of the Ugandan people benefited from the introduction of the 'modern' economy of the colonial state. The character of the colonial economy meant the economic enslavement of Uganda as a dependent state – hence its underdevelopment whose seeds were sown during the stipulated period. For purposes of exploitation, colonial administration and local bureaucracies were established and the masses of the Ugandan people were forced to pay to maintain the colonial system.[17] It was for this purpose that the British used feudal rulers – oppressive rulers who were not answerable to the people – to plunder Uganda's resources.

Thus the real character of the colonial economy entailed the following points identified by R Mukherjee.[18] First was the economic subjugation of the Ugandan societies; this was a prerequisite for the introduction of a colonial economy. Second was the emergence of cotton production as the basis of the colonial economy following some prior experiments on colonial exploitation. Third was the policy of commodity production of crops (mainly cotton) by the Ugandan Africans. This transformed the character of the economy of pre-colonial Ugandan societies from subsistence to production for the external market. Fourth, Britain's control over the economy was evident from the commercialization of crops and the one-sided development of colonial economy depended heavily on cotton export. Fifth, the fallacy of Britain's economic aid indicated how the import of machines and their accessories into Uganda was meant primarily for a more determined exploitation of Uganda's resources and labour so as to realize maximum profit for the British bourgeoisie. Sixth, the dynamics of the colonial economy revealed how all-embracing the control of the British capitalists was over the economic life of Uganda. Seventh, there was an economic drain on Uganda resulting from an adverse balance of trade. Eighth, an analysis of the internal economy of the colonial state reveals that Ugandan peasants and workers worked so as to fill the coffers of foreign monopolists and their resident and local agents. It also shows how even the small sum which was formally given to them as primary producers of the raw materials needed by the foreign capitalists, was taken back, virtually entirely via the administrative and commercial channel controlled by the foreigners.

Enough information has been given here to give a picture of the political-economy of Uganda during the stipulated period. We now turn to the equally crucial subject of culture and curriculum during the same period in order to focus on the main theme of this chapter.

CULTURE AND CURRICULUM WITHIN THE COLONIAL EDUCATIONAL SYSTEM

Like colonial administration and economy, education served the interests of the colonizers. The introduction of Western-type education at the beginning of this century brought with it Western cultures and ideologies, which were alien to the indigenous peoples. However, before a full discussion of these is entered into, it is necessary to examine the kind of schools that were introduced.

The pioneers of Western education in Uganda were Christian missionaries. Until 1925, virtually all school education was controlled by the missionaries, with the exception of Makerere. At Makerere, the colonial regime established a technical school in 1922 for carpenters, mechanics and junior medical personnel.[19]

Namilyango was the first missionary school established in 1902, by the Mill Hill Fathers,[20] and the students of this school were sons of Catholic chiefs. Numerous schools of the Namilyango type were established in and around Kampala. Among them were: Mengo High School founded in 1903 for Anglicans (in Uganda they are called Protestants); King's College, Budo, founded in 1905 for sons of Protestant chiefs and the Buganda royal family members[21]; Gayaza High School founded in 1905 for daughters of leading Protestants[22]; St Mary's College, Kisubi, originally St Mary's School, Rubaga, founded in 1906 for sons of devoted Baganda Catholics and Goans (a group of Catholic Indians residing in Uganda).[23]

This school pattern meant that Catholic parents had to send their children to either Kisubi or Namilyango and not to Budo or Mengo. It also meant that Protestant parents had to send their children to Budo and Gayaza and not to Kisubi or Namilyango. Clearly then, this school pattern reveals that education was denominational. We do not intend to discuss the history of this education in any detail because it has been adequately covered elsewhere. It is sufficient only to raise a few points regarding the introduction and development of Western education, which though missionary, was simultaneously colonial in character. The missionaries insulated their students against Ugandan traditional education. They seem to have operated on the false assumption that they brought education to absolutely 'uneducated' Africans, a typically racist view. However the missionaries in particular, and the colonizers in general did not introduce education into Uganda or Africa;

they only introduced a new set of formal educational institutions which partly supplemented and partly replaced those which were there before. As Jomo Kenyatta[24] argued, in the African traditional educational system the fireplace was the classroom; the homestead was the school; the elders were the teachers; the seasons were the terms; and things taught included African history–stories of war heroes; African geography – African rivers, lakes, mountains; African music, dance and drama. And as Walter Rodney[25] has observed, in Egypt there was the Al-Azhar University, in Morocco there was the University of Fez, and in Mali there was the University of Timbuktu – all testimony to the standard of education achieved in Africa before the colonial intrusion of which the missionaries were the vehicles.

The purpose of the colonial school system was to train Africans to help man the local administration at the lowest ranks and to staff the private firms owned by Europeans. In effect, this meant selecting a few Africans to participate in the domination and exploitation of Uganda and Africa as a whole. It was not an educational system that grew out of the Ugandan environment; neither was it one designed to promote the most rational use of material and social resources. It was not an educational system designed to give young Ugandans confidence and pride as members of the Ugandan society; but one that sought to instil a sense of deference towards all that was European and capitalist. Colonial schooling was 'education for subordination, exploitation, the creation of mental confusion, and the development of underdevelopment'.[26]

However, most of what emerged from the colonial educational system was not unique. This is for the simple reason that educational systems are designed to function as props to a given society and the products of such educational systems automatically carry over their values when time comes to make decisions in the society. In Uganda the colonizers were training low-level administrators, teachers, non-commissioned officers, railway booking clerks, messengers, carpenters, mechanics, etc., for the preservation of colonial relations. In these relations racism was paramount. Specific theories that claimed to be based on 'thorough' empirical investigations were produced and taught in schools. Absurd claims were made to the effect that the African had no logic, no capacity to think or to attain rationality, no real knowledge, no real religion or philosophy, no real language, only dialects;[27] that there was a causal link between tropical climate and savagery or between lack of a strong climatic challenge and absence of civilization.[28] In terms of psychology, Africans were said to be children who had no 'real' political institutions and were incapable of self-government; that an African was a *homo sexus*, *homo emotionalis*, and *homo pigere* (or *homo ignoravus*).[29] Because of these bogus theories, and through assimilation, paternalism and indirect rule, imperialism carried out a planned systematic, and destructive process of cultural alienation and domination. Imperialism concentrated on the process of *negating* the personality, identity and dignity of the colonized people. The motive was nothing less than to create a 'zombie' who would be dominated, manipulated, exploited and oppressed. This process culminated in the production of people with a perpetual inferiority complex, people who harboured attitudes of subservience, timidity and cowardice, uncreativity, unimaginativeness, idealism and romanticism.[30] It generally produced a slave mentality which negated the people's effective appreciation of their conditions of oppression, exploitation and domination.

Among the institutions that played the greatest role in the process of cultural alienation and domination was the church. To the colonizers, the African had no religion, and knew not of God. He was taken to be ungodly and superstitious. In schools it was taught that there was only one God who happened to be white, his angels were white, but the devil was black, his angels were black, and sin itself was black. The church and European teachers glorified Christianity as the real vanguard of civilization. They claimed that Christianity was godly, rational and culturally universally beneficial to all peoples. This racist argument neglected the fact that African religions had qualitatively developed alongside the modes of economic production and distribution to whose development those religions contributed both directly and indirectly.[31] The negation of African religions paralysed the development of people's national productive forces. Through numerous religious rites Ugandan nationalities celebrated their successful and plentiful harvests, giving thanks to God and honouring the achievements of the people whose hard work and perseverance had yielded so plentifully.[32] Equally celebrated through religion were successful adventures in the blacksmith industry; and so were successful hunting expeditions and warfare. But when Christianity came it inculcated the attitudes of fear, subservience, individualism, laziness, contempt for labour and the enslavement of the mind.[33] Christianity even denied that the African had a right to his name. Thus, the African convert had to discard his/her African name and adopt Christian names such as Smith, Welensky, Verwoerd, Robert, James, Julius, Ironmonger, Winterbottom, Elizabeth, Mary, Margaret, Summer and Winter.[34] This exercise of acquiring new names is rooted in slavery where the slave dealer branded the slave with his own mark and gave him his name so that he would forever be known as that master's property.[35]

The church also used the school to destroy Ugandan music, dance, drama and modes of dress, in support of imperialism. Indigenous songs, dances and dresses were suppressed and European ones were popularized. In illustrated books on Africa authored by intellectuals of colonialism, the European colonizer occupied the central stage of action and drama with light radiating outwards from him.[36] The African occupied the background and merged with darkness and natural scenery at the outer edges of the action.[37]

The colonial educational system stressed European languages and European literatures. African languages were relegated to the periphery – at best they were described as vernaculars, meaning the languages of slaves or merely barbaric tongues.[38] Education, therefore, served the purpose of enhancing cultural imperialism in Uganda. From the nursery, English was compulsory within school bounds. Whenever the children of the colonized were caught speaking their mother tongue they were ridiculed and punished. However, when they spoke English, which they were encouraged to speak, they were rewarded. The idea was to make the children despise their indigenous languages, hence the values in those languages, and by extension despise themselves and others who spoke them. Similarly, they were made to admire English and other European languages and the values they carried.[39]

The literature taught in schools was European literature. In the literature books, the good African was one who collaborated with colonialism. (In Alan Paton's book, *Cry the Beloved Country*, such an African, subservient of imperialism, was the Reverend Steven Kumalo.) On the other hand, the 'bad native' was that African who rejected colonial occupation and struggled for freedom and the recovery of his land and wealth. Such an African was portrayed in a most revolting manner. The history taught was also European; African students were taught that Africa had no history of its own; that African history started with the arrival of European explorers, that Africa was discovered by Europe. Students were made to learn of the 'great' European explorers who travelled in Africa which was referred to as the 'Dark Continent'. They learnt of English queens and kings, Napoleon and others. In the field of geography, the syllabus centred on European geography. Students learnt about the Alps mountains, the River Rhine, the British Isles, dairy farming in Western Europe, European seasons, and the like. They were made aware of the river Nile, Lake Victoria, Mount Kilimanjaro, the Sahara desert and the great African Rift Valley, only in regard to which European 'discovered' (or the first European to see) them. Even science, technology and medicine, were all taught to produce specialists who worshipped European inventions and advancements and despised African achievements and initiatives. This process produced people who feared modern technology – instead they preferred to beg such technology from the West. These imperialist compradors assisted in stifling and destroying local industries.

Before the advent of colonialism in Uganda, the medical industry had developed technique and technology for connecting broken bones, curing snake bites, delivering babies and purging constipation.[40] Similarly, the military- and agricultural-oriented technological industries produced spears, including the Karamojong spear which could be manipulated by the thrower with the aid of the wind. They also produced axes, grinding stones, hoes, animal traps and irrigation technology.[41] These industries were either destroyed or paralysed by imperialism, and in their place European technology took over.

Like the other disciplines, law was also taught with a European bias. The legal system of Uganda was a replica or an extension of the British legal system. The media, press, legislative, judiciary, the state itself and its other institutions were all effective apparatuses of cultural and ideological domination. Through these imperialist cultural and ideological processes, there emerged a Ugandan society of contradictory classes and class ramifications. For instance, a *petit bourgeoisie* (mainly an educated elite) was developed by and with the greatest alienating cultural, ideological and economic effects across the numerous and divergent nationalities.

In all these disciplines, colonial curriculum designers wanted African learners to act like physicists, biologists, historians, geographers, with a view to becoming specialists who admired European advancements and yet despised their own. There was too much compartmentalization of disciplines even if they were European based. Indeed, during the stipulated period, colonial education emphasized a subject curriculum. In this regard, the subject matter was selected and organized before the teaching situation, and the curriculum was entirely controlled by the teacher (someone representing authority external to the learning situation). This period saw the teaching of 'facts'; imparting information and acquiring knowledge for its own sake. Teaching was such that emphasis was laid upon teaching specific habits and skills as separate and isolated aspects of learning. Emphasis was also laid on uniformity of learning results. In other words, colonial teachers considered education as conforming to the patterns set by the school curriculum and its various associated instruments, and education was wholly equated with schooling.[43] This subject centred curriculum harboured several serious weaknesses. We highlight only a few of them. One weakness of this approach was the failure to give sufficient attention to integrative objectives. Pupils were unable to relate one discipline to another and to see how the content of the discipline could be brought to bear on the complex problems of modern life not answerable to a single discipline. Two steps could have been taken to help overcome this weakness.[42] First, an emphasis could have been placed on 'integrated' studies in which input from several disciplines could have been applied to important social problems in the Ugandan society and other societies in Europe and elsewhere. The second step, the teaching of knowledge in a way that learners would acquire a range of perspectives to understand their experiences. Another weakness in the academic concept of curriculum was the tendency to impose on the pupils colonial adult views on the subject matter. Colonial teachers often gave insufficient attention to the prevailing interests and backgrounds of particular learners. They could have used those interests as stimulants through which learners could acquire the effective intellectual organization of learning. As an example of another weakness, science education did not meet the personal, social and career needs of the learners. In other words, the curriculum was organized around the structure of separate disciplines, with only marginal emphasis being given to the personal applications of knowledge.[44] Yet another weakness was that teaching was based on acquiring knowledge for its own sake, as we have seen. It would have been better if emphasis had been placed on teaching meanings which would function immediately in qualitatively improving the life of the people. Therefore, meaningful teaching must be based on building habits and skills as integral components of larger experiences. Equally important, emphasis should be placed on variability in exposure to learning and variability in the results expected and achieved rather than on uniformity of exposure to learning.[45]

Another weakness was the assumption that education was schooling, rather than viewing education as aiding the learner to build a socially creative individuality. Education could be seen to mean rather a continuous intelligent and progressive process of growth and maturity.

As a consequence of these attitudes and actions, the self-image of black Ugandans derived from the colonial experience of education was such that they were British in all but colour. Although this cultural imperialism was shown to perpetuate colonial exploitation in Uganda, it ended up establishing a yardstick (for those who went to school and those who did not) for measuring later aesthetical, epistemological and metaphysical standards in the country. Henceforth it became 'common knowledge' that an 'intelligent' and productive Ugandan was one who went to school, obtained a certificate and possibly had a chance to travel to Europe or North America.

Thus, colonial education marked the divide between 'traditional' and 'modern' values. As we observed earlier, Ugandan schoolchildren were literally uprooted from the experiences and values which their ancestors had tested over time. These 'new' Ugandans were moulded to think that they were a separate and distinct entity that was not to be spoilt by the forces of traditionalism.[46] Colonial education created in its products a sense of superiority over those Ugandans who did not attend school. And colonial education created an equally strong sense of inferiority among the so-called uneducated. This had the effect of widening the elite–mass gap.

Due to the scarcity of funds and lack of willing British administrators, there was an acute shortage of colonial administrators in Uganda. To overcome this difficulty, the British embarked on a policy of training selected Ugandans as 'future administrators'. This was a disastrous start for the self-image of 'educated' Ugandans. From the beginning, colonial education gave a signal to those who passed through the system and to onlookers alike, that it was a breeding ground for Ugandan clerks and administrators who would tow the British imperialist line. Colonial education was for a 'white collar' job and nothing else.[47]

The legacy of the 'white collar' job attitude derived from colonial education haunted Ugandan elites even after independence. The view prevailed that the end-product of education was a luxurious office, a good car, a big house, housekeepers and fine living. This kind of mentality made the graduates of the Ugandan school system 'roam' urban areas looking for 'white collar' jobs – often not available. Failure to acquire such jobs frequently led to disillusionment, frustration and bad habits like excessive drinking, drug abuse, stealing and prostitution. Such graduates failed to come down to earth. They also failed to learn that an asserted aim of education is to provide one with skills to earn a living.[48] Because of the great pressure to produce colonial administrators, then, colonial education emphasized literacy rather than acquiring practical knowledge. Most of the schools such as Kisubi, Budo, Namilyango and others, devoted more time to academic than to practical subjects. Thus, when technical schools such as that at Makerere were established, they merely acted as an outlet for academic 'dropouts'. A brilliant student automatically became one who could memorize his/her subjects well, pass examinations and continue with further studies. Consequently, Ugandan elites harboured the misconceived view that technical subjects were for 'fools'. This view, inevitably, created a serious shortfall in the supply of technicians. The task of decolonizing the mind of the African in this respect remains a formidable one.

It should be stressed yet again that colonial education emphasized formal learning where learners were gathered and isolated in specific schools under a European or European-tailored African supervisor or assistant. This created the impression that learning could only occur in a school. Education equated with schooling had dangerous consequences. Education was reduced to the mere acquisition of certificates, regardless of whether or not they were relevant to society and its needs and demands. Those who did not attend school were automatically labelled 'stupid'.

By equating knowledge with formal schooling, the colonial educational system created a pompous and arrogant attitude in its products. More than that, however, it made the 'new' Ugandans lose time-tested skills which the elders had developed as a result of careful study of the indigenous environment. Overnight, children lost respect for elders (who had, moreover, paid the children's school fees) simply because they despised these elders who had not gone to school.[49]

For much of the colonial period agriculture was under-emphasized as a discipline in the colonial school system. This was partly because peasant agriculture had been more successful than settler farming.[50] Where agriculture was taught, theory was emphasized at the expense of practice. In the same vein, digging was reserved as punishment for culprits of the school system. This act of deliberate omission meant two things. First, it meant that agriculture was a 'punishment' for those who were 'uneducated', the majority of whom were peasants. Second, the education available was not meant for rural life. In this way, education was perceived as a step toward escaping the 'hardships' of the peasant *modus vivendi*. As a corollary, colonial education was regarded as a means of achieving the luxury of urban life.

As already observed, for colonialism to be effective, it was necessary that the minds of Ugandans had also to be colonized. Through school indoctrination, an educated Ugandan was expected to be one that dressed, ate, behaved, thought and spoke like an educated Englishman. Language was, of course, a major area where British cultural imperialism was all-pervasive. The various pre-colonial Ugandan nationalities had distinct languages which the imperialists chose to call 'dialects'. With the consolidation of British hegemony, English became the medium of instruction, as well as the official language of Uganda. What emerged was that a literate and 'respected' Ugandan became one who spoke English. Indigenous languages were considered the 'dialects' of 'primitive' and 'backward' peoples. English was the language of 'civilization'.

Colonial education also had an impact on the religious outlook of Ugandan elites. In the missionary schools, inevitably Ugandans were lectured on the 'benevolence' of the only 'true' God and the 'wickedness' of African gods.[51] Christianization gained unprecedented impetus becaue of the dominant role schools played; they were agents of imperialism and colonialism. On the establishment of the first missionary schools, baptism became the *sine qua non* for admission to these schools. Thus, to many Ugandans, whether schooled or not, the possession of Christian names was itself a sign of 'modernization' or 'civilization'.

In pre-colonial Ugandan societies, music played a central role in the daily life of the people. However, with the establishment of colonial rule and colonial educational system, the teaching of African music was prohibited because the missionaries claimed that it was part of 'paganism'. As a result, school attendants played Christian music on piano, flute, violin and sometimes guitar.[52] Ultimately for Ugandan elites music could be good only if European instruments were used; and dances were attractive only in the European style. The dislike of indigenous music and the preference for 'English' music played in the 'English' way, persisted into the post-colonial era. Thus, traditional music was only occasionally played.

Those black Ugandans, therefore, who experienced colonial education were frequently systematically and effectively dispossessed of their cultural heritage as a matter of course. Irrelevant education, materialistic ambitions, linguistic and artistic alienation adversely affected the creation of a confident identity. However, it should not be overlooked that those black Ugandans who did not directly experience colonial education were not immune to its influence. Equally it affected the construction of their identities!

CONCLUSION

The so-called modern state in Uganda was established by British imperialism to cater for its own selfish interests. Once the colonial state had been etablished, forms of cultural and ideological domination ensued. These included the destruction of cultures and ideologies of the Ugandan nationalities and the establishment instead of European cultures and forms of ideology. Colonial education was fundamental to this exercise.

Colonial teachers taught bourgeois culture and capitalist values right from the early stages of education. To a large extent, colonial teachers thoughtlessly applied their own curricula without reference to Ugandan conditions; on the other hand, quite often they deliberately did so on the basis of racism – with the intent to dominate, control and mystify. Furthermore, they employed a subject currriculum which harboured serious weaknesses. However, the central inadequacy of the colonial educational system unquestionably was the too common transmission of image of the black learner as backward, limited, inadequate and incapable of advanced learning. Not only was the education Eurocentred but the perceptions of the educationalists were ethnocentric.

Ideally, education should promote progressive social change in a society: colonial education did the opposite in Uganda. Education is an important component of national integration and development, but colonial education encouraged disintegration and underdevelopment. Education is a critical factor in the alleviation of individual ignorance and servility. Colonial education was the opposite; it maintained ignorance and promoted servility. Education has the potential to foster the knowledge, values and skills necessary for productive activity. Indeed, education contributes to political development by creating an informed and participant citizenry. It also contributes to socio-economic development by equipping the masses for new roles associated with an expanding range of occupations. Colonial education performed few, if any, of the above functions. It certainly created social classes and accelerated social stratification based on economic factors. It created different categories of schools to further the colonial policy of divide and rule. Essentially, colonial education was irrelevant to the people of Uganda. It never had close links with indigenous cultural life, neither in a material nor in a spiritual sense.

In the African tradition, education must be collective in nature, rather than individualistic. Uganda's educational system must now de-emphasize the separation of education and productive activity and there should be no division between manual and intellectual education. Our educational system should match the realities of Uganda and should produce confident, capable, well-rounded personalities to fit into the Ugandan society. At present it does not do so. This is in large measure a colonial heritage. This is because 'the colonial school system educated far too many fools and clowns, fascinated by the ideas and way of the European capitalist class. Some reached a point of total estrangement from African conditions and the African way of life, and . . . they chirped happily that they were and would always be "European"'.[53]

10 Rulers and ruled

Racial perceptions, curriculum and schooling in colonial Malaya and Singapore

Keith Watson

INTRODUCTION

Although it is now generally accepted that colonial educational penetration was a form of cultural imperialism[1] it is often forgotten that, in the British context at least, there was no universal policy. This varied between, and even within, individual colonial territories either according to the educational and social background of individual administrators, who frequently developed their own policy on the spot[2] or according to the racial and ethnic composition of the territory concerned. Many territories only became racially mixed as a direct consequence of colonial intervention, as for example, through the importation of indented labourers, usually from India. As a result, amongst the most lasting legacies of colonialism are the different perceptions of these different groups towards each other.[3] Colonial Malaya is an interesting case in point.

A study of the Colonial Office and Malayan Education Service documents reveals a fascinating account of the different views of British colonial administrators towards the different races in what we know today as Malaysia and Singapore. Some views were highly idiosyncratic and resulted from agonized debate and deeply held convictions or prejudices, on the part of individual administrators. Others were shaped by the educational and religious background of the official concerned.[4] These in turn shaped the educational and language policies accorded to different races and social classes. Thus, while Malay rulers were accorded considerable privileges, the rural Malay peasant, the *bumiputras* (sons of the soil) were to be 'protected' from the worst effects of colonial penetration. The Chinese were tolerated, but largely left to their own devices until they were perceived to be politically subversive. The Indians were largely ignored until a social conscience persuaded the colonial authorities to become interested in their plight. At no time before the Second World War, except in a few government-aided schools, were there any attempts to use the education system as a means of bringing together the different races in a sense of national harmony.

The curriculum and the textbooks used, especially in the English-medium schools, sought to portray the British rulers as benefactors, traditional

Malay society was idyllic, but backward and the other races as of little consequence except for their economic contribution. The patronizing treatment of different Malay groups, the Sultans, the peasants and teachers was to leave a lasting impression on Malay Society. The training of Malayan teachers in England was a part of this belief in British superiority. The cynical economic exploitation of Chinese and Indians and the lack of concern about a harmonious multi-racial society were to leave deep-rooted scars which are still in evidence. It is little wonder that Tun Abdul Razak should have made the curriculum a central plank of education policy for the newly independent Federation of Malaya in 1957.

THE MALAYSIAN CONTEXT

Present day Malaysia and Singapore gradually came under British control from the late eighteenth century onwards. While their present economic standing within the Association of South East Asian Nations (ASEAN) can be directly attributable to the economic legacy of the British (see Table 10.1) these figures belie the economic and racial complexity of both nations.

In 1786 Penang was purchased on behalf of the East India Company by Sir Francis Light. In 1795, during the Napoleonic Wars, the Dutch voluntarily ceded Malacca to the British for fear of the port falling into French hands. This transfer was finally agreed by the Treaty of London of 1824, by which the British ceded Bencoolen in Java in exchange for Malacca. Singapore was acquired in 1819 by Sir Stamford Raffles, also on behalf of the East India Company.[5] From 1826, until the creation of the Federation of Malaya in 1957 and the Republic of Singapore in 1959, these three territories were known as the Straits Settlements (SS). Until 1858 they were loosely administered by the East India Company, first from Penang, then from Calcutta, eventually from Signapore. In 1867 ultimate control was transferred to the British Government in London.

British penetration into the Malay peninsula began in earnest in 1874 with the signing of the Pangkor Engagement between Britain and the Sultan of Perak, by which the British authorities agreed to help restore law and order in the tin mining areas between rival Chinese gangs and indigenous Malays[6] in return for an agreement

> to receive and provide a suitable residence for a British officer, to be called a Resident, who shall be accredited to his Court and whose advice must also be asked and acted upon in all questions other than those touching Malay religion and custom.[7]

Similar agreements were signed with the Sultans of Selangor, Pahang and Negri Sembilan, which, in 1896, were constituted as the Federated Malay States (FMS). Gradually schools, hospitals, postal services, roads, railways and an administrative infrastructure were developed where none

Table 10.1 Basic indicators of South East Asian nations 1990

	Country	World basic ranking*	Population (millions 1988)	Area (1,000km²)	GNP per capital (1988)	GNP growth (% 1965–88)	Inflation (% 1980–8)	Life expectancy (1988)	Adult numeracy (% 1985)
L/G	Indonesia	34	174.8	1,905	440	4.3	8.5	61	26
	Myanmar (Burma)	38	40.0	677	–	–	–	60	–
	Vietnam	42	64.2	330	–	–	–	66	–
M/G	Philippines	44	59.9	300	630	1.6	15.6	64	14
	Thailand	57	54.5	513	1,000	4.0	3.1	65	9
	Malaysia	74	16.9	330	1,940	4.0	1.3	70	27
H/G	Singapore	101	2.6	1	9,070	7.2	1.2	74	14

Source: The World Bank (1990) World Development Report 1990, Washington D.C.
Note: *The poorest country is Mozambique (1), the richest is Switzerland (121).

had existed before and the British Residents acquired *de facto* administrative and educational control. According to Wicks

> The early British administrators opted for a cautious preservation of the Malay social order, respected the fundamental division between rulers and ruled, developed formal education programs which served to perpetuate this division, and sought to avoid the creation of unrealizable Malay aspirations within a colonial context. Such an approach also accorded with nineteenth century British practices of differential elite and mass education.[8]

Not all states, however, were administered in the same way. Four northern states, Kedah, Perlis, Trenganu and Kalantan, acknowledged the suzerainty of Siam (not known as Thailand until 1946) and recognized the role of Siamese advisers! In 1902 the British authorities persuaded the Siamese to allow British advisers to replace the Thais and in 1909, in return for a financial loan for railway and bridge building, the Thai monarchy yielded its claims to suzerainty and British advisers took up residence. While British 'advisers' were accepted all four Sultans refused to join the FMS and became known as the Unfederated Malay States (UMS). In 1914, the Sultan of Johore made a similar agreement. These arrangements lasted until 1957. Although the authority of the British 'adviser' was somewhat less than that of the Residents in the FMS their advice 'was no more than a euphemism for control and the British became the real masters of the whole of Malaya'.[9]

The results of the British intervention were to have far-reaching implications for Malaysia in terms of population growth and ethnic diversity. Both were inextricably interwoven because, by allowing unlimited immigration from China during the period 1890–1920,[10] and by encouraging indentured labour from India to work in the rubber plantations,[11] not only did the population rise from 0.5 million in 1850 to 4.9 million by 1947 and 6.2 million by 1957 (see Table 10.2), but Malays increasingly felt alienated in their own country, especially from the urban areas (see Table 10.3). The basic economic, ethnic, political and urban/rural cleavages that have persisted to this day were also established, largely through colonial educational policies.[12]

Because the numerous treaties and agreements reached between the British authorities and the Malay rulers guaranteed a special status to the Malays[13] not only were the rural Malays, whose homeland it was, left largely undisturbed and unaffected by the economic, urban and population changes that were taking place but the Christian missionaries, who were largely responsible for developing formal secular education in the country, were debarred from proselytization amongst the Malays and thus from establishing Western-type schools amongst them. The result was the establishment of an education policy which allowed four parallel school systems to develop, largely along ethnic lines,[14] with the prestigious English-medium, grant-aided schools, mostly being opened in urban areas and mainly benefiting the Chinese, a smaller number of Indians and only a fraction of Malays, since barely 15 per cent of them lived in urban

Table 10.2 Racial composition of the population of the Malaysian peninsula, 1921-70

All Races	1921 Number (1,000s)	1921 %	1931 Number (1,000s)	1931 %	1947 Number (1,000s)	1947 %	1957 Number (1,000s)	1957 %	1970 Number (1,000s)	1970 %
Malay	1,569	54.0	1,864	49.2	2,428	49.5	3,125	49.8	4,669	53.0
Chinese	856	29.4	1,285	33.9	1,885	38.4	2,334	37.2	3,136	35.6
Indian	439	15.1	571	15.1	531	10.8	707	11.3	934	10.6
Other	43	1.5	68	1.8	65	1.3	112	1.8	70.	0.8
Total	2,907	100.0	3,788	100.0	4,909	100.0	6,278	100.0	8,809	100.0

Source: D.Z. Fernandez, *et al.* (1975) *The Population of Malaysia,* Paris, Table 1.4.

Table 10.3 Urbanization by ethnic group in the Malaysian peninsula

	1947		1957		1970	
Ethnic group	*Urban*	*Rural*	*Urban*	*Rural*	*Urban*	*Rural*
Malay	7.3	52.7	11.2	88.8	14.9	85.1
Chinese	31.1	68.9	44.7	55.3	47.4	52.6
Indian	25.8	74.2	30.6	69.4	34.7	65.3

areas.[15] As Chai Hon Chai has observed, the effects of these developments 'was to keep the vast majority of Malays in a socially and economically depressed position'.[16] Jayasuriya is even more damning:

> British economic and educational policies contributed in substantial measure to the creation and perpetuation of Malay disadvantage of such dimensions that restitutional measures extending over several decades are necessary for the achievement of a fair racial balance in enjoying the fruits of economic progress. The dominance of the Chinese in the economy makes racial balance the overriding issue in society and politics.[17]

How this situation came about is the focus of the remainder of this chapter.

ATTITUDES AND POLICIES TOWARDS EDUCATION

Chamberlain, commenting on the growth of imperialism in the nineteenth century, has observed that:

> The whole imperialist movement was conditioned by the fact that at this time Europe had a long technological lead over the rest of the world and genuinely believed its civilization to be superior to any other.[18]

These views of European superiority were certainly to colour the attitudes of many colonial leaders in Malaya, though perceptions differed markedly towards different ethnic groups. Initially, however, the colonial authorities were more concerned with law and order, defence and economic development, than with education provision. This *laissez-faire* approach and indifference resulted from 'an absence of any clear educational ideas as well as from a lack of belief in education'[19] and there was certainly no clear cut policy before the First World War.[20]

Education can have one of two main thrusts. It is either designed to preserve the status quo, as was the position with the traditional Koranic school, or it can introduce new values and attitudes which are likely to lead to social discontinuity and change. Part of the problem facing British rulers in Malaya is that they could not readily resolve this dichotomy. Many wished to preserve the status quo on the part of the rural Malays as far as possible but wished to develop new attitudes on the part of urban dwellers.[21] Thus British policy in the SS, for example, formulated by Raffles was that schooling (i.e. Western-type secular/formal schools) should be for the sons of Malay rulers and for other people but not for the Malays.[22] Raffles hoped for a 'trickle down' effect of modernization which would help to ensure British political influence and control by reinforcing the existing social status quo. On the other hand, the need to find clerks and administrators for the colonial administrative hierarchy meant that in due course schooling had to be provided for other ethnic groups, the Chinese and the Indians.

At the time of the British arrival in Malaya existing schooling was designed to maintain the status quo. There were essentially three sorts of schooling: the *Koranic schools*, where the rudiments of Arabic were taught so that boys could memorize and recite large chunks of the Koran;[23] *Chinese writing schools*, where Chinese boys were taught the classics and rudiments of reading, writing and recitation;[24] and 'education based on a system of *apprenticeship* to parents and others'.[25] None of them was universal. Descriptions of each tell us as much about the observers as about the education provided. For example, R.J. Wilkinson, one of the first British administrators to take a keen interest in the Malays, their language, literature and customs, and who, shortly after his appointment as Federal Inspector of Schools in 1903, began to develop a Romanized form of the Malay script (*rumi*), wrote:

> Education was based upon a sort of apprenticeship. Most boys picked up a good deal of industrial knowledge by assisting their parents in the work of agriculture, fishing and trapping. They acquired manual dexterity by working in wood and rattan ... They also learnt to be observant. A few youths of exceptional gifts would go further and learn something of art and metal working by giving occasional help to a village craftsman; a few more might specialise in reading and writing, either for religious purposes or with a view to becoming doctors, diviners, sorcerers and letter-writers.[26]

An ideal picture of Islamic education can be seen from the following description:

> Muslims learnt reading and writing in order to read the Qu'uran; they also learnt arithmetic to enable themselves to calculate the tithe, the accurate prayer times and feast days; grammar to avoid mistakes while reciting the verses of the Qu'uran; interpretation and jurisprudence to understand the tenets of religion and its legal provisions. Finally, they learnt philosophy and logic to defend their religion and its creed. Education was thus a means to spread religion and direct the morals of the people.[27]

On the other hand, Islamic education came in for considerable criticism from the British administrators who felt that many of the teachers did not understand what they were teaching or because they felt that it failed to offer any intellectual stimulus. There was also an implied anti-Islamic bias. The following official comment illustrates this sense of disdain admirably:

> Not a few of these men teaches, day after day, long passages of the Koran in the Arabic, which they do not understand and with the most patient efforts to impart the correct pronounciation, intonation and phraseology, although they cannot either read or write in their own Jawi character, or indeed, in any other, the names of the pupils in their classes.[28]

This scorn for the worthlessness of traditional Koranic education was repeated in many of the early official reports on education in the FMS, though only subsequently did this lead to resentment.

Chinese schools fared only marginally better. Wherever they existed they were noisy, overcrowded and repetitious but respect was accorded to their sense of earnestness.[29] For example, Cheeseman, one of the leading British Education officers, writing in 1931 had this to say:

> The interest of the Chinese in education is proverbial. Their record in Malaya does them the greatest credit ... In almost every village, even in the remotest districts, there is a Chinese school to be found, usually entirely financed by locally collected funds, to which it is not uncommon for every member of the community to be a willing and regular contributor.[30]

Enthusiasm, however, did not imply quality and the Director of Education for Singapore wrote in the Annual Report of 1917 that Chinese schools were poorly staffed and equipped, that they seemed to take a greater interest in military exercises than in learning and that they were apparently controlled by the Chinese government with scant regard for any local British authority.

Education never came high on the list of priorities of the colonial authorities and until the Colonial Office assumed responsibility for administering the Straits Settlements in 1867 there was no official education policy. With the appointment of an Inspector of Schools for the Straits Settlements in 1872 there began an attempt at some co-ordination of policy in the colony. Prior to that, however, the position with regard to education must be regarded as *laissez-faire* and of only minor importance. What education did take place was either of the indigenous sort outlined above or it very much depended on the interests and time of individual governors such as Blundell and Cavenagh in the Straits Settlements[31] and individual Residents in each of the Malay states. One official document observed that education only began

> on the initiative of the British Resident who directs its [the State's] affairs and could only be undertaken when order and honest administration had been evolved out of the chaos and corruption that had previously existed in each state.[32]

It was not until the creation of the FMS in 1896 that any form of co-ordination was attempted. Thereafter, however, followed in quick succession the 1899

Education Code, the 1902 Education Ordinance and the creation of a Director of Education post for the SS (1901) and the FMS (1906). The primary function of government under British rule was the maintenance of law and order and financial administration. Education was seen as of incidental importance and only available if there was political stability and a surplus of funds. This view was admirably summed up in the Report of the Retrenchment Commission of 1932:

> However desirable cheap or free education may be, it must be remembered that there can be no state-aided education at all except under the conditions of a stable administration – and the cost of education and of the social and development services generally must be met from what we may describe as a residual fund, that is, from money left over after the costs of services necessary for the maintenance of the fabric of the state have been provided.

Another view has been expressed as follows:

> The essential characteristic of British Malaya was that of the marketplace, what the majority of the inhabitants chiefly required was a form of government which could regulate and control lawlessness and provide the services necessary for the maintenance of reasonable living conditions with the minimum of interference in commercial activities. This the administration supplied in good measure. [33]

Such views partly account for why so little was done to develop any form of coherent educational policy which would have embraced all the different ethnic groups.

As has been previously mentioned, throughout the early period of British rule in Malaya there were conflicting views about the place of education in colonial society. Loh (1975) has described the two positions as conservationist versus diffusionist.[34] The former view was held by orientalists who sought to preserve what was good in traditional Malay society by developing vernacular education, especially at the primary level, and this became the focus for much of the ecducational and social policy towards the Malays throughout British colonial rule. The second view, held by liberals from the 1830s onwards, was that the superiority of English-medium education should be acknowledged as the best vehicle for modernization and the diffusion of Western knowledge and values to the masses. This view was strongly influenced by Macaulay's famous 'Minute of 1835' to the Board of Directors of the East India Co.,

> We must at present do our best to form a class who may be interpreters between us and the millions we govern – a class of persons Indian in blood and colour, but English in tastes, in opinions, in morals and in intellect.

It has been suggested, however, that the diffusionists would have won the day in spite of Macaulay, though the results in Malaya were not as strong as in India.[35] Whereas the diffusionist view led to the development of elite

English-medium schools, especially the Malay College, 'The Star of the East', in the FMS, the conservationists' view prevailed amongst many of the FMS administrators, especially men like Swettenham, who, as resident of Perak in 1890, feared that the spread of English education would not only be seditious but would undermine the traditional culture of the rural Malay.

> The one danger to guard against is an attempt to teach English indiscriminately. It could not be well taught except in a very few schools and I do not think it is at all advisable to attempt to give the children of an agricultural population an indifferent knowledge of a language that to all but the very few would only unfit them for the duties of life and make them discontented with anything like manual labour. At present, the large majority of Malay boys and girls have little or no opportunity of learning their own language, and if the government undertakes to teach them this, the Koran, and something about figures and geography (especially of the Malay peninsular and archipelego) this knowledge, and the habits of industry, punctuality and obedience that they will gain by regular attendance at school will be of material advantage to them, and assist them to earn a livelihood in any vocation, while they will be likely to prove better citizens and more useful members of the community than if imbued with a smattering of English ideas which they would find could not be realised.[36]

The result of this fear of revolutionary change was a very slow growth of English schools in Perak. Indeed the policy that evolved in the FMS was largely designed to keep the Malays in a position of quiet subservience. As Wicks has observed:

> the official British position sought to avoid any challenge to colonial rule from an English-educated indigenous group by concentrating on the provision of rural-based vernacular education.[37]

Indeed Swettenham wrote in 1894 that 'whilst we teach children to read and write and count in their own language, or in Malay . . . we are safe'.[38] This was reiterated with regard to all the Protected Malay States in 1895.[39]

As can be seen, several policy options were available to colonial administrators. They could refrain from any kind of educational intervention. They could support the rulers, the Sultans, and offer them and their children, one form of education or they could develop schooling for both rulers and ruled. They could have imposed a British type of education regardless of the consequences. They could have provided a common education for Malays and other ethnic groups which would have concentrated on Malay education only. As it turned out several of these options were developed: vernacular education for Malays, support for limited English-medium education which brought together different ethnic groups, especially at secondary level, and, until the 1920s and 1930s at least, relative indifference towards the education of non-indigenous groups, the Indians and Chinese. It must be stressed, however, that the policies that evolved gradually, over time, came largely from men on the spot, and not from the Colonial Office which took little or no active interest in defining educational policy except to endorse, or criticize those views that were expressed by the Residents and Advisers.[40]

It must also be stressed that British officials in Malaya were largely influenced by their own conservative, traditional upbringing, by current developments in England and by what they perceived to be happening in British India. The result was the development of a four-language system of education – maintained Malay vernacular primary schools, mostly in the Malay States; assisted or maintained English-medium primary and secondary schools, mostly in urban areas; private Tamil-medium primary schools and private Chinese-medium primary and secondary schools, though in time many of these came to be supported or assisted by the government. Although by the 1920s/1930s, when it was apparent that the ethnic composition of the country had been transformed, the government could have consciously set about developing multi-ethnic harmony by developing a monolingual (Malay) or bilingual (English and Malay) education system: sadly, the government chose not to do so, partly because of a deep-rooted mind-set which argued that the responsibility of the colonial authorities was towards the Malays only and was not towards other ethnic groups. The effects of these decisions were to persist throughout the twentieth century.

The 1870s mark a watershed in the developments of educational history in Malaya. Prior to then one of the few people to have made any pronouncements on education had been Sir Stamford Raffles, who, in the 1820s, had sought to establish a new Institution in Singapore which would have combined the best in Malay and English education and would have been for the children of Malay chiefs and for rich Chinese merchants. Raffles had had to return to the UK in 1823 before this elitist institution got beyond the foundation stone, with the result that the concept died. However, the Report of the Woolley Committee (1870) on education in the SS led to the appointment of a Director of Schools, an Inspector of Schools and a growing sense of responsibility on the part of the colonial authorities to provide some kind of education, at least for the children of aristocracy and wealthy merchants. The result was that in the period prior to the First World War, the government developed a dual policy towards the Malays, described by one observer as 'protective and paternalistic'[41] with conciliation and training for leadership for the Malay ruling classes, minimum interference towards Malay villagers and comparative indifference towards other vernacular schools. These views were expressed in several annual reports. Sir George Maxwell, the Chief Secretary of the FMS for example, wrote in 1920

the aim of the Government is not to turn out a few well educated youths, nor a number of less well educated boys: rather it is to improve the bulk of the people and to make the son of the fisherman or the peasant a more intelligent fisherman or peasant than his father had been, and a man whose education will enable him to undersand how his own lot in life fits in with the scheme of life around him.[42]

Such paternalistic and morally superior views towards the indigenous population were not uncommon amongst many of the colonial bureaucrats. For
example, shortly before his retirement in 1928 Maxwell had this to say:

> our policy in regard to the Malay peasants is to give them as good an
> education as can be obtained in their own language. The last thing that
> we want to do is to take them away from the land.[43]

The Annual Education Report of the SS in 1903 was equally patronizing,
arguing that the only level of education necessary was

> the bestowal of elementary education such as will enable a villager to keep
> his simple records and to so protect himself against petty swindlers who,
> in our mixed population, are ever ready to prey upon ignorance[44]

The Annual Report for Kedah in 1913 noted that:

> The aim of the Education Department so far as vernacular schools are
> concerned, should, I think always be to teach the young *rai'at* to be an
> intelligent *rai'at*; not to make him something else than the padi planter
> which his forefathers have been.[45]

Indeed the policy throughout the FMS reiterated this viewpoint as can be seen
from the Special Report of 1905:

> The curriculum of work will be seen – to be very elementary but it is
> sufficient for the ordinary requirements of Malay boys, who will become
> bullock-wagon drivers, padi-growers, fishermen etc. and enable them by
> the time they have passed the fourth standard to read or write the simple
> literature of their tongue either in Javi or Roman character, to keep accounts
> if they become small shopkeepers and to work simple problems in the money
> currency, weights and measures of their country.[46]

As we shall see this emphasis on 'simple literature' was to create problems
for the British authorities in the years between the World Wars. The real
problem, however, was that by 'preserving' the Malays in a rural time warp
the British authorities failed to prepare them for political change and kept
them in educationally inferior positions *vis-à-vis* other ethnic groups, who
tended to be urban dwellers. The legacy of this approach has been that
subsequent independent Malaysian governments have had to use policies of
positive discrimination in order to redress the economic imbalance against
the rural Malay.

Although there was somewhat greater emphasis on mission and government-
assisted English-medium schools in the Straits Settlements, the same patronizing
perceptions can be seen in the 1921 Annual Report on Education:

> Malay vernacular education has broadly three functions to perform:
> (a) to teach the dull boy enough reading, writing and arithmetic to
> help him keep his accounts with the village shopkeeper or his employer;

(b) to prepare the intelligent boy for that English education which is necessary if he is to aspire to well paid business or government posts: (c) to give the bright boy with a bent for manual work the groundwork for prosecuting such work profitably.[47]

There were a number of reasons put forward for these patronizing and negative views. One was undoubtedly financial. As has been observed education came low down on the scale of colonial administrators as an unnecessary luxury, even though huge sums of money were beginning to be received from tin and rubber extraction, as can be seen from Table 10.4.

Table 10.4 Expenditure on education in the Federated Malay States, 1875–1900

	Total revenue ($)	*Expenditure on education ($)*
1875	409,394	–
1896	8,434,083	–
1898	9,364,467	96,699
1899	13,486,410	106,588
1900	15,609,807	139,059

Source: The System of Education in Federated Malay States (1902)

The government was more than content to exploit the missionary societies and get education on the cheap.[48] A report of 1892, for example, highlighted the status of education in the following manner:

What we spend on education at present is too small a proportion of our revenue, but until the railways under construction are completed, I fear we cannot greatly increase the expenditure on other services.[49]

As has already been shown, even as late as 1932 the Retrenchment Committee pointed out that education was only possible after other services had been provided. Indeed, one of the main weapons of control over education during the colonial period was exercised through a system of grants-in-aid. Such aid was governed by three main principles – charity, partnership and duty. The first applied to mission schools, the second to the Free Schools (i.e. government-aided English-medium schools) and the third to government vernacular schools.

There were several reasons for this approach. The economic situation that developed towards the end of the nineteenth century, with a thriving tin industry largely in the hands of the Chinese, provided the British authorities with a lucrative source of revenue without their being forced to tax the Malays. In any case the subsistence economy pursued by the many widely scattered Malay Communities would have made revenue collection exceedingly difficult and hardly cost effective. Besides, many administrators regarded Malay Society as idyllic[50] and Malays as 'gentlemen'[51] and they did not wish to upset the Malays' social system. They therefore sought to 'protect' the Malays from the immigrant groups, the Chinese and the Indians and to prevent a repetition of the situation that had developed in India, namely the appearance of the semi-literate Babu.[52] Others, such as Maxwell, feared that too much education, especially in English, would lead to political subversion. A speech by a Mr Arthur Kenion to the Federal Council of the FMS in 1915 summed up these views admirably:

> You can teach your Malays so that they remain in the padi fields and so that they do not lose their skill and craft in fishing and jungle work. Teach them the dignity of manual labour, so that they do not all become Kramis, and I am sure that you will not have the trouble which has arisen in India through over education.[53]

These views, of course, were not only patronizing and paternalistic, but were designed to keep the Malays in a position of subservience as is beautifully summarized by the British Resident in Negri Sembilian in 1898:

> Vernacular education is the teaching of Malay boys to read and write Malay, arithmetic, geography and Romanised Malay. This much education teaches them to be regular, obedient and clearly fits them for appointments as Policemen, Peons, Customs Clerks, Forest Rangers and Mining Overseers. So far it is good.[54]

In other words the Malays had to know exactly what was their social and economic position within a British colonial-dominated society. That they were not consulted about what kind of society they wanted or what kind of education they preferred hardly occurred to the 'benevolent' administrators. The British knew what was best for the Malays without having to ask them. Thus, from the 1890s onwards the British authorities actually made 'a conscious attempt to freeze the status quo and prevent any social or economic change in the Malay village community'.[55] They did so 'as an act of political and administrative expediency' though it represented for many of the administrators 'the attainment of a social ideal'.

If one looks at the views expressed by British officials at the time, as we have been doing in this section, it is easy to realize why so much of Malay education led to a dead end.[56] Ironically as will be shown subsequently, it was this policy of preservation of the Malay status quo that was eventually to lead to the development of Malay nationalism, which was antagonistic both towards the British and the immigrant communities, especially the Chinese. Because Malay teachers trained in the Sultan Idris Training College in Malacca, and later at Kirby in England, were made aware of the changes taking place in their country away from the villages through their own observations, rather than through what they learnt in the curriculum, they began to take the message back into the villages (*Kampongs*) that they were an ethnic group who were increasingly being marginalized. The result was that from the 1930s onwards there was a growing sense of frustration, which was to spill over into Malay nationalism.

Initially, the Malays' response to vernacular secular education was largely one of indifference, suspicion or resentment, either because of fears of proselytization, expense, inconvenience or loss of earnings of their sons; all good reasons why many rural people were, until recently, still uncertain about formal secular education. The authorities used fines, compulsory attendance legislation and eventually the co-operation of the rulers to extend Malay vernacular education, but no amount of propaganda could conceal the fact that the school system on offer was inferior and was designed to breed ethnic inferiority. The rural Malay school, therefore, conveyed some very powerful images into the Malay community for it became apparent that Malay education was conservative, designed to maintain the social cohesion of rural society and tended to isolate the majority of the Malay community from the mainstream of social and economic developments taking place elsewhere in the country, especially as it consisted of a meagre four years of primary schooling. Except for teacher training and some vocational education, there was no Malay-medium secondary education until after independence in 1957.

The exception to this state of affairs was the treatment of the Malay rulers. During the 1890s attempts were made to develop an English-medium school for the sons of rajas, but it was not until the 1903 Rulers' Conference had stressed anxiety at how few Malays there were in the administrative Civil Service that plans were developed to open the special, prestigious, English-medium Malay College, the 'Eton of the East'.[57] The Malay College that opened in Kuala Kangsar in 1905 was geared to a political objective, rather than an educational one – 'to give to future Sultans, Malay chiefs and the traditional Malay elite an approximate English public school education which could prepare them for participatory roles within the British administration.[58] By the 1920s preferential treatment for the Malay upper classes in public service was not only recognized but was claimed as a right by Malay leaders. This policy of support for the Malay leadership and the suppression of the rural Malays, the *bumiputras*, or 'sons of the soil' was to have long-term implications for the country's development. In spite of positive discrimination and preferential treatment under the New Economic Policy, the inferiority of the rural Malay remained compared with their more sophisticated and better educated urban colleagues. One group of rulers might have replaced another at the time of independence, but the plight of the ruled, in the rural areas at least, remains [1991][59]

The non-indigenous immigrant groups fared even less favourably than the Malays, for although government policy was vaguely to encourage Malay vernacular education it was to avoid as far as possible involvement in providing other vernacular schools. Initially, at least, there was a clear avoidance of any responsibility for any group other than Malays. The federal inspectors of schools in the FMS summed up this attitude in 1898.

I can see no reason why the Government of these States should educate children to make them suitable citizens for China or southern India apart from what services they may be able to render here as Chinese or Tamil interpreters.[60]

Hugh Low, Third Resident of Perak, was supposed to 'dislike' the Chinese,[61] though this was not a view shared by Swettenham or Clifford, other Residents in the FMS.[62]

The view of the early Residents was to perceive the Chinese in the Western Malay States as essentially alien, transient and potentially disruptive 'birds of passage'.[63]

It was not so much that the Chinese were unimportant – they were not in an economic sense – it was that they were treated with disdain, and any sense of government responsibility towards them was lacking. As a result, they were expected to provide their own education if they so wanted.[64] When a proposal was made by the inspector of schools for Perak to establish a government-financed Chinese school, this was openly opposed by J. Driver, the inspector of schools for the FMS.[65] The result was that the British authorities adopted a *laissez-faire* approach, leaving the Chinese to develop their own school system, which they did quite effectively, especially after the reforms in China began to filter through to overseas Chinese settlers.[66] However, it was the strong links between China and the overseas Chinese, both financially and politically, that were to make the British authorities take a greater interest in developments. The development of the Kuo-yu, or National Language Movement in 1917 and the decision to adopt Mandarin as the medium of instruction for all schools in China and overseas, using a common curriculum, raised fears of subversion. This fear was especially strong following the riots of 1919 sparked off as a result of the Treaty of Versailles' cessation of former German territories in Shantung province to the Japanese. Thereafter British colonial government officials not only began to take an interest in Chinese schooling to ensure that 'teaching shall not be of such a kind that it is against the interests of the government of the colony', but the passing of the 1920 Regulation of Schools Ordinance demanded the registration of schools, managers, staff and textbooks. Although the Ordinance was aimed at all schools its specific target was the Chinese schools. Thereafter followed a series of measures designed to curb the political aspects of Chinese schools, in return for grants-in-aid, and to bring them under strict government inspection. Even so, although by 1938 over 82 per cent of Chinese pupils were enrolled in Chinese schools, they received only 5.19 per cent of government educational expenditure. Government responsibility might lie in the area of regulation of schools; as yet it did not stretch to generous funding of them.

Tamil schools fared even less well, although government interest was shown far earlier. By 1905 the government felt it ought to establish Tamil schools as and when the need arose, though it preferred to leave provision to estate managers or to private individuals. The result was that there was no such thing as a Tamil school system. Schools opened and closed with alarming regularity and standards varied considerably. The 1923 Labour Code placed the responsibility for establishing schools for plantation workers' children firmly on to the shoulders of the plantation managers, who became 'the reluctant custodians of the education of the vast majority of Indian children'.[67] Standards were usually only as good as the standard of the teachers, and although grants-in-aid were made available from the 1930s onwards, little attempt was made to control the curriculum or to carry out inspections. It is little wonder that Tamil schools have been described as a mockery and the Cinderella of the systems.[68] As one writer has observed, however, what else could be expected since

> the Tamil school was an instrument of welfare, and also made economic sense on the ground that the immigrant labourer must inculcate the ideas of sanctity of contract and of ordinary honesty to the employers.[69]

The attitudes of the colonial authorities to the different ethnic groups would, in modern parlance, have been perceived as racist. There was a sense of moral obligation to provide some schooling for the rural Malays in order to improve their social lot, but this was very much seen in terms of social welfare and the preservation of social cohesion. The development of English-medium urban schools for all groups was based on economic expediency – the need for English educated clerks and junior civil servants. The special provision of the Malay College at Kuala Kangsar for the sons of the aristocracy was an attempt to preserve the indigenous social hierarchy and to win the co-operation of the Malay Sultans. After all, they were seen as part of the ruling class. It is the most contemptuous dismissal of the immigrant groups that is, in hindsight, so amazing. Instead of seeing the Chinese as descendants of an ancient civilization, they were regarded as rude and barbarous, coolies, cheap labour, whose cultural, social and educational needs were definitely not the responsibility of the colonial authorities. Only when, as a group, they were perceived as being potentially politically subversive, were any Mandarin speaking British officials appointed and was there some attempt at 'controlling' the group, though in effect there were, and are, many diverse Chinese groups.[70] The treatment of the Tamil labour force was degrading. Seen as transitory labour, working on the many diverse rubber plantations, the Tamils were very much left to the mercy of the plantation owners. It was not until the inter-war period that the colonial authorities sought to regulate some form of schooling for the children of estate workers, but this was never little more than child-minding. As for the indigenous tribal peoples, no attempt was made to interfere with their daily lives let alone provide schooling.

The images of the different ethnic groups of Malaya and Singapore in the eyes of the British colonial authorities were, therefore, based on a mixture of social responsibility, prejudice and economic necessity. The images the different groups had of themselves in relation to others, however, were somewhat different. The Malay rulers, the Sultans and the aristocracy, collaborated with and generally related well to the British. They treated with some disdain the rural Malays and the Tamils, and with fear and suspicion, the Chinese. The rural Malays gradually came to see themselves in a position of economic, political and educational inferiority and eventually were to seek to reassert their rights. The Chinese believed that their economic contribution to the country's well-being justified their position and they tended to see themselves as superior to the Malays and the Tamils, especially as they excelled in the education system. The Tamils developed highly negative perceptions of themselves. Many of these images, stereotyped though they may be, were reinforced by the curriculum and the textbooks used in the different school systems.

THE CURRICULUM AND TEXTBOOKS

While there is little doubt that the fourfold education system that was developed by the British authorities, together with the policies that shaped these structures, have had a profound influence on shaping the future developments of both Malaysia and Singapore, the curriculum that was permitted and the textbooks that were used also profoundly influenced the psychological perceptions of the teachers and the pupils taught. In the inter-war years, for example, the Chinese schools 'gave their pupils a Chinese education and brought them up to regard themselves as subjects of the Republic of China in a foreign country'[71] and although a system was worked out between the government and the schools regarding textbooks imported from Shanghai, 'there was no mention in them of Malaya's history, geography, trade, commerce or its mixed population'.[72] Instead the emphasis was on identification with China. The Tamil schools merely emphasized basic literacy and numeracy with little attempt to stretch the mental horizons of their pupils. After all why should plantation owners, who needed docile and obedient workers, wish to arouse discontent amongst their employees by giving them a broad education? Even today the images of the Tamil estate workers as the poor of society are widely held.

The schools that helped to break down racial distinctions were undoubtedly the urban English-medium schools, predominantly run by missionary groups. According to Wong their chief aim 'was to provide a general education and a better standard of moral life based on the tenets of Christianity'[73] rather than specific proselytization. In this way they must be judged as highly successful. Their most constructive role was to bring together different ethnic groups under one roof and to teach them as individuals. As the Annual Education Report for 1954 observed

> the English schools everywhere co-operated to create that feeling of education between the different races of the country which is the best hope for the emergence of one nation.[74]

The pity is that the system was not more widely extended. The English-medium schools were predominantly urban, had developed under the auspices of missionaries or private individuals and were open to all, regardless of race, creed or colour, provided they could pay the fees. Because of government policies, English schools were beyond the reach of most rural Malays even if they could pay or wanted to attend.

As Jayasuriya has cryptically noted

> the British did less than justice to the Malays in denying them access to English education. The situation was compounded by the fact that it was the missions that supplemented official efforts at providing English education. The reluctance of Malays on religious grounds to patronise mission schools has been pointed out earlier ... The non Malays profited not only from the few English schools set up by the government but also from missionary schools, several of which turned out to be prestigious institutions, prominent even at the present time. The mission schools received grants from the government, and in this sense revenue derived from Malays helped more in the education of non-Malays than of Malays.[75]

This is not the place to assess the role of the mission schools – this has been done elsewhere[76], but in terms of curriculum, both Protestant and Roman Catholic boys schools offered a basic core of English, French, Chinese, Malay, arithmetic, book-keeping and drawing, while the girls were offered reading, writing, Malay, English and needlework. Both offered a fairly traditional Western type of curriculum. A few schools offered commercial education, typing and shorthand. Religious instruction was regarded as a separate subject and was not always compulsory. The government-aided English schools offered reading, English (oral and written), recitation, spelling and dictation, writing, arithmetic, geography, hygiene, history, art and handiwork, needlework and physical training.[77]

Many of the books used would have been produced by Longmans, Oxford University Press, Heinemann and Nelson and were little more than modifications of texts used in English schools in the UK of that time, though a number of examples were taken from the local situation. The history syllabus of standard II, for example, while identifying an element of world history was concerned with

> Stories, told simply, and illustrated by pictures and portraits where possible, of the lives of men who have had some connection with local history, such as Confucius, Buddha, Alexander the Great, Muhammed, Marco Polo, Magellan, D'Alburquerque, St Francis Xavier, Drake, Light, Raffles and others. [By Standard IV concern was on] the nations of Europe, World discoveries, the growth of the British Empire ... An outline of Malayan history should be included, describing in particular, the growth of Malayan contact with western people. [At Standards VI and VII, the syllabus was] A two years course on the History of the British people, the pre-Tudor period being much abridged. Emphasis should be laid on social and

economic aspects and on overseas expansion, rather than upon political events. Some attention should also be paid to constitutional development.[78]

Three widely used textbooks were W.S. Morgan's *The Story of Malaya* (Wheaton and Co. Exeter), N.J. Ryan's *Malaya through four Centuries: An Anthology 1500–1900* (Oxford UP), and Philip Nazareth's *The Malayan Story* (Macmillan and Peter Chong, Singapore). They all lay stress on different people of the region, the coming of the Portuguese, the Dutch and eventually the British; as if the process was both inevitable and legitimate. In each case well over half the pages are devoted to the British involvement.

While there is an attempt at being dispassionate, there is also a strong emphasis on the benevolence of the British. Take this example of Morgan's eulogy of Raffles,

> With such a character, Raffles was bound to stand out as a man born to do great things . . . In a short time he could write and speak Malay easily, and he was always studying the customs and history of the Malays. He welcomed them all from all parts to talk to him of their lives and their homes, and amongst them he made many good friends. In him there grew a love and enthusiasm for the Malay world, so that it became the ambition of his life to bring to it all the good that lay in his power as a servant of the Company . . .
>
> Raffles dreamed of the British becoming the overlords of the whole Malay world. He read that in ancient times all the Malay Sultans had acknowledged an overlord, or protector, who had the title of 'Bitana'. Why should not the British become the 'Bitana' of the Malays? He disliked the Dutch and their ways of government. Their desire to grab all the trade, and their bleeding of the island for the sake of profit, had brought no good but only bankruptcy to their Company and poverty and discontent to the Malays. Everywhere there was slavery and the seas were filled with pirates. In Raffles' eyes the Dutch had failed, and he wanted the British to take their place . . . Slavery and forced labour, piracy and lawlessness should be ended. Native traders should be free to buy and sell where they pleased, and the people to reap the fruits of their toil without being forever ground down under their rulers like slaves.[79]

Such views were designed to show the British not only as superior to the Dutch, but as benevolent, abolishers of slavery, enablers of free trade, 'improvers of the lot of the people'[80] and Raffles, in these extracts, is portrayed as being deeply loved by his people and servants.

> Raffles' true memorial is in Singapore, now grown into one of the great ports of the earth, and in the Malay world, where, as he once hoped, slavery, piracy and lawlessness have given way to order and peace.[81]

Recognition is, however, given to the Chinese whose 'labour has made possible the prosperity of Singapore and Penang . . . the most industrious and useful part of the population,[82] but they had only become that way because the benevolent rule of the British brought about peace and prosperity. The following extract highlights this:

> What brought the Chinese was the chance of making their fortunes under the safe protection of British government. It neither ill treated them as helpless strangers in a foreign land, nor did it bleed them with heavy taxes. It suited them to be left free to work hard and make money, while the British did the job of governing and keeping order.[83]

This latter view hardly accorded with the facts, but it sought to justify why the British largely ignored the social and educational needs of the Chinese.

With regard to the Malays, not only were they shown to be a bunch of pirates before the Europeans arrived and brought peace, but the Malay states were shown to be constantly at war with one another. While there is much truth in both these contentions, the situation was exaggerated in order to portray the British in a better light, though it needs to be acknowledged that the failures of the East India Company administration were also highlighted. Here is a description of a Malay State:

> A Malay State in the past was very different from what it is today ... A state was a collection of riverside villages, such as might be found along the River Selangor or Perak or Penang. The Sultan was the head of the State ... Sometimes the Sultan was a strong man and villages lived in peace, but usually he was weak and unable to control his chiefs. He made no laws and employed no officials, no police and no magistrates to give justice and to carry out his command. Each chief was a law unto himself. If we were to tell the story of each Malay State it would be a long, dull one of wars and quarrels between one Sultan and another, between the Sultans and their chiefs, and between the chiefs themselves, who raided each others' villages and built stockades to plunder passing traders. The peninsula was a land of disorder, where might was right, where a *Kris* [a small knife] was worth more than a legal document, and where every man went about armed for his own protection.[84]

Children were taught how the Residential system was brought about, how taxation, law and order, justice and good government followed and 'the days of lawlessness were at an end, and Krises were hung on the wall'.[85] In other words the presence of British rule had led to the creation of peace, harmony and stability.

Another view is that:

> the history of Malaya after 1896 is the story of steady development towards unity, prosperity and eventual self-government. Malaya's history, which in the preceding centuries had been colourful and turbulent, became more prosaic and peaceful ...

The Portuguese introduced the Western world to Malaya, bringing new and revolutionary contacts. The Dutch provided little of permanent value. . . . The Chinese showed the great advantages of trade and the importance of the internal resources of the country. Finally, the British in their pursuit of trade brought, perhaps unconsciously, the ideas of parliamentary government which were to grow out of justice and free speech.[86]

Interesting judgements were also made about the racial composition of the country; the tribal peoples, the Malays themselves and the immigrant peoples, the Chinese and the Indians. Observations such as those that follow were not unusual:

Scholars who study races, can tell the tale of a man's ancestry by the shape of his head, his colour, his height and, best of all, by his hair. They have agreed that mankind is divided into three great families – the woolly-haired, the wavy-haired and the straight-haired. Men of all three families came here in the past, and their descendants can still be recognised to-day . . .

The earliest people to live in this part of the world were tiny negroes, with woolly hair, very dark skins, broad noses and thick lips . . . They are called Samang in the West and Pangan in the East . . . They lead a very simple life . . . They can only count up to two . . . The early woolly-haired men were followed from the north by much taller men with wavy hair and light brown skins . . . In Malaya these tribes are called the Senoi who belong to the wavy-haired family.[87]

The Negritos are small negro-like people with round faces, flat noses, thick lips, dark chocolate brown skins and crinkly hair . . . The Senoi are slightly taller than the Negritos and have slim bodies, wavy hair and brown skins . . . The Senoi are pagans. They speak a Mon-Annan dialect . . . The Aboriginal Malays are the most advanced of the Malayan aborigines and most of them live in Kampongs in the usual Malay-type atap houses.[88]

The Malays belong to the Mongolian race, which has straight, black hair and narrow eyes . . . The modern Malay is a very different kind of man from the simple Jakun, though they once had the same ancestors and were of the same race. Men have measured the skulls of the Malays, and they say the Malay has a bigger skull than the other races of the peninsula. Thus he has a bigger brain and is more intelligent. This is because the Malay, as a dweller and wanderer in the Archipelego, has mixed with other people.[89]

Intelligent or not, great stress was placed on the fact that the Europeans (i.e. the British) had brought law and order and good government, thus enabling the growth of economic prosperity, the Chinese and Indians had developed the country economically, while the Malays allowed it all to happen. These stereotyped images have lasted on throughout much of this century and the following extract brings out clearly how and why such images were formed.

The peace and order which the Malay states began to have after 1873 enabled not only the Malay *rayats* to till their fields in peace, but also the Chinese to make their living without fear of losing their lives and savings . . . Without the Chinese the Malay States would have remained poor. Their labour did most of the work of opening up the land. They were the charcoal burners and wood cutters, the carpenters and bricklayers, the shopkeepers and traders . . . As contractors they made the roads, railways, bridges and public buildings. They are the chief town dwellers and tin miners, and many find employment on the rubber estates . . .

Of the Indians who live in the peninsula . . . a small number of these are educated, and since the days when it was hard to get men of education in Malaya, they have done much useful work as government servants, doctors, schoolmasters and lawyers . . .

~ The Malays have played only a small part in Malaya's rise to prosperity through trade, rubber and tin. That is because they have refused to become workers on estates and mines. They have no desire to perspire for hours on end and day after day in order to save a little money, and they are not interested in using their energy in the ceaseless drudgery and worry of buying and selling things. The Malay is content to leave that to the Chinese, Indians and Europeans. In this he shows that he has a character and wisdom of his own . . . He is easy going and he values his hours of leisure more than those of work.[90]

Not only are the different perceptions of the different groups that go to make up Malaysia clearly highlighted, but these images persisted well after independence. Such was the Malay frustration that they had only 'played a small part in Malaya's rise to prosperity' and that they were perceived as lazy and easygoing by other groups, that the government sought to redress the economic and educational imbalance of the country through the New Economic Policy of the 1970s and 1980s. Nevertheless, before independence it was perhaps as well that the urban English-medium schools were mostly filled with Chinese, Indians and Europeans! Other textbooks, for example, in English, Science, Mathematics and Civics were far less overtly racist in tone and few would quibble with their content or style, given similar books in use in the UK at the time. The Civics syllabuses for Singapore, [91] might surprise us by their firm emphasis on the community, racial co-operation, ethical rectitude, cleanliness, kindness, politeness, truthfulness, helpfulness, fairness, self-control etc., but only in so far as this has never been central to English education. Such views were reinforced in School Assemblies which took passages from all the Great Religions[92] and which could act as models for many multi-racial and religiously plural schools in England to-day.

As for education of the Malays this was intitially predominantly based on teaching the Koran and the Malay language and was very different in tone, purpose and thrust from the English-medium schooling offered. Only gradually was the curriculum diversified to include other subjects, but even so 'Malayan education in the Kampong was so restricted in content that the rural Malay was isolated and even divided from the minority who were English educated'.[93]

Because of fear of Western secular education there was great reluctance for children to participate in Malay schools. The result was that different attempts made to enforce compulsory education had to be passed in different States. By 1929, however, attendance at Malay schools had reached 90 per cent and the need for coercion was no longer necessary. Even so 'for the majority of Malays vernacular education was designed to lead them back to the padi fields or to swell the rank of manual labourers'.[94] In spite of changes and in spite of a steady increase in the number of schools (see Table 10.5) and enrolments, so that by 1938 there were 1,169 Malay vernacular primary schools with an enrolment of over 57,000 pupils, they typified the negation of educational development for the Malays until after the Second World War. After all, if the Malay 'is easy going and values his hours of leisure more than those of work' what was the point of providing anything more than the basic rudiments of schooling? Indeed, as Sellah has observed, 'the aim of Malay vernacular schools was never beyond that of the eradication of illiteracy'.[95]

Table 10.5 Number of Malay schools in the Straits Settlements, Federated Malay States and unfederated Malay states, 1924, 1931, 1938

Straits settlements	1924	1931	1938
Straits Settlements			
Singapore	21	25	–
Penang	98	102	–
Malacca	88	87	–
	207	214	219
Federated Malay States			
Perak	238	274	–
Selangor	73	87	–
Negri Sembilen	77	88	–
Pahang	54	85	–
	442	534	569
Unfederated Malay States			
Johore	72	113	155
Kedah	67	88	111
Perlis	16	23	25
Kelantan	24	62	63
Trengganu	12	20	27
	191	306	381
Total	840	1054	1169

Source: Various Annual Reports, cited in J.E. Jayasuriya, (1983) *Dynamics of Nation-building in Malaysia*, Colombo. Associated Education Publishers, p. 15.

By the 1930s, the curriculum consisted of the three Rs as well as hygiene, physical education, basketry and gardening, designed to give the schools a rural bias. According to Winstedt, one of the Education Officers in the FMS, 'English and Malay should be taught simultaneously or, alternatively, there should be classes in Malay for Malay boys attached to some of the English schools.'[96] As it happened, English was not taught until after the Second World War. As the Annual Report for the FMS (1922) stated, 'For the majority of the boys who attend the vernacular schools an English education is not, at all events, in the present stage of development of the country, a necessity.'[97] Winstedt even went further by suggesting that 'the educationalist has to beware lest vernacular education may give a pupil a smattering of book learning and rob him of his alert interest in his surroundings'.[98] As a result the curriculum had a remarkably narrow focus. Geography, for example, was based on the local environment with some knowledge of the Malay peninsula, and the Malay archipelago; natural science was basically physiology and hygiene. History, interestingly enough, was not enouraged, the argument being that it was pointless teaching the history of Europe because the concept was too difficult to grasp and it was futile teaching Malayan history because 'the fairy tales that stand for history in the Malay chronicles were founded on evidence too debatable' to consider.[99] It was, however, taught and both history and geography were based on R.J. Wilkinson's series of papers on Malay subjects which he translated into Malay. Malay was based on the standardized Roman script. Other subjects included elementary agriculture (i.e. school gardening), basketry and needlework.

One of the difficulties facing Malay vernacular education was finding a sufficient number of teachers. Initially the solution was found by offering reasonably good salaries, but it was gradually solved by providing teacher training. The earliest Teacher Training Institute was at Taiping where part of the curriculum was 'a course of manual instruction in carpentry and bamboo and canework for the native teacher'.[100] The Training College at Malacca, however, was concerned that the curriculum:

> should render students conversant with the best literature of their country and the principles of arithmetic, to instruct them in the principles and practice of school management, the element of drawing some manual work, especially carpentry.[101]

The curriculum of the Malay Women's Training College at Malacca was more explicitly geared for domestic science and domestic life, with the curriculum concentrating on arithmetic, reading, writing, composition, history, geography, nature study, domestic science, hygiene, principles of teaching, religious knowledge, singing, drill and games, drawing, serving and craftwork.

Ultimately these colleges were to merge into one central college, Sultan Idris Teacher Training College (SITTC) in 1922, on the grounds of providing uniformity, efficiency and cheapness. Emphasis was placed on elementary agriculture, handicrafts common to rural village life (basketry, carpentry, cotton printing, pottery, silver work, net-making, sunblind-making, watch repairing, lampshade-making, bookbinding and weaving), religious knowledge, arithmetic, Malay language and literature, history and geography. The College was designed deliberately not to copy European methods and ideas for fear of generating 'a restless desire for change'.[102]

Amongst the textbooks used were a series of arithmetic textbooks, *Kitab Hisab* II, III and IV, based on past Overseas Cambridge arithmetic papers; a series of Malay books based on traditional stories; a history of the Malay world, *Sejarah Alam Melayu* (I-V) and *Tawarik Melayu*, written by an Englishman, R.J. Wilkinson. Ironically it was this interpretation of history that was, as much as anything else, to lead to the growth of Malay nationalism. A translation bureau translated into Jawi many books from well-known Western authors – fairy tales, Greek fables, stories from the *Arabian Nights* etc. – published as the Malay Home Library Series and the Malay School Series.[103]

One of the main criticisms was that the level of books used was juvenile and not designed to stretch the students' mental abilities. One writer and former teacher at SITTC wrote:

> The books read by children did not offer them any meaning. The books, instead, made the children feel small, humble and inferior, resulting in them having no ambition in life and adopting a feeling as if they were slaves.[104]

Indeed the Commission on Higher Education in Malaya (the McLean Commission, 1939, pp. 116–17) condemned not only the low standard of teacher training at SITTC but also the poor standard of textbooks used:

> they have standard no higher than that equivalent to the Junior Cambridge Examination. A few of them know some English but most of them have virtually no acquaintance with this language . . . Their educational reading must be confined to the few textbooks translated from English into Malay by the Translation Bureau, and their general reading to the few translations in the Malay Home Library Series and to Malay newspapers. Yet to these teachers falls the important task of training the students who are to teach in the Malay vernacular schools.

There were other criticisms. There was no library. No English was taught. The College was 'modelled on the lines of an English public school', situated in an isolated part of the country. The one principal, O.T. Dussek (1920–36), who encouraged the students to take an interest in things wider than rural kampongs, in race, language and religion, to assert themselves in their own land before it was too late, to take a pride in being Malay, etc., was pensioned off early because of fears by the British authorities that he was subverting the system. There seems little doubt that the rulers intended to patronize and denigrate the Malays: SITTC was one instrument designed to keep the ruled in a position of subservience. Ironically, however, far from accepting the level of training offered many teachers were to become ardent Malay nationalists working in the kampongs while urging the overthrow of British colonial rule.

Perhaps the last word should go to Sellah, who has made a study of SITTC. He argues that while many of the British bureaucrats, Wilkinson, Winstedt, Maxwell, Cheeseman, had an interest in Malaya and all that they believed was good in it, and although they wrote and published widely,

> They looked at the Malay way of life, not as a system, but as a culture so different from the one with which they were familiar and from which they came. It was a new world that they discovered – a world that was so romantic. This romantic world must be preserved or it would soon be lost.[105]

He describes them as paternal bureaucrats, not educationalists. The policies they pursued were deliberate because they believed them to be the best for the Malays.

CONCLUSIONS

Although the Japanese occupation of Malaya and Singapore during the Second World War and events following the war were to lead to changed attitudes, moves towards greater racial harmonization and eventual independence for both Malaya and Singapore as separate nation states, the educational framework and patterns of thought had been laid down by the time war broke out. What therefore can be said of the British colonial legacy?

British involvement in Malaya and Singapore changed the political, economic, and ethnic shape of both countries irrevocably. By developing a four-language educational policy, linked as it was with economic opportunities, by deliberately confining Malay vernacular education to the primary level only, except for the sons of the ruling classes, and by failing to pursue an even-handed approach for all ethnic groups at least three forms of pluralism were created – social, cultural and economic. Social pluralism came about because English-medium education, leading to the most prestigious social positions, was available only to the Malay aristocracy and urban dwellers, while Malay-only education was available to the subject and largely rural classes. By not encouraging a sense of loyalty amongst the Indians and Chinese to their country of adoption the British helped create social divisions along ethnic lines. Cultural pluralism and separatism were brought about because of the four-language media, reinforced by the textbooks used in the different medium schools.

Only the English-medium schools sought to bring the different groups together, but they created the third kind of pluralism, economic, because they conferred socioeconomic advantage on those who attended. In trying to 'preserve' the Malays from the impact of modernization and in keeping them in a position of subservience, the British colonial authorities inevitably disadvantaged them *vis-à-vis* the other groups. Successive governments since independence have sought to redress this imbalance firstly through the school curriculum, then through the National Language policy and finally through the New Economic Policy. In spite of these efforts and in spite of policies of positive discrimination in favour of the Malays, many, especially in rural areas, continue to be socially and economically deprived. The politics of rulers and ruled continue to have repercussions in Malaysian society, but above all the images that were created as a result of educational policies and the content of schooling during colonial times have persisted even into the 1990s.

11 'English in taste, in opinions, in words and intellect'

Indoctrinating the Indian through textbook, curriculum and education

Suresh Chandra Ghosh

PROLOGUE

The East India Company formed in 1709 to trade in the Eastern Seas did not introduce English education to demonstrate the superiority of Western civilization and culture to a pagan civilization in India until Britain became an imperial power, by the beginning of the nineteenth century. Before the start of the nineteenth century the East India Company's settlements in India were confined to Calcutta, Madras, Bombay and Surat and the English in India were one of the many European powers, all competing for the India trade, all equally dependent on Indian governmental favour. The headquarters of the Company were located in London and its executive body was the Court of Directors consisting of twenty-four members, who used to manage the affairs of the Company abroad.[1] For each of the settlements in India, they appointed a Governor who was assisted by a Council consisting of senior merchants of the settlement. Below the Governor's Council came the senior and junior merchants, the factors and the writers. Outside the ranks of the Company's servants came a sprinkling of free merchants. Apart from the Company's servants and the free merchants, the only representatives of the professions were the Company's chaplains and surgeons. The hospital and the punchhouses frequented by soldiers and sailors complete the picture of the early settlements in India.[2]

In pre-Plassey days, the servants of the Company in these settlements used to live in dark and damp lodgings in the Fort, amid the warehouses and offices in which they spent their working days, receiving goods from up-country and despatching them to Europe. They met for dinner and supper at a common table, taking their seats according to their rank, presided over by the Governor of the settlement and at night the gates of the Fort shut upon them.[3] Their life thus bore a strong resemblance to that of an Oxford or Cambridge College, or to that of a great merchant household in London, where the master slept with his family over his place of business, 'servants and prentices above in the garrets and porters and messengers packed away anywhere in cellarage and warehouses'.[4]

The servants of the Company scarcely went abroad from their own settlements except from one factory to another and as occasional ambassadors to the Mughal Court. They had little social intercourse with Indians as equals – the men they saw were either agents like the *dubashes* of Madras or the *banians* (Hindu traders) of Calcutta and *shroffs* (bankers or money-changers) of Bombay, servants and slaves or superiors like an occasional Mughal Governor who might visit the factory. They were frequently ignorant of the country's languages and conducted their business in the debased Portuguese spoken round the coast, or by means of interpreters. Generally speaking they kept apart and aloof from Indian life, thought they had developed no contempt for Indian social customs or political power. They had no prejudice against adopting any Indian fashion or custom which made life in an alien climate more comfortable or more luxurious. Englishmen in India took the *zenana* (womens' quarters) from Muslim society without themselves becoming Muslim and adopted various current Hindu superstitions and practices without ever absorbing any Hindu philosophic ideas. They remained what they were and they were proud of being so. There was no trace of racial feeling or talk of inferiority, though there was no great attraction for either race to the other.

The position of the servants of the Company began to change after the battle of Plassey in 1757 when they played the role of king-makers in Bengal and became *zamindars* (landlords) after the grant of the *Diwani* in 1765 by the Mughal Emperor, Shah Alam II.[5] The Company had now become a power in Bengal and had come in close contact with the Muslim and Hindu princes. The latter on their side ceased to regard the Company as troublesome traders and began to display an increasing interest in European methods, in order to discover the secret of European success. At that time, the tide of racialism was quite unperceived in the cross-current of mutual contact and interest; and there ensued a period of cosmopolitan intercourse which blossomed in European appreciation of oriental learning and literature among the higher officials of the Company in Bengal.

Thus Warren Hastings who came to Bengal in 1750 developed a great love for Indo-Persian culture. With his encouragement as Governor-General of Bengal, Nathaniel Halted wrote *A Code of Gentoo Laws* in 1776 and a Bengali grammar in 1778, in 1779 Charles Wilkins brought out his Sanskrit grammar and Francis Gladwin wrote *Institutes of the Emperor Akbar* in 1783. In 1781, Hastings established the Calcutta Madrassa (centre for Islamic teaching) at the request of a Muslim deputation. The main object was to 'qualify the sons of the Mohamadan gentlemen for responsible and lucrative offices in the state, even at that time largely monopolised by the Hindus'. The institution was very popular and attracted scholars from far-off places. The period of study extended over seven years and scholars received stipends. The courses included natural philosophy, Koranic theology, law, geometry, arithmetic, logic and grammar – all on Islamic lines. The medium of instruction was Arabic. Hastings purchased a site and laid the foundation of the Madrassa on his own account and asked the Court of Directors to assign 'the rents of the one or more villages' near Calcutta as an endowment for the college. The Directors later sanctioned this and reimbursed Hastings.[6]

With the arrival of Sir William Jones at Calcutta in September 1783, a new impulse and a new organization was given to Indo-British orientalism. Jones was already an accomplished Persian scholar, whose *Grammar of the Persian Language* and translation of the Persian poets, published in 1771 and 1773, had won him a European reputation. He now applied his own enthusiasm to the organization of scholarly effort in Bengal. But he soon realized that without 'the united efforts of many' he could not achieve his ambition of knowing India 'better than any other European ever knew it' (as he later said to Lord Althorp). He had been elected a Fellow of the Royal Society in London in 1773 and he set out to create a similar learned society in Calcutta, with as its aim 'enquiry into the history and antiquities, arts, sciences and literature of Asia'. Not long after his arrival in Bengal he addressed a meeting of thirty Englishmen, the elite of Calcutta society, in the Grand Jury room of the Supreme Court, under the presidency of Robert Chambers, the Chief Justice and an old fellow of University College, Oxford. Jones asked his audience to utilize their leisure hours in learning to know Asia, 'the nurse of science, the inventress of delightful and useful arts, the scene of glorious action, fertile in the production of human genius, abounding in natural wonders, and infinitely diversified in the forms of religion and government, in the laws, manners, customs, and complexions of men'. History, science, and art; Jones called upon men to study all three and on 15 January 1784, the Asiatic Society of Bengal was formed to pursue these aims. Warren Hastings and the members of the Supreme Council acted as patrons, Sir William Jones as President and J.H. Harrington as Secretary of the Society, the foundation of humanistic study of 'Man and Nature' in Bengali.[7]

While the Asiatic Society under Sir William Jones's impulse was busy unlocking India for Europe, involving the co-operation of Indian with English scholars, Jonathan Duncan, Resident at Benares, obtained in 1792 the permission of Cornwallis, the Governor-General, to establish a Sanskrit College at Benares, for preserving and cultivating the laws and literatures of the Hindus. In this college, as in the Calcutta Madrassa, the students were not only taught *gratis*, but were also given stipends. Finally, Wellesley set up the Fort William College at Calcutta in 1800 to train the British civilians as administrators and included in the curriculum, courses on oriental learning and appointed *Pandits* or oriental experts to teach them.[8]

These measures taken to revive an interest in oriental culture and literature may not be construed here as the beginning of a definite education policy endorsing the classical Indian system of education (*tols* for Hindus and *madrassas* for Muslims at the higher level and the village *patshalas* and *maktal* at the elementary level) by the East India Company in Bengal. They owed their origin to individual enterprises and were undertaken mainly for the preservation of ancient Indian culture. There were also political and administrative needs to be considered. Not only was it necessary to conciliate the feelings of both communities, Hindus and Muslims, but it was felt to be useful to understand their languages and customs for better governance by the Company officials, who were being increasingly called upon to assist the East India Company in the administration of the territories acquired by it. There was no trace or intention on the part of the Company to impose on the Indians an alien culture and civilization through the introduction of the English language.

CHARLES GRANT

By the end of the eighteenth century there was a change in the status of the East India Company in India and the transformation of the British from merchants to rulers was almost complete. The battle of Plassey (1757) followed by the battle of Buxar (1764) and the grant of the *Diwani* (1765) helped the British merchants to acquire territorial interests in Bengal and by 1803 they were also successful in defeating their own European rivals as well as curbing the power of Indian rulers like Oudh, Mysore and the Peshawa. In Bengal, Bombay and Madras there had been considerable increases in the number of civil servants, and a dramatic increase in the number and quality of its military servants, and an influx of women who brought with them their insular whims and prejudices, which no official contact with Indians or iron compulsion of loneliness ever tempted them to abandon. The Company still managed a large and expanding trade and the commercial branch, with its headquarters at the Board of Trade in Calcutta and its commercial residents up-country, still sorted and baled cottons and silks, and shipped out saltpetre from Patna as before. But the commercial branch was now overshadowed by a civil service responsible, as collectors and magistrates, or as judges of the district courts, for the administration of an empire which stretched from Chittagong and Cuttack as far as Delhi. It was from the revenues of these territories and the profits of the China trade that the commerce between India and England was sustained. The handful of European troops, maintained as guards up-country and as garrison in Calcutta, Bombay and Madras had also grown to an army of several thousand men in each place, with a further considerable army of European-officered native battalions, and a number of royal regiments serving in India for a few years only with a maximum of national pride and a minimum desire to understand the country. As the higher posts of the government were filled with appointments from England, its designs became more imperial and its attitude more haughty and aloof. The gulf between the two races so dissimilar in character, in culture and in institutions as the English and the Indian, which Muslim Nawabs and English *bon viveurs*, diplomatic *pandits* and English scholars had for a time bridged, began ominously to widen again. With it, the attitude of the average Englishman changed also from one of disapproval of Hindu 'superstition' and Muslim 'bigotry', or philosophic interest in Hindu mythology, the Golden Age and the histories of Mughal glory into one of contempt for an inferior and conquered people. A 'superiority complex' was forming which regarded India not only as a country whose institutions were bad and whose people were corrupted, but one which was by its nature incapable of ever becoming any better. Colour was all too simple a symbol of such disapproval. Colour was already associated with the idea of inferiority in the case of the Africans. How easy to pass from saying 'The Indians, who are coloured, have a civilization inferior to ours' to the thought 'The Indian civilization is inferior because Indians are coloured'.

The foremost among the Company officials who found the Indian society degraded and incapable of any improvement by itself was Charles Grant. Grant had come to India in 1767, acquired an immense fortune, and had a hectic life until 1786 when, through family mishaps and close contact with David Brown, one of the Company's chaplains, and George Udny of the Company's civil service, a great change came over him. In 1790 he returned home and two years later completed the first draft of his treatise: *Observations on the state of society among the Asiatic subjects of Great Britain, particularly in respect to morals; and on the means of improving it*. He charged the Hindus with dishonesty, corruption, fraud, mutual hatred and distrust and described their customs such as *suttee* as barbarous and the Muslims with haughtiness, perfidy, licentiousness and lawlessness. He asserted that the intercourse of the two communities had led to the further debasement of both because each had imbibed the vices of the other.

Grant blamed the East India Company for viewing these grave evils with apathy and contended that it was under no obligation to protect the creed of the Hindus which was monstrous and 'subversive of the first principles of reason, morality and religion'. He came forward with a suggestion to help Indian society improve itself from within by a 'healing principle'. This involved the supercession of the existing Hindu and Muslim religion by Christianity through the dissemination of the science and literature of Europe, 'a key which would at once open a world of new ideas' to them. Grant explained that the long intercourse between the Indians and the Europeans in Bengal rendered it feasible to use the English language as the medium of instruction. Moreover, as he said, a knowledge of the English language would immediately place the whole range of European knowledge within their reach, while translation of English books into the Indian languages would take a long time and would be less efficacious. Grant also urged the substitution of English for Persian as the official language because that would induce the Indians to learn it. He urged the establishment of English schools under teachers 'of good moral character', hoping that very soon the pupils taught in these schools would themselves become the teachers of English to their countrymen. In conclusion, he triumphantly asserted 'the true cure of darkness is light. The Hindus err because they are ignorant and their errors have never been fairly laid before them'.[9]

Grant's observations on Indian society were a reflex of the forces at home – one unplanned, the other purposeful – the Industrial Revolution and the Evangelical Movement, setting forward new social values.[10] The Industrial Revolution created a new class of men with power and authority to set aside the old aristocratic land-owning leadership. Where the latter had depended upon inheritance in a fixed hierarchical society and had set an example of grand, even extravagant living, the new men rose by personal effort, by hard work and by frugality. A new economic order developed a new code of social values and behaviour in answer to its unspoken need.[11] Contemporaneously, a religious revival affected England, which though it had its starting point in vital religion, in personal conversion, also served to promote such social virtues as frugality, sobriety and industry. Among the lower orders of society it was Methodism which inspired 'the civilization, the industry and sobriety of great numbers of the labouring part of the country'.[12] Among the upper classes, the impulse was provided by the Evangelicals and by such persons as Hannah More. They numbered in their ranks men such as Milner of Queen's College or Simeon of King's College, Cambridge, the merchant Zachary Macaulay, William Wilberforce, Henry Thornton the banker and James Stephen the lawyer,[13] men of the class from which many of the Company's servants were drawn. In 1793, Wilberforce and Hannah More gathered round Joseph Venn, rector of Clapham. They were there joined by Charles Grant, by Sir John Shore, Stephen, Thornton, Macaulay and others.[14] These Claphamites were, perhaps, social conservatives in their acceptance of the order of society, but they were radical in their determination to secure a reformation of manners and a new righteousness in the upper ranks of society.[15]

Charles Grant belonged to an age which in Europe was called the Age of Reason. The intellectual revolution of the late seventeenth century hinged upon the emancipation of reason from authority and its application to the study of man and nature. The eighteenth-century intellectual in Europe thought that the application of the principle of reason made indefinite social and intellectual progress possible. When other civilizations were examined in the light of this idea, it was noted that they all seemed to be imprisoned in authority, in custom and in tradition. From this it was deduced that they were stagnant or dormant societies. Only the West had found the secret of progress; therefore, Western culture was superior to others in quality and forging even further ahead in achievement. When the Mughals were seen to have lost their power and the Marathas not to have inherited it, both Muslims and Hindus fell in cultural as well as political estimation as the East India Company, with the help of Western technical progress, became a *paramount power* in India.

When Henry Dundas, the President of the Board of Control, was shown the manuscript of Grant, he asked his Secretary, William Cabell, to write a note on it. Cabell emphasized the political advantages that could be derived from developing a system of education based on Grant's *Observations*. He mentioned that a common language would draw the ruler and the ruled into closer contact, and the introduction of European education would lead to the removal of many abuses from which people were suffering, due to their 'false system of beliefs and a total want of right instruction among them'. However, when the subject was debated on the occasion of the renewal of the Company's Charter in 1793, the Attorney-General and the Solicitor-General explicitly stated in a bill that the real end sought was to send missionaries and schoolmasters to India for the ultimate conversion of Indians. This was considered fully detrimental to the trading interests of the Company, dominated by men with long experience in India, who considered any such move would result in political unrest in that country. They condemned the bill and through some of their connections in both the Houses of Parliament, they manoeuvred to defeat it.[16] Thus ended Grant's hope of improving the character of Indian civilization with the imported know-how of Western civilization.

THOMAS BABINGTON MACAULAY

The idea of introducing a European education as a gift from an imperial power to improve a pagan civilization in India was vigorously revived three decades after the failure of the Grant Plan. At that time Bentinck, a utilitarian, was Governor-General of India and Thomas Babington Macaulay, another utilitarian was the Law Member of his Council, while still another utilitarian, James Mill and his more famous son, John Stuart Mill held influential offices in the headquarters of the East India Company in London. By that time, the East India Company had become a paramount power and its territories now extended over a large part of India. It had assumed responsibility, mainly because of pressure from missionary societies in England and Scotland, for the education of the people of India in 1813 when the Charter Act of the Company was renewed. The Act which for the first time officially permitted the missionaries to proselytize in British India included a clause (no. 43) which empowered the Governor-General to appropriate 'a sum of not less that one lac of rupees' in each year out of 'the surplus territorial revenues' for the revival and improvement of literature and the encouragement of the learned natives of India, and for the introduction and promotion of a knowledge of the sciences among the inhabitants of the British territories in India.[17] The first part of clause 43 was obviously based on Minto's 'Minute' written in 1811 drawing the attention of the Court of Directors to the dilapidated and decaying condition of Oriental institutions and learning in India, while the debates in both Houses of Parliament made it clear that, by 'sciences' was meant 'Western sciences'.

It was in 1823 that one lakh of rupees was available 'out of the surplus territorial revenues', a General Committee of Public Instruction was formed and the money was placed at its disposal for expenditure on education. Since the Committee, consisting of ten members, was largely dominated by persons with great admiration for Sanskrit and Arabic literature, they began to spend it quite in keeping with the first part of clause 43 in the revival of Oriental learning and institutions. However, in 1820s, the British Parliament was being increasingly influenced by Whig Liberalism, its policies of conserving the indigenous traditions of the colonies were losing favour and the imperial urge to govern and 'civilize' the colonies according to British ideas was becoming stronger. The entry in 1820 of James Mill, and a little later of his son, John Stuart Mill, to the Examiner's office in India House which housed the executive body of the East India Company brought about an era of utilitarian educational concern at the Home Office. The utilitarians were interested in the teaching of the sciences, history and philosophy, not literature and poetry. Mill reacted to the activities of the General Committee of Public Instruction by sending to India a strongly worded despatch on 18 February 1824:

> We apprehend that the plan of the institutions to the improvement of which our attention is now directed was originally and fundamentally erroneous. The great end should not have been to teach Hindu learning, but useful learning ... In professing, on the other hand, to establishment of seminaries for the purpose of teaching mere Hindu or mere Mohamedan literature, you bound yourselves to teach a great deal of what was frivolous, not a little of what was purely mischievous and a small remainer indeed in which utility was in any way concerned.[18]

As more and more young men imbued with the utilitarian ideas [19] joined the services of the East India Company and some of them replaced the either dead or retiring members of the General Committee of Public Instruction in Calcutta, the activities of the Committee almost came to a standstill. There were often 'recurring and inconvenient discussions' at meetings without any decisions being made, though Holt Mackenzie, an erstwhile member of the General Committee of Public Instruction, wrote in his report to Parliament in 1832, 'Of late years, it has been the policy of the Government to extend [teaching of] the English language'.[20]

It was almost at this juncture that Thomas Babington Macaulay, the man commonly credited with the introduction of English education came to the forefront of affairs. Macaulay came to India as a member of the Governor-General's Council in December 1834 and though his main preoccupation was to be the composition of the Indian Penal Code, he was also appointed by virtue of his known intellectual stature, President of the General Committee of Public Instruction (now clearly divided between the Anglicists and the Orientalists).

Macaulay, whose interest in consolidating the British Empire by the propagation of English laws and English culture grew up, being the son of Zachary Macaulay, in the circle of the Clapham Evangelists. Zachary Macaulay had been governor of the British colony, Sierra Leone, and believed that the true basis of the British Empire was to be built through the dissemination of British civilization by means of English education. The son shared in the belief of the father and one year before he came out to India, he gave a speech to the British Parliament, on 10 July 1833, a speech that was full of brilliant rhetoric and foreshadowed his 'minute' of 2 February 1835 in India. In that Parliamentary speech, Macaulay's triumphant rhetoric gave to nineteenth-century British imperialism the halo of political altruism, to which he added a cultural sentiment, the greatness and glory of the renascent British nation. The speech, which in fact was a special pleading for the continuance of the Company's administration of India, glorified the Government of India as 'an enlightened and paternal despotism' bent on bringing good government and civilization to India. It also gave to the imperialist ambition of Britain the glorious pretensions of philanthropy.

> It is scarcely possible to calculate the benefits which we might derive from the diffusion of European civilisation among the vast population of the East ... What is power worth if it is founded on vice, on ignorance, and on misery, if we can hold it only by violating the most sacred duties which as governors we owe to the governed, and which, as a people blessed with far more than ordinary measure of political liberty and of intellectual light, we owe to a race debased by three thousand years of despotism and priestcraft? We are free, we are civilised to little purpose, if we grudge to any portion of the human race an equal measure of freedom and civilisation.[21]

In India as President of the General Committee of Public Instruction, Macaulay did not take part in the controversy of the Committee which was then sharply divided between the Anglicists and the Orientalists. It was when the Orientalists as well as the Anglicists decided to approach Bentinck, after their failure to come to a decision on the future education policy of the East India Company in India, occasioned by the question of converting the Calcutta Madrassa into an institution of Western learning as well as reorganizing the Agra College on the model of the Hindu College in Calcutta, that he drew up on 2 February 1835 a long and elaborate minute. This championed the cause of English education in his usual characteristic prose, marked by rhetoric and antithesis.

Macaulay argued that the word 'literature' occuring under clause 43 of the Charter Act of 1813 could be interpreted to mean English literature; that the epithet of a 'learned native of India' could also be applied to a person versed in the philosophy of Locke or the poetry of Milton; and that the object of promoting a knowledge of sciences could only be accomplished by the adoption of English as the medium of instruction. If this interpretation were not accepted, he was willing to propose an Act rescinding clause 43 of the Charter. He was against the continuance of the institutions of Oriental learning and suggested these should be closed as they did not serve any useful purpose: 'We found a sanatorium on a spot which we suppose to be healthy. Do we thereby pledge ourselves to keep a sanatorium there if the result should not answer our expectations?' On the subject of the medium of instruction Macaulay pointed out that all parties agreed

> that the dialects commonly spoken among the natives of this part of India contain neither literary nor scientific information, and are moreover so poor and rude that until they are enriched from some other quarter, it will not be easy to translate any valuable work into them. It seems to be admitted on all sides, that the intellectual improvement of those classes of the people who have the means of pursuing higher studies can at

present be effected only by means of some languge not vernacular amongst them.

The choice of the medium of instruction was naturally left between Sanskrit and Arabic on the one hand and English on the other. Macaulay who admittedly did not have a 'knowledge of either Sanskrit or Arabic' brushed aside the claims of these two languages to be the medium of instruction by observing that 'a single shelf of a good European library was worth the whole native literature of India and Arabia'. On the other hand the claims of English could hardly be necessary to recapitulate. As he said:

> It stands pre-eminent among the languages of the West . . . whoever knows that language has already access to all the vast intellectual wealth which all the wisest nations of earth have created and hoarded in the course of ninety generations. It may safely be said that the literature now extant in that language is of greater value than all the literature which three hundred years ago was extant in all the languages of the world together . . . In India, English is the language spoken by the ruling class. It is spoken by the higher class of natives at the seats of Government. It is likely to become the language of commerce throughout the seas of the East.

He referred to the alleged prejudices of the Indian people against English education and argued that it was the duty of England to teach Indians what was good for their health, and not what was palatable to their taste. He further pointed out that the Indians themselves preferred an English education to their own – as the crowding of the Hindu College and the Scottish Church College in Calcutta and the comparative desertion of the Sanskrit College and the Madrassa in the same city, in spite of its stipends, showed. He also mentioned that while the Committee of Public Instruction was finding it hard to dispose of the Oriental publications, the English books of the Calcutta School Book Society were selling in thousands. Macaulay observed

> The question now before us is simply whether when it is in our power to teach this language, we shall teach languages in which, by universal experience, there are no books on any subject which deserve to be compared to our own; whether, when we can teach European science, we shall teach systems which, by universal confession, wherever they differ from those of Europe, differ for the worse; and whether, when we can patronize school philosophy and true history, we shall countenance, at the public expense, medical doctrines which would disgrace an English farrier, astronomy which would move laughter in girls at an English boarding house, history abounding in kings thirty feet high and reigns thirty thousand years long, and geography made of seas of treacle and seas of butter.

Macaulay suggested that the government should not incur any heavy expenditure on the maintenance of the Oriental institutions of learning which could be used for the promotion of English education. If Sanskrit and Arabic were essential as the languages of the law and religion of the people, government should start codifying Hindu and Muslim laws in English. In one respect Macaulay agreed with his opponents – he admitted that it was impossible to train the mass of the population. He contended,

> We must at present do our best to form a class who may be interpreters between us and the millions whom we govern, a class of persons Indian in blood and colour, but English in taste, in opinions, in morals and intellect. To that class we may leave it to refine the vernacular dialects of the country, to enrich these dialects with terms of science borrowed from the Western nomenclature and to render them by degrees fit vehicles for conveying knowledge to the great mass of the population.

Macaulay, however, was ready to respect some of the existing interests but would like to 'strike at the root of the bad system which has hitherto been fostered by us'. He advocated that the printing of the Oriental works should be stopped, all Oriental colleges, except those at Delhi and Benares, they being chief seats of Oriental learning, should be abolished and all stipends should be discontinued. Macaulay loosened his last shaft at Oriental education by declaring that 'the present system stands not to accelerate the progress of truth but delay the natural death of expiring errors' and threatened to resign if his suggestions were not approved.[22]

Bentinck gave his 'entire concurrence' to the sentiment expressed by Macaulay despite Prinsep's note of 15 February answering some of the observations made by Macaulay on Oriental institutions and learning.[23] In a resolution of 7 March 1835, Bentinck passed the following order:

First: His Lordship is of the opinion that the great object of the British Government ought to be the promotion of European literature and science amongst the natives of India and that all the funds appropriated for the purposes of education would be best employed on English education.

Second: But it is not the intention of His Lordship in Council to abolish any college or school of native learning while the native population shall appear to be inclined to avail themselves of the advantages it affords, and His Lordship in Council directs that all the existing professors and students at all the institutions under the superintendence of the Committee shall continue to receive their stipends.

Third: It has come to the knowledge of the Governor-General in Council that a large sum has been expended by the Committee in the printing of Oriental works. His Lordship in Council directs that no portion of the funds shall hereafter be so employed.

Fourth: His Lordship in Council directs that all the funds which these reforms will leave at the disposal of the Committee be henceforth employed in imparting to the native population a knowledge of English literature and science, through the medium of the English language.[24]

Thus was taken the most momentous decision in the history of India, not to speak of the history of education in India. Since Bentinck took the decision a few weeks after receiving the papers from the General Committee of Public Instruction, it was clear that the Governor-General did not have the necessary time to obtain the required sanction of the Court of Directors. It is to be remembered that these were the days of steamship navigation, when a despatch from Calcutta used to take not less than three *months* to reach London. This simple fact does not need the scholarship of a Spear[25] or a Ballhatchet[26] to prove or disprove that Bentinck acted without the authority of the East India Company in London. Also, given the image of Bentinck that has emerged through recent researches, that of a true product of his age,[27] it does not seem plausible that Bentinck took the decision without reading Macaulay's 'Minute' and that he was motivated solely by Macaulay's threat to resign, as Arthur Mayhew writing on the subject more than a hundred years later in *The Education of India* would have us believe.[28]

THE ENGLISH-EDUCATED INDIANS

While enlightened Indians like Raja Ram Mohan Roy saw in the introduction of English education an opportunity to deliver his countrymen from obscurantism and barbarous superstitions,[29] the majority of young Indians saw in it an opportunity to gain employment in various British establishments, official as well as non-official, that were then emerging in metropolitan cities such as Calcutta, Bombay and Madras and up-country in British India. Though the officials of the East India Company, writers and cadets as they were then called, were always recruited in London, there was always demand for local hands to assist them in the administration of the growing British establishments. The East India Company authorized the Indian administration to make local appointments for very lowly paid jobs and those young men who had knowledge of the English language, though not necessarily of English literature, were ideal for such appointments. The number of colleges in the metropolitan cities of British India imparting Western education and the number of students attending them was not large. Many, like the Hindu School of 1817 which became the Presidency College in 1853 when Dalhousie reformed it, grew out of schools teaching the alphabet along with 'Shakespeare, the Calculus, Smith's *Wealth of Nations*, and the Ramayana'.[30] Students taught in these colleges could easily be absorbed into the services of the East India Company and other British establishments. They were docile, submissive and active participants in the British administration and because of the opportunities offered by an English education, there was a great demand for it, particularly in Bombay, Calcutta and Madras. This led F.J. Mouat, Secretary to the Council of Education in Bengal to actually submit a plan for university education in India in 1845. These groups of Indians formed the nucleus of the Indian middle classes. They were not critics, but admirers of the British Raj because of the benefits they derived from the British administration. So when the revolt of the sepoys swept India in 1857, they remained quiet and silent spectators to it. They had actually become a class of people very much after the vision of Macaulay in 1835: ' class of persons Indian in blood and colour, but English in taste, in opinions, in morals and intellect'.

This situation started to change during the mid-1850s and the starting point of this change may he said to have been marked by the establishment of the three universities at Calcutta, Bombay and Madras in 1857. Henceforth colleges became an integral part of the university system in India and they could admit such students as had passed the entrance or matriculation examination held by the universities to which they were affiliated and impart instruction according to such courses only as had been prescribed by the universities. Contrary to Canning's expectation in 1857, that the universities in India would become 'an aristocratic institution' which would be mainly attended by the children of 'the nobility and upper classes of India', they became 'popular institutions'[31] attended largely by the children of the new middle classes that had been emerging ever since the beginning of the nineteenth century. Because of the material advantages of holding university degrees, a very large number of those who passed the matriculation sought admission to these universities. The number of colleges which was 27 in 1857 rose to 55 in 1873 and the number of students rose from 219 in 1857 to 4,449 in 1873.[32] In 1881 the coresponding figures were 85 and 7,582 respectively.[33] The number of students who succeeded in their examinations in the years which followed the establishment of the universities was also considerable. Between 1857 and 1873, for example, the number of successful candidates from matriculation onwards was 12,392 at Calcutta, 5,502 at Madras and 2,703 at Bombay.[34] The annual output of the recipients of the bachelors degree also increased in the early years from 1857 so that there were 175 graduates by 1870, 404 by 1880 and 470 by 1884.[35] Failures of the 'First Arts' Examinations in 1870 were 570, in 1880, 1,110 and in 1884, 1289.[36] The number of persons educated in English can be obtained for the period 1857 to 1884 by taking the total number of successful candidates for 1857 First Arts and BA diplomas and degrees and adding it to the number of successful final candidates. Henry Maine estimated five time 5,000 BAs and MAs from 1853 to 1883 or a total of 25,000 out of an estimated population of 250,000,000.[37]

Having received a good secondary school education up to the level of matriculation and having attended a university, these men were certainly very educated compared to the illiterate town-dwellers or village ryots (farmers). They themselves were very much aware of this difference. What prospects were open to the large number of students who were thus able to receive higher education? For one thing, a career in the Indian Civil Service was virtually never open to talent, though the principle had been asserted time and again in the Charter Act of 1833 and the Queen's Proclamation of 1858 after the Mutiny. Some avenues like army and politics were closed altogether. In those days, agriculture offered no temptation to an educated person and neither did manufacturing and commerce, for the latter was almost impossible to enter without skill, capital and equality in terms of competition with European businessmen.

As a matter of fact, the very nature of the course, with its 'unique and disproportionate attention' to English literature and philosophy,[38] compared with physical and cognate branches of practical instruction, tended to limit the choice of a career to either the service of government or similar employment.[39] 'What also can he do but qualify himself', lamented a Calcutta newspaper, 'or if he is father, train his son for the public service or one of the learned professions?'[40] In theory, the covenanted civil service[41] was open to the Indians since 1853 but in practice difficulties stood in their way – the early upper age-limit for the examination, the content of the syllabus, the expense of going to London where the examination was held, the Hindu prejudice against crossing the 'blackwater', and the official reluctance of the British to admit Indians into this vital service. The educated Indians could only avail themselves of the posts at the lower level of the uncovenanted service which continued to remain open to them. Here the salaries were very poor, prospects for promotions negligible and conditions of service very bad.[42]

Since men were not often employed outside their own provinces, less than two thousand posts were available in the uncovenanted executive and judicial branches in Bengal, Bombay and Madras for the graduates of the universities in these areas. Not all of them were given to the educated: in Bombay and in Madras less than half of the uncovenanted civilians had qualifications in the new education while in the North Western Provinces and in the Punjab most of these posts went to those who had no qualifications at all.[43] The creation of nine departments of education by 1879 as per the provision of the Education Despatch of 1854 and the gradual development of a graded Indian educational service to man these departments and the colleges under them opened new vistas for employment in British India – but the posts in this uncovenanted service were not normally open to the educated Indians, but to the European with qualifications from British universities, particularly from Oxford and Cambridge. In the whole of British India while there were only five educated Indians serving in this uncovenanted service, the number of Europeans serving in it by 1879 was 95.[44]

The paucity of suitable openings in the public service naturally compelled many to turn to independent professions such as teaching, law, journalism and medicine. Unlike the government servants who were inhibited by their dependence on the goodwill of the government which employed them, in these professions there was greater opportunity to take part in public life. By the end of the 1870s, there was hardly any important town in India which did not possess a sprinkling of teachers, lawyers, journalists and physicians who took a very lively interest in the social, political, economic and religious questions of the day.[45] It was this group of people who later formed the backbone of the Indian National Congress, and because of their complaints against the government they were often distrusted and ridiculed by the European officials and the English press.[46].

It is thus obvious that the moderate difficulties of the 1850s in finding suitable employment for the English-educated Indians, had become a major problem in the 1870s. A year before the establishment of the universities in India, The *Friend of India* had warned of the problem: 'Native education had gone so far that it has become one of the most serious problems of the day. What to do with our educated men.'[47] Since 1857 when higher education in India started expanding by leaps and bounds, the problem also became aggravated. By 1877 it reached such dimensions that Sir Richard Temple, the Lieutenant-Governor of Bengal, did not hesitate to record a minute on it:

It is melancholy to see young men, who once appeared to receive their honours in the university convocation now applying for some lowly-paid appointment, almost begging from office to office, from department to department, or struggling for the practice of petty practitioner, and after all this returning baffled and disheartened to a poverty stricken home, and then to reflect how far happier their lot might have been had they, while at school or college, been able to move in a healthier atmosphere of thought and freer walks of life. Nevertheless, with these examples before their eyes, hundreds, perhaps thousands of young men persist in embarking on the same course, which can lead only to the same sad ending.[48]

The incidence of unemployment among the educated Indians made them discontented with the British Raj which not only gave them no relief or sympathy, but even excluded them from higher posts in the army, education and the civil service. They saw the grand spectacle of thousands of foreigners being given precedence in appointments to all the best places in the administration. In the press and on the platform, the professionals joined the educated unemployed in waging an acrimonious war of criticism on the Government of India as being responsible for the prevailing unemployment. The attack against the government was on two grounds; first, the system of education provided by the government and second, its failure to employ those who had been trained by it. In 1882, the very year which saw the appointment of an education Commission, Dadabhai Naoroji wrote to the Secretary of State for India on the subject of unemployment among the educated Indians:

The thousands that are being sent out by the universities every year find themselves in a most anomalous position. There is no place for them in their motherland. They may beg in the streets, or break stones in roads for aught the rulers seem to care for their natural rights, position and duties in their own country. They may perish or do what they like or can, but scores of Europeans must go from this country to take up what belongs to them, and that in spite of every profession for years and years past and up to the present day, of English statesman, that they must govern India for India's good by the words of the august Sovereign herself.[49]

The next year, the contributor to the *Indian Spectator* brought out more clearly the differences between the prospects of an educated Indian and that of an Englishman:

How many university graduates go without work? The luckiest of them is often too glad to begin life as a *Mamlatdar's*[50] clerk. Now look at his English contemporary. The very first appointment he holds is that of Assistant Judge or Collector. What a difference when both had worked equally hard! The native graduate knows his importance, he feels his neglect all the more bitterly. He has the power to do the harm, and may exercise that power. The uneducated does not feel neglect, he can get some work or other which he is not too proud. Not so that educated youth. He knows his marketable value and when neglected, he frets and fumes.[51]

Such criticisms were likely to arouse the suspicions of the Government of India, the provincial authorities and the British press. As the *Englishman* wrote in 1870:

The number of thinly veneered, but highly polished, students who are every year turned adrift into the world from our Anglo-Indian schools and colleges is perfectly appalling. Puffed up with a notion of superiority to the rest of their countrymen, they are no longer content to apply themselves to the industrial pursuits of their forefathers but demand employments more suited to the educational aroma with which they are imbued. Failing this, they spread abroad over the land, diffusing a feeling of discontent wherever they settle down, and stirring up, disaffection to the very Government whose fond weakness has given them whatever strength they possess.[52]

In the same year that the *Englishman* made these comments, official scepticism about the value of the spread of higher education began. It was presumably provoked by the fact that in 1869 three Indians had successfully competed in the civil service examination.[53] If more money were spent on higher education, many more Indians would be able to enter the civil service, hitherto a European preserve. In May 1870 the *Supplement* to the *Gazetteer of India* carried a resolution by the Government of India from the Finance Department, dated 31 March 1870. After having referred to the resolution of 8 September 1869 which spoke about the withdrawal of financial assistance by the State for the instruction of the people of Bengal in the English language, the resolution of 31 March 1870 went further to declare that the motives which induced people to seek instruction in the English language were *prima facie* sufficient for its rapid development without any contribution from the Imperial finances, whereas the desire for vernacular education required much artificial stimulus and encouragement. Therefore, 'it should be, in accordance with the view expressed by successive Secretaries of State, the constant aim of the Supreme and the Local Governments . . . to reduce to the utmost the charge upon the state of English education in the view of rendering it as self-supporting as possible.'[54]

The publication of this resolution was the signal for an agitation in Bengal which was unprecedented in intensity and magnitude. Without government assistance most of the Indian high schools and colleges which mostly drew their students from the middle- and lower-income groups and depended for their existence on the grants-in-aid system, would have to close down. The Bengali press raised the cry of 'higher education in danger' and in view of the agitation carried out by the British Indian Association at Calcutta and in the *mofussil* (suburbs), the Government withdrew the resolution and reassured the public by denying that it had any intention of stopping its assistance to higher education. All the while, the English-language press owned and managed by the Europeans, severely criticized the government's policy of supporting higher education. It pointed to the existence of a reaction against it among the Englishman in India and in Great Britain including those who had earlier supported the spread of English education in India. The press openly said that the time would soon come when the Government of India would have to revise its policy respecting the education in English for Indians.

However, that time for the revision of its policy towards English education did not come until the end of the 1870s when a movement sprang up in many parts of India to fight the reduction of the maximum age at which the Indian civil service examinations could be taken by the candidates from 21 to 19. This lowering of the age limit by Lord Salisbury in 1876 was primarily aimed at making it more difficult for Indians to come and compete in London. As early as 1866, educated Indians had opposed the reduction of the maximum age limit from 22 to 21 because they thought it was injurious to Indian aspirants; the further reduction from 21 to 19 was even more unacceptable to them. They looked upon it as a manoeuvre on the part of the Government of India to thwart the ambition of Indians to enter the civil service. Under the leadership of Surendra Nath Banerjea, they decided to organize a national protest which would invoke the Charter Act of 1833 and the Queen's proclamation of 1858 in which the rights of the Indians for service in the administration, irrespective of class, creed, caste and colour had been proclaimed. On 24 March 1877, a public meeting was held at the Albert Hall, Calcutta, and a committee consisting of the representatives of educated sections of the Indian community in Calcutta was appointed to write a memorial drawing attention to the principles and pledges contained in the Charter Act of 1833 and the Queen's Proclamation of 1858 and to forward it to Parliament. Surendra Nath Banerjea was assigned the task of travelling all over the country in order to gain support for the memorial. In April 1879, Lal Mohan Ghose was asked by the Indian Association to go to Great Britain as its representative to lay before the British public the grievances of the Indian people regarding access to apppointments in the civil service and other questions as well.[55] This agitation which was supported by educated Indians throughout the country was organized and conducted with such care and in such a constitutional manner that it drew admiration from Europeans. 'The really remarkable feature of the whole movement', wrote *The Times of India* on 24 December 1877, 'is the moderation, the good sense, and political tact which have distinguished it from first to last ... A race that can conduct a political campaign with such ability has already won half the battle.'[56] The option and gradual extension of Western methods of agitation and organization acquired through universities by the educated Indians posed a 'real danger to our rule in India', as Hamilton pointed out decades later to Curzon.[57]

The commotion in Indian public opinion gave pause to the Government of India and induced it to consider the revision of its policy towards the education of Indians in the present system. 'The present system', wrote the Rev. James Johnston in *Our Educational Policy in India* in 1880, 'is raising a number of discontented and disloyal subjects'.[58] Against this battleground, a liberal Viceroy, Lord Ripon, took the most bold step of appointing the first education commission in 1882 – called the Hunter Commission – to review the whole field of primary and secondary education in India. Its president, Sir William Hunter, thought that governmentally supported education was producing a revolt among the educated Indians against three principles which represented the deepest wants of human nature – the principle of discipline, the principle of religion, the principle of contentment.[59] On the recommendations of the Commission, the Government of India withdrew from activity in higher education, nominally as a measure of economy and it encouraged private enterprise in the field. It directed the local governments to close down or hand over to 'a suitable agency, public or private', control over some of the *mofussil* (suburban) government colleges while deciding to continue financially supporting the Presidency colleges 'on which the higher education of the country mainly depends'.[60] A stronger reason for the withdrawal was more political than economic. Lord Ripon in his convocation address at the University of Bombay in 1884 intimated, rather sympathetically to the Indian cause,

> that it is little short of folly that we should throw open to increasing numbers of the rich stores of Western learning; that we should inspire them with European ideas, and bring them into the closest contact with English thought, and that then we should as it were, pay no heed to the growth of those aspirations which we have ourselves created, and the pride of those ambitions we have ourselves called forth.[61]

EPILOGUE

In the years following the recommendations of the Hunter Commission, as the government moved out of the field of English education, Indians moved in and English education instead of showing any signs of decline went on expanding every year. The expansion of English education was accompanied by a similar explosion of the problem of unemployment among the English-educated Indians. The growing unemployment among the English-educated Indians and the latter's disillusionment with the British Raj's policy towards the problem was increasingly adding fuel to the nationalistic sentiments that had been growing ever since the middle of the nineteenth century. In 1885 when the Indian National Congress, which Hume saw as 'a safety-valve' to the growing discontent with the alien rule was formed,[62] it adopted 'wider employment of the people in the public service' as one of 'the three important questions' constituting 'the chief planks in the Congress platform'[63] and hardly any annual session of the Indian National Congress took place without discussing the subject of employment and passing resolutions on it.[64] In one such session in 1900 Surendra Nath Banerjea, an English-educated young man, ascribed racial considerations to the exclusion of English-educated Indians from the services of the British Raj in India,

> If you look at the statistics connected with these Departments, you will find that the higher offices, the bulk of the higher offices – I should not be guilty of the smallest exaggeration if I say that at least 90 per cent of the higher offices – are filled by Europeans and Anglo-Indians ... Imperialists, somebody says, they may be imperialists or not but at any rate, these Departments constitute the close preserve, the absolute monopoly of these gentlemen. We are excluded. And why? Because of our race. Our colour is our disqualification.[65]

All English-educated Indians seemed to echo Banerjea's views and it was gradually realized by the Raj that the decision to promote English education since the days of Macaulay was 'a story of grave political miscalculation' containing a lesson 'that has its signficance for other nations which have undertaken a similar enterprise'.[66] English education in India had over the years given birth to a tone of mind and to a type of character that was 'ill regulated, averse from discipline, discontented and in some cases actually disloyal'.[67] Macaulay and others associated with the introduction of English education in India came to be increasingly identified with Erasmus who when reproached with having laid the egg from which came forth the Reformation had thus replied: 'Yes, but I laid a hen's egg and Luther had hatched a fighting cock'.[68]

12 Historical discourses, racist mythology and education in twentieth-century South Africa

Peter Kallaway

South Africa has been the archetypal racist state where class and colour coincide in a colonial and post-colonial context to define the boundaries of privilege and domination, power and dependency, affluence and poverty. The ideology embraced by the major traditions of historical scholarship in this society, and the history taught in schools during this century, are clearly a reflection of those power relations. It is therefore not surprising that South Africa provides a fascinating comparative laboratory for the exploration of racist mythology, racist ideology and racist educational practices.[1] This chapter will attempt to provide a brief overview of the complexities and implications of those issues in regard to the specific area of history education in schools.

The apartheid state of the post-1948 era was in many ways the epitomy of institutional racism that had its origins in the nineteenth-century colonial context. Yet apartheid had distinctive features which represented the ascendancy of a particular tendency in white politics from the 1930s. It is of great significance to stress that South African history should not be reduced to the simplistic notion that everything that happened prior to 1948 was simply a rehearsal for the era of apartheid. The writing of history has its own history (historiography), the milestones of its progress being discernable, in the main, by the changing ideological affiliations and attitudes of those who set the pace of scholarship in the subject. That is not to say that all history is necessarily characterizable as being biased – there are after all standards of good and bad scholarship in South Africa as elsewhere – but it is to say that the impetus behind historians and the emphases they give to their work reflects the ideological construction of the world in which they live and the way in which they interpret that knowledge.

In the context of South Africa various forms of racism came together to provide a potent brew. All of them, whether deriving from the British jingoistic traditions of the late nineteenth century (Social Darwinism mixed with the unique forms of British classism), or the racism of Central Europe (the Fascist traditions taken up by the Purified National Party in the 1930s), or elements of Southern racist policies in education derived from the Post Civil War era,[2] helped to shape political and educational policies in the area of race relations.

In this context 'racism' has had at least two significant meanings in South Africa during the period under consideration. In the first place, in a region where British imperialism had powerful white enemies during the early part of the twentieth century, 'the race question' in public discourse referred to the question of relations between English-speaking settlers and the Dutch/Boer/Afrikaans inhabitants. British jingoism was rampant during the heyday of imperialism prior to the First World War, and it gave rise to its opposite, 'Boer' or Afrikaner Nationalism. This was the demand by the emergent Afrikaner 'nationalists' for their own independent states in the north prior to 1900 (the South African Republic and the Orange Free State), and thereafter, within the context of a British dominated sub-continent or a Union under the Union Jack, a demand for their own culture and language to be recognized, for political and economic rights, and at times, for a renewal of their republican independence. The content and circumstances of those demands differed substantially in the contexts of the independent Boer republics and the British Colonies of the sub-continent, and it changed over time. 'Racism' and racist mythology in this context therefore referred to arguments about the rights and wrongs of British political and economic power on the sub-continent. What was racist in one interpretation, was and is the defence of 'own' cultural traditions, language and interests to its proponents.

The other meaning given to the concept of 'the race question', which has a more familiar ring at the present time, is of course the evolution of the ideology and politics of conquest, segregation and apartheid aimed at maintaining the distinction between the settlers and the indigenous peoples. This also bred its opposite, a powerful Africanism which propounded resistance to the colonial state, and in its more extreme forms, the rejection of all forms of co-operation with the 'white oppressor' including liberals and radicals who propounded the politics of non-racism and opposition to apartheid. Whereas the state increasingly evolved a set of institutions designed to entrench institutional racism in the law and in political practice, the fight for a non-racial economic and political dispensation which emphasized equal rights for white and black inhabitants – the colonizers and the colonized – gradually gained momentum by the mid-century in keeping with developments elsewhere in Africa. Yet it is only in the last decade of the twentieth century that the prospect of a non-racial democratic state has dawned in which the individual will be protected from racist practices.

This sketch provides the backdrop to the development of the historiography of this society and the way in which young South Africans have been told the story of their past. In the context of a racially segregated educational system, the teaching of history in schools has always provided an extremely significant testing-ground for the legitimacy of that education. The launching of a new educational system free of racism in the near future, brings with it the urgent need for a new history education which can eradicate the shameful past in the area of school history and this provides a significant challenge to historians and educationalists at the present time. This chapter is an attempt to summarize the complex background to such policy debates against which the evolution of racist history, mythology and racist educational practices are to be understood in order to overcome them.

In order to undertake that task we will briefly explore the nature of South African historiography, and attempt to relate this to the creation of a schools' history curriculum during this century. The critique of schools' history under apartheid will follow. Attempts to counteract the influence of that syllabus and document initiatives aimed at changing the practices of teachers within the present system during the 1970s and 1980s will be recorded. Finally there will be an attempt to draw a sketch of the current situation and understand what might be necessary for a school history devoid of racism and racist ideology in an age where the merits of multi-cultural education and ethnic assertion are being universally pronounced.

TRADITIONS IN SOUTH AFRICAN HISTORIOGRAPHY

For convenience I shall divide this section into four aspects: phase 1: British jingoism versus Afrikaner nationalism; phase 2: colonial history; phase 3: the liberal tradition; phase 4: the revisionists: Africanists and Marxists.

Phase 1: British jingoes versus Afrikaner nationalists

Before 1910 the British colonies of the Cape and Natal tended to develop educational policies which paralleled those in the 'mother country'. The curriculum content and educational philosophy were imbued with the rhetoric of late nineteenth century British jingoism and imperial ideology with little regard for critical analysis. The subject matter, as in colonial Africa up until the era of independence in the 1960s, uncritically emphasized the heroic story of the British nation and the British Empire – of noble deeds, battles, heroes and institutions – that constituted the defence of the realm or what subsequently became known as the 'Whig Interpretation of History'. The purpose of studying such history was never questioned by educationalists who assumed the benefits of British rule for all the inhabitants and the consequent benefits of a command of patriotic history and culture. Afrikaners or Blacks were judged on the scale of 'civilization' in terms of the extent to which they could speak English or adapt to the norms and standards of lower middle-class Victorian England. A command of imperial history was an important element in that socializing process.

Not surprisingly, towards the end of the nineteenth century, liberal Afrikaners in the Cape Colony, who were coming to show increasing political sympathy with their northern countrymen after the Jameson Raid (1895), demonstrated their dislike for the history that was taught in the schools. In the last decade of the century, steps were taken to remedy this situation as part of an overall development of Dutch political consciousness. In doing so they came to develop a distinctive heroic history which provided a counterweight to the English version. This was the heroic story of the Afrikaner people (they did not yet call themselves that) for survival in Africa in the context of a hostile physical environment, the threat of indigenous (African) enemies and, above all, their resistance in the face of the repeated attempts of the British colonial power to subdue the spirit of cultural and political independence of the new 'nation'. Dominee S.J. Du Toit of the Genootskap van Regte Afrikaners wrote *Die Geskiedenis van Ons Land in die Taal van Ons Volk* (1877) as an expression of his people's desire for the recognition of their heritage. It was no less polemical.

The interpretations of history that developed in this context have endured into the latter part of the twentieth century as part of the cumulative reconstruction of a specific interpretation of history. This interpretation became a key element of the ideology of the Purified National Party which emerged to defend the racist politics of what came to be called *apartheid* after 1948. These interpretations relate to the heroic nature of the frontiersmen and their 'commitment to Christianity and Freedom'; the romanticization of the Great Trek; the conquest of the African kingdoms, in particular the Zulu king Dingane at the Battle of Blood River (1837); the valiant struggles of the First and Second *Vryheidsorloe* (Freedom Wars) [the Anglo-Boer Wars of 1877–8 and 1899–1902]; and in the twentieth century industrial urban context, the defence of the class interests of white workers in the context of the 'poor white' struggles, the campaign to maintain the colour bar in industry, the heroic rise of Afrikaner nationalism leading up to the victory of the National Party in 1948 and the regaining of 'independence' with the achievement of a Republic in 1961.

On this interpretation, peripheral treatment is given to other groups or historical actors in Southern Africa, or other interpretations of the past. There is a neglect of the internal divisions amongst Afrikaners – on political, social or economic grounds – and a myopic concentration on establishment political and constitutional history from the time of Union in 1910.[3] Even as late as 1969, Professor C.F.J. Muller's *500 Years* dealt with the history of the black peoples of Southern Africa in a pseudo anthropological twenty page appendix; elsewhere, as Shula Marks points out, Africans only appear in the text 'on such occasions when they are "restless"; "impudent", "fractious"; "truculent" or otherwise "causing difficulties".'

As long as these are viewed as avowedly polemical writings, linked to the specific defence of a particular political programme, they provide rich insights into a key aspect of South African history. This approach could be understood and appreciated in the context of 1877, or even as the polemical wing of the National Party. Yet it is totally inadequate for understanding the complexities of twentieth-century history, for history is not just the story of the temporarily successful! In the current drive to find an adequate reinterpretation of South African history for schools that lesson will have to be well learned.

Phase 2: The founding fathers of a colonial history: Theal and Cory

During the early twentieth century an indigenous settler history began to emerge which had links with the developments outlined in Phase 1, but really constituted a new 'professional' stream of historical writing. G.M. Theal (*History of South Africa*, in eleven volumes published over the period 1898–1919) and G.E. Cory (*The Rise of South Africa*, five volumes, 1910–1930) have often been considered to be the founding fathers of historical research in South Africa. Theal has also been seen as the 'frontiersman's historian'. Although he had strong sympathies with the frontiersmen, he did not ignore the 'other side' of that frontier to the same degree as many of this disciples. In keeping with the political climate of 'reconciliation' after the South African War and Union, these scholars were concerned to create a new 'national history' for all white South Africans. This perspective was often anti-imperialist and generally anti-black. It is perhaps appropriate to characterize these works as a curious blend of appreciation for indigenous African tradition and racist paternalism.

This was the great tradition which was taken up by educationalists and school textbook writers. In striving to produce an indigenous history they helped to provide the holy grail for whole generations of school textbook writers up to the present day. Hardy annuals like Fowler and Smit,[4] which passed through the hands of generations of schoolchildren in the middle of the century, inducted them in a history which emphasized the trials and tribulations of the colonists, the wrongs of the imperial government and the threat of the African peoples of Southern Africa during the nineteenth century. They stressed the civilizing mission of the colonists, their 'realism', and their heroic struggle to 'preserve' Western culture and build a modern industrial nation on the basis of the diamonds and gold discoveries at the end of the nineteenth century.

Phase 3: The liberal tradition

The above developments set the scene for a new school of 'liberal' historians who began to have an influence in the 1920s and 1930s. E.A. Walker was one of the first to write a really comprehensive *History of Southern Africa* (1928), which, despite its lack of criticism of the imperial government, did signify an important benchmark in the evolution of historical scholarship in South Africa and is still one of the most reliable basic texts. The titles of his other publications give an insight into Walker's essentially Cape liberal sympathies – *Lord de Villiers and his Times* (1925) and *W.P. Schreiner: a South African* (1937).

The focus that now emerged from the work of the emerging 'liberal' school highlighted not only the conflict and co-operation between the white population groups, but also expressed a deep concern with the historical dimension of race relations between blacks and whites. In the evolving urban industrial context these historical themes reflected the earlier debates of the frontier. The physical frontiers of the nineteenth century were giving way to the class frontiers of colour bar politics in the twentieth century. This research generated themes and agendas for an entire generation of scholars and set the stage for many of our present-day debates. A re-examination of inter-white history was set against the backdrop of historical relations between black and white.

The frontier came in for detailed consideration in Walker's *The Frontier Tradition in South Africa* (1930) and the *Great Trek* (1934); J.S. Macmillan's *Bantu, Boer and Briton* (1929) and J.S. Marais's *Maynier and the First Boer Republics* (1944). This naturally led to the examination of the role of other actors in nineteenth-century history, with Macmillan's *Cape Coloured Question* (1927) and Marais's *The Cape Coloured People* (1939) breaking important new ground. Macmillan was particularly interested in the role of the philanthropic missionary, Dr John Philip in shaping the race relations of the Eastern Frontier. The interaction between the British government's policies and the development of indigenous political traditions was also examined in detail in C.W. de Kiewiet's *The Imperial Factor in South Africa* (1937), T.R.H. Davenport's *The Afrikaner Bond* (1966) and D. Welsh's *The Roots of Segregation* (1971). Important contributions were also made in the interdisciplinary studies of some scholars, in particular C.W. de Kiewiet's *A History of South Africa: Social and Economic* (1941) and Leo Marquard's *Peoples and Policies in South Africa* (1960). A particularly significant innovation in the light of the future growth of labour history was an attempt to link race relations more firmly with economics in Sheila van der Horst's *Native Labour in South Africa* (1941).

The book that is often regarded as the apex of the liberal tradition was the *Oxford History of South Africa* (hereafter referred to as *OHSA*), published in two volumes in the period 1969–71 edited by Monica Wilson and Leonard Thompson. A supplementary volume in the form of Leonard Thompson's *African Societies in Southern Africa* (1969) included the work of a variety of new researchers in the field of African history. These invaluable collections, with their emphasis on 'interaction between peoples of divers origins, languages, technologies, social systems, meeting on South African soil', embraced the beginnings of African history south of the Limpopo, with an important focus on pre-colonial history, and an innovative attempt to promote interdisciplinary enquiry by blending history with social anthropology, economics and sociology. Chapters by Monica Wilson on the 'Growth of peasant communities' (*OHSA* II, ch. 2), Francis Wilson on 'Farming 1866–1966' (*OHSA* II, ch. 3) and David Welsh on 'The growth of towns' (*OHSA* II, ch. 4) broke new ground for historians and were well reviewed.

Liberal historical scholarship had a profound effect on the way in which South Africans understood their past. Christopher Saunder's recent overview of the accomplishments and limitations of the tradition is essential reading for anyone interested in South African historiography.[5] Here was a history that stood outside of traditional British imperialist and Afrikaner nationalist interpretations or settler apologia, but within the broad stream of liberal internationalism of the inter-war and post Second World War era. The development of this tradition had the profoundest implications for the understanding of racist mythology. For the first time there was a historical mechanism for understanding the ideology of historical writing, and an attempt to interrogate the assumptions of the earlier traditions. In retrospect from the 1990s, it often seems that these historians were paternalistic, too uncritical of 'the role of the missionaries (and commerce) in conquest', and naive regarding the motives of liberals or reformers. Their inability to critically debate the policies, practices and social consequences of the advance of industrial capitalism places them in their own ideological context. Yet here were the elements of a tradition that laid the basis for a South African historiographical tradition which was never co-opted to the segregationist politics of the times, and capable of withstanding the winters of the apartheid era.

A major identifying feature of this tradition was its opposition to racism. As such it provided a mode of critique for those who opposed segregation and apartheid – and provided the empirical and ideological underpinning for a staunch critique of those policies. As such this tradition had a negligent impact on the version of history embodied in school textbooks either prior to 1948 or thereafter. Indeed, it was a key element of the education necessary for any oppositional history in the early days of apartheid. The indictment of history under apartheid education for its lack of objectivity and the call for its revision in the works of Auerbach, Cornevin and Dean *et al.* all rested heavily on the assumption that the liberal version was indeed the objective version of history, and as such should be promoted in schools because of its 'scientific standing' and correctness in terms of facts presented. To put it the other way around, much public debate in the early years of the apartheid era seemed to assume that all that was wrong with apartheid history in schools was that it failed to incorporate the liberal perspective. The Afrikaner nationalists had 'falsified' history, and the liberals offered the antidote. While this was in part true, and in part hopelessly positivist, the whole nature of South African historiography was to undergo a fundamental shift during the 1970s and this was to add a number of new equations to the problem of constructing an adequate school history.

Phase 4: The revisionists: Africanists and Marxists

As a reaction to the imperialist, settler and the Afrikaner nationalist versions of South African history, and to the liberal interpretations, came a two-pronged intellectual attack from those scholars who were influenced by African history in the 1960s, which highlighted *resistance* as a key organizing concept, and those who spurned the racial/colonialist interpretations in favour of an emphasis on class analysis. It is not always easy to distinguish between these schools or interpretations, and it might even be argued that it is counter-productive to attempt to do so. For convenience I have nevertheless made some attempt.

The rise of African nationalism linked to the decolonizing of Africa during the 1950s and 1960s gave rise to a whole school of African history that slowly came to influence the writing of South African historians. The rise of a radical tradition of resistance to white rule in South Africa which crystallized in the massacre at Sharpeville in 1960, complemented this development in the academic field and gave rise to initial attempts by black intellectuals to frame a history of the colonized people. The autobiographical genre of Nkrumah's *I Speak for Freedom* (1961) and Kenyatta's *Facing Mount Kenya* (1953) was taken up in South Africa by Albert Luthuli, the leader of the African National Congress in *Let My People Go* (1962) and Nelson Mandela's *No Easy Walk to Freedom* (1965), while the Pondoland Revolt of 1960 was documented in Govan Mbeki's *The Peasants' Revolt in South Africa* (1964). In an earlier era, Sol Plaatjie had used fiction in an attempt to capture the other side of frontier life in *Mhudi: An Epic of South African Native Life a Hundred Years Ago* (1930), and others had followed his path.

A range of research on African history broke new ground from the 1960s. John Omer-Cooper's *Zulu Aftermath* (1966) opened exciting new perspectives to young historians. This was followed by a range of other studies of pre-Colonial Africa that transformed the discipline. They introduced a range of new theoretical perspectives and research techniques that were inititally viewed with apprehension by the establishment historians who had served their time in the archives. Thus oral evidence, archaeology, the collection of songs and stories, and sociological theory all entered the picture. The harvest of research of the 1970s was largely the result of a generation of historians who studied at British and American universities, and thus came into contact with the new Africanist and Marxist winds of change that were sweeping through the discipline internationally.[6] The exploration of the history of modern African resistance and the political movements of the twentieth century were also given increasing emphasis by scholars.[7]

Secondly, Marxists of various stripes, particularly members of the Communist Party of South Africa (CPSA), and the Unity Movement, introduced a new conceptual perspective by presenting the struggle for racial freedom in South Africa in terms of imperialism, class analysis and working class struggles. Jack and Ray Simons's *Class and Colour in South Africa: 1850–1950* (1969) and Brian Bunting's *The Rise of the South African Reich* (1964) were classics in this tradition. Other tendencies within the Marxist camp were represented by Edward Roux's excellent worker history *Time Longer Than Rope* (1948) Mnguni *Three Hundred Years* (1952), and N. Majeke (Dora Taylor) *The Role of the Missionary in Conquest* (1952). The influence of the Unity movement in the field of historical writing is carefully reviewed by Bill Nasson in the *Radical History Review*'s special edition on the writing of history in South Africa.[8]

This tradition gave sustenance to the neo-Marxist 'revisionist' history of the 1970s and 1980s. The revival of Marxist studies in Europe had the effect of stimulating a new school of historical scholarship relating to South Africa. The focus of research moved away from the liberal concern with race relations and the optimistic assumptions that in the long run economic growth and industrialization would tend towards the evolution of a 'rational', 'just' and 'equitable' society that would inevitably erode and replace the 'outdated' politics of apartheid. This new generation of scholars sought to re-evaluate a whole range of assumptions regarding the social and economic fabric of South African society from pre-colonial times to the present. Such questions led scholars toward a reappraisal of contemporary history and politics as well as a re-examination of the dynamics of contact and conflict between pre-colonial societies and the growth of capitalism. African responses to the new market economy were examined, both in terms of cash-crop production and in terms of the labour market.[9]

Researchers like Martin Legassick, Rick Johnstone,[10] and H. Wolpe sought to demonstrate that segregation and apartheid had been extremely 'rational' to the capitalist order and to the political projects of successive white minority governments, challenging the growth model of the liberals. The edited papers of the Institute of Commonwealth Studies South Africa seminar in London provide benchmarks for a study of the changing historiography of this era.[11]

By the 1980s the influence of the neo-Marxist structuralists began to ebb and give way to the influence of the social history associated with the History Workshop tradition in Great Britain. This prolific school has been very influential during the 1980s, C. van Onselen's social history of the early Witwatersrand being one of the most significant contributions.[12]

The sheer volume of research that has been characteristic of the last two decades means that any attempt to categorize it is fraught with difficulties, and the above attempt should not in any way be seen as definitive, rather as a means of entry into the debates. This is in any case not the appropriate place to attempt such an exercise.

Suffice to say that little of the history of the liberal tradition, let alone the more radical Africanist or Marxist traditions, which challenged the racial stereotypes or mythologies of pre- or post-1948 South Africa, was allowed to intrude on or affect the nature of the school curriculum or the school textbooks. The system of administrative control over the school curriculum development process effectively precluded such initiatives, though some efforts have been made during the 1970s and 1980s to bring about changes on a small scale, focusing on the possibilities presented for individual initiatives in the classroom, school or community, through the work of groups of motivated teachers. The rest of this chapter will attempt to outline a number of such initiatives in the 1970s and 1980s which were aimed at breaking the mould that the apartheid political order had established in the realm of school history. This will in part represent an autobiographical account of attempts to influence such changes in the teaching and learning of history in high school.

These initiatives provide a background for the current context in which we are engaged in attempting to research a new curriculum development procedure and give content to a new history for schools for a post-apartheid society.

HISTORY EDUCATION UNDER APARTHEID: THE FOCUS ON RACISM AND BIAS

The need for fundamental change in the area of history education in South Africa is uncontested at the present time. The desire to move away from apartheid history and produce a school history that is in keeping with the political climate of the times is an essential element of a transformative education. While we certainly need a new school history that will provide a platform for nation-building in the broadest sense, the temptation to once again make school history the handmaiden of political ideology must be resisted at all costs. That is not to make an old-fashioned appeal for objective history, whatever that might be, but to recognize the ideological nature of the subject and use it to develop critical capabilities and analytical skills to enable children to make sense of history and of the complex political, social and economic changes through which they will live in the 'new' South Africa.

The area of history education has long been one of the most contested and publicized aspects of apartheid education. A long, if not particularly rigorous, debate has been conducted in newspapers and other public forums ever since the 1960s on what was usually referred to as the 'bias of school history' and its exclusive focus on the perspective of Afrikaner nationalist historiography. There was also some academic research on the topic, notably by Frans Auerbach,[13] Paddy Mulholland,[14] and UNESCO researchers Marianne Cornevan and E. Dean *et al.*,[15] but given the centrality of this educational issue in the political arena it is very surprising that it did not receive more attention from liberal, Marxist or Africanist scholars. This is not the place to explore why this was the case, but it presents an important area for further enquiry.

Suffice to say that up to the late 1980s school history was a topic that attracted a great deal of negative criticism and generated a lot of heat in public debate. Any educational gathering of black South Africans was likely to focus on this as a key aspect of the ideological agenda of inferior education associated with apartheid. Within the People's Education movement (c. 1986–88), the call for People's History was very prominent. Yet it is of some significance that this emphasis has died away completely in the context of the 'new politics' of post-2 February, 1990.

The move from resistance politics to the politics of negotiation seems to have side-lined school history as a significant site of protest and contestation. Again, the reasons for this are by no means clear, but for present purposes it is sufficient to note this fact.

Of course we need to move away as rapidly as possible from apartheid education – the exclusive focus on Afrikaner nationalist history, colonial history, or white history – whatever it might be called, and engage with new historiographical perspectives outlined above which will provide a new content for the syllabus. Precisely what that will look like and how it will be defined and arrived at is part of the problem I wish to raise here. Equally important, yet often neglected in the past, is the whole question of the educational objectives, curriculum development procedures, methodologies and forms of evaluation to be recommended for the area of history education in the future, a part of the effort to get away from the racist ideological legacy. Emphasis must be given to the development of critical skills and conceptual development in the planning of educational objectives. Teachers, teacher educators and educational administrators must recognize the importance of emphasizing these objectives in the syllabus and in the classroom. The pedagogy and learning methodologies promoted by the school and the forms of assessment used to evaluate teaching and learning must reflect these values. All this needs a great deal of clarification and research in conjunction with the task of formulating a new syllabus content. In short, many of the critics of apartheid history in the schools have been concerned to ensure that reform does not simply lead to a change of content from Afrikaner nationalist history to African nationalist history (though this is of course a necessary part of the change). As the whole nature of history education in the schools comes under review it is necessary to ensure that the subject regains its educational legitimacy and credibility in the eyes of the public.

Once these issues have become part of a public debate it will be possible to turn to the area of textbook and resource development, and the priority need for in-service courses for teachers to promote such policies. Evidence drawn from international sources indicates that teacher education is vital to the development of the total curriculum package, as it is only through the participation of teachers in the overall curriculum development process that meaningful changes will occur and the nature of the educational process will be significantly influenced.

It is against the broad background sketched out above that the need arises to address the situation facing educators and teachers in the area of history education at the present time, and appeal for a public and professional debate on history education as a significant part of the overall quest for new educational policies.

SMALL ATTEMPTS TO SHAPE A CULTURE OF CRITIQUE IN SCHOOL HISTORY UNDER APARTHEID DURING THE 1970s: A POSSIBLE FOUNDATION FROM WHICH TO BUILD?

The background to these remarks needs to be briefly alluded to as a part of an introduction to my own participation in the process of change in this area. Four elements of such a foundation are considered below.

First, during the 1970s a small group of teachers, many of them graduates of Johannesburg College of Education (JCE) or the Department of Education at the University of the Witwatersrand, began a process of experimentation aimed at transforming history education in their classrooms. These initiatives were largely based on the (Schools) History Workshop and drew much of their inspiration from the work of the 'New History Movement' and the Schools Council History Project in Great Britain.[16] Teacher seminars on African history and the new neo-Marxist historiography, as well as the introduction of 'New History' methodology, which emphasized the acquisition of critical skills and historical understanding as against the memorization of content, broke the ground for teacher involvement in the production of resource materials on a modest scale. Most of these materials were circulated locally for teacher use and proved to be the beginning of a culture of 'alternative history' for teachers. Prior to 1976 Soweto teachers were enthusiastic participants, and a number of meetings were held at Orlando West High School at that time.

The overall lesson of these developments was, however, that the energy put into such projects very seldom justified the rewards. Limited markets for the materials, teacher shyness of new methods, the controls which black teachers were subjected to in the course of their work, limited funds and facilities for copying materials, and simply pressure to 'get through the syllabus' all militated against the use of alternative materials in the classroom. Indeed the children themselves were often most resistant to 'alternative history', especially when it was seen as irrelevant to the dreaded final examinations that were looming.

The second aspect of innovation in the 1970s was associated with the area of public examinations. I was one of a team of examiners for the Joint Matriculation Board (JMB) history examination between 1977 and 1981 and was able to participate in the introduction of an exciting new assessment procedure developed for this external public examination. For the first time in South Africa, this examination focuses on the evaluation of the candidate's critical understanding of the syllabus and assumed that the purpose of teaching history was to develop critical skills and understanding. By changing the nature of the external examination paper and marking process it was possible to influence school pedagogy. In this small area of relative freedom from the large educational bureaucracies we were able to set out the elements of a policy that would promote a new kind of history evaluation free from the bias and selection of the present system. Here we helped to lay down the elements of a process of evaluation that will hopefully inform future history evaluation in South Africa.

Third, despondent about the gains to be made by attempting to get direct access to teachers for workshops in the volatile political climate of the late 1970s and early 1980s and disheartened by the possibilities of developing alternative resources for the history classroom while locked out of possible influence on the educational bureaucracy, the offer in 1985, by a small publisher, of the opportunity to produce an 'alternative' textbook for schools presented an exciting set of possibilities. In the context of the curriculum revisions this seemed to present a novel opportunity for getting a new kind of content and a new pedagogy into the schools and into the hands of teachers.

The *History Alive* textbook series covered the full range from Standard 1 to Standard 10 by 1988. It was welcomed by a number of teacher organizations and very well reviewed by the press. The team I was associated with worked on the Std 9 and Std 10 volumes.[17] Our goal was to produce textbooks that would conform to the formal requirements of the syllabus but encapsulate a challenge to the Afrikaner Nationalist/Christian National Education paradigm that has dominated school history. We were particularly concerned to produce a workbook for teachers and students who wanted to explore beyond the confines of conventional history teaching in the senior school and included revisionist perspectives. Although we were constrained by the content of the core syllabus as laid down by the JMB, we agreed to do only the bare minimum to fulfil the needs of the formal syllabus. Indeed we wished to challenge many of the assumptions, both about content and methodology, built into that code.

All the work drew heavily on the methodologies developed by the Schools Council History Project in Britain which emphasized skills-based learning as outlined above. The text was organized in an interrogative manner rather than the conventional direct narrative. An explanatory, rather than a chronological or narrative approach, was our goal. So far as possible, through the use of documents, diagrams, pictures and extracts, we attempted to raise issues of interpretation and translation in the context of exercises included in the text and through skills development exercises.

A full evaluation of the project still remains to be completed, but preliminary findings, where the texts were most used in the Natal Education Department (NED) and the House of Delegates (Indian) schools, would seem to indicate a favourable response. Some teachers found the content unfamiliar and difficult, others used the book mainly as a teacher aid, many thought that it was an exciting initiative but were wary of using it in the context of Std 10 external examinations, where the conventional modes of examining encouraged teachers to be cautious and use the generally accepted texts.[18]

On the completion of the *History Alive* series the members of the team who lived in Cape Town continued their informal involvement with these issues by establishing a History Education Group (HEG), based on the School of Education at UCT, and the History Teachers Society of the Western Cape. The aim was to keep in contact with developments in the field and seek opportunities to develop our strategies more fully. This group is still functioning and, in association with members of the UCT History Department, seeking to influence future developments. The thinking in this Chapter is representative of the deliberations and challenges we are seeking to address. Above all, the question that has faced us for some time is how best to proceed in the current phase of political transition?

PEOPLE'S EDUCATION AND PEOPLE'S HISTORY: NECC HISTORY COMMISSION 1987–88

Prior to the changes of 1990, the period of educational crisis during 1987–88 led to the emergence of the whole discourse around People's Education, which was coupled to a period of intense activity in popular politics. In that context the NECC (National Education Crisis Committee) People's History Commission was set up to investigate the needs of this area of education and make recommendations. The committee, under the leadership of Professor Colin Bundy of the University of Cape Town, was comprised mainly of academics from UCT (University of Cape Town) and University of the Western Cape, and also drew on the membership of the History Workshop in Johannesburg.

Although the campaign for People's History was fundamentally associated with political mobilization rather than the revision of schools history, this provided a unique space for considering the nature of the history that should find its way into the national curriculum in the future. Although there was no sense at that time that these debates would transform themselves into policy issues within the schools in such a short space of time, this provided an invaluable framework for future debate of the issue of history education in the schools. African history and the history of the liberation movements was given a position of prominence, and the issue of methodology and interpretation was highlighted in the publication of the group that emerged at the beginning of 1988.[19] Yet the intitiative failed to really make much headway with regard to school history as the alternative materials failed to arrive in the schools, suffering much the same fate as the earlier attempts described above, to introduce alternative materials. Once again the DET (the Department of Education and Training (African Education)) refused permission for the publications of the NECC to enter its educational institutions. The political moment was not right for such a move into the schools, whatever significance the People's Education campaign had for the general purposes of political conscientization. By 1988 the Committee had effectively ceased to function.

It needs to be mentioned in this context that the 1980s gave rise to a crop of independent projects which were aimed at the production of popular history for popular consumption. These included worker histories (the best known of these is Luli Callinicos's *Gold and Workers* (1982)) and the innovative readers published by the Foundation of Education with Production – Gay Seidman's *Working for the Future* (1985) and Judy Seidman's *In Our Own Image* (1990).

HSRC INVESTIGATION INTO THE TEACHING OF HISTORY IN SCHOOL IN THE RSA 1988–91

Another major opportunity that presented itself between 1988 and 1991 was the chance to engage in the investigation into History Education initiated by the HSRC's (Human Sciences Research Council) Education Research Programme. We were at first wary of the exercise as the influential HSRC report on *Provision of Education in the RSA* (1981) (the De Lange Committee report), which formed the background to this investigation, had been heavily criticized in the early 1980s as a front for reformist National Party thinking in education.[20]

Yet after consultation with members of the defunct NECC History Commission and members of the NECC executive we opted to attend the meetings held in Pretoria to test the water. After further doubts about the merits of participating we decided to stay with the exercise on the grounds that it provided us with the opportunity and resources to proceed with the kinds of work we were already engaged in, without tying us to a specific outcome.

We chose to focus on the area of Evaluation in history education in the belief that changes in the examination and assessment procedures would inevitably have a backwash effect on the teaching and learning of the subject as a whole. If examinations tested critical thinking and understanding, along with insights into the modes of investigation common to the historical discipline, the transformation of teaching and learning of the subject in the classroom would follow. Teachers would then automatically be provided with the space for experimentation and teaching for critical understanding. This would be a powerful lever for promoting a break with the practices of apartheid education. Three other reports were also produced, which together with our own, helped to stake out the territory for future policy debate.

A full account of this exercise has been documented elsewhere.[21] Nevertheless, a number of remarks need to be made which are germane to the current exercise. Despite the rhetoric of scientific enquiry and objectivity that surrounded the HSRC exercise, it was quite clear to us that there was from the outset a strong current of the De Lange methodology in the Work Committee. The desire of the chairman for consensus research had to be repeatedly contested. The attempt by some members of the Committee to pre-empt the debate on syllabus content by launching their own '*konsept syllabus*', based on notions of multi-cultural education which emphasized group rights and cultural identities, seemed to reflect National Party tactics in the general political arena. These seemed to be elements of a strategy to perpetuate aspects of apartheid history in the schools through an appeal to the democratic rights of racial (cultural or ethnic) communities, based on the rationales developed in other, mainly First World, contexts, without an appropriate recognition of the legacy of apartheid or the power relations embedded in such recommendations. Such a strategy sought to emphasize the merits of a policy of multi-cultural education as an aspect of the democratic rights of groups in a multi-ethnic society. What had been enforced by autocratic government under apartheid was now claimed in terms of democratic rights in the new South Africa. In practice it means that Afrikaner, or Zulu 'communities' (the only examples offered by the protoganists) would be able to opt for an education, or at least a history syllabus, which promoted their 'cultural identity'. To many of us this looked like apartheid in new clothes, even if we recognize that the question of cultural diversity will need to be taken seriously.

At the time of writing these conflicts have not been resolved. Though there is a clear need for a history syllabus which embraces the need for a strategy of nation-building, it is clear that the conflicts do not lend themselves to easy solutions. Yet the gains recognized so far could be measured by the extent of agreement on the criteria for history education in schools in terms of educational objectives, methodologies, skills promotion and modes of assessment to be used, amongst the restricted membership of that committee. While there is as yet no substantive debate about the content of the new syllabus for a future South Africa, this did mark the beginning of a process to establish a foundation for such policy. We argued that the compiling of a future content syllabus could not be undertaken outside of a broader public debate and considerable research on the topic. Within the context of the HSRC Work Committee we sought to postpone that debate for other times and circumstances. In the end the Chairman agreed to simply allow the reports to be published in their original forms, and not seek to condense them or seek consensus for the purpose of publication. On that basis we are at present (November 1991) in the process of preparing the final draft of the report.

HISTORY EDUCATION AS AN ASPECT OF THE BROADER EDUCATIONAL DEBATE OF 1991

Syllabus revision on the old formula?

During 1991 the government and the NECC prepared new educational scenarios for South Africa after apartheid. Since the latter half of the previous year the NECC's National Education Policy Investigation (NEPI) has been constituted to map out the policy terrain and research guidelines for future policy alternatives. On the side of the National Party and the existing educational bureaucracy, there has been a concerted attempt to pre-empt policy reform by tabling elaborate policy guidelines in the interim or transition period of macro-politics. New draft syllabi have been tabled for a number of subjects, in line with regular revision of syllabuses scheduled for the present time. In this manner the new Draft Core Syllabus for History for the Department of Education and Culture: Administration House of Assembly appeared at the end of 1990. This was intended for implementation in 1992/3 and would have fixed policy for the next six years.

During 1991 there were two major initiatives on the part of the government and the administration of the Department of National Education in the direction of educational reform. These comprised the *Educational Renewal Strategy* and a discussion document on Curriculum Planning.[22] The first of these is concerned to lay down broad guidelines for discussion on the area of 'educational renewal'. Although it gives considerable attention to the issue of orientating educational policy towards the needs of the workplace, in the wake of the De Lange recommendations, it does not really develop specific recommendations for curriculum policy. The other, more recent report, of November 1991, promotes skill development and the cultivation of intellectual skills (including logical, independent, creative and critical thought) but does not give details regarding curriculum content, although it does imply a multi-cultural curriculum model.

From apartheid history in schools – to what?

In attempting to assess the current babel of policy discourse, a number of issues seem to stand out. Firstly, there is wide acceptance of the need for change in the current educational curriculum as part of the overall political transition that is upon us. Apartheid and racism are formally rejected by all the major parties, including the National Party. At the same time the meaning of that assertion in relation to the shaping of a new history syllabus or curriculum development procedure is liable to different interpretations from different parties in different circumstances. Although there is little detailed public discussion on the specific area of history education, the legacy of opposition to apartheid history makes it safe to assume that this inevitably places a degree of priority on this area of policy. Secondly, although there is agreement on the need for change, there is little agreement on the detailed route to follow to bring about the best possible policies in keeping with the educational and political demands of the politics of transformation, but a beginning has been made to laying the foundation for criteria or 'norms and standards' for the subject. A skills-based, conceptually focused curriculum development strategy is broadly accepted as the best way to ensure a sound policy for the future. Only after extensive consultation with academics, educators, community groups and students will it be possible to gain clarity on further development like the *process* of curriculum development and the selection of content. These are issues that must receive urgent attention.

To what extent must the syllabus reflect the demand for school history to be an introduction to a mode of critical thinking and analysis, and how far must the demand for specific content(s) be recognized? Is multi-cultural education an acceptable replacement for apartheid education? What would it mean in a South African context? What objectives should be encouraged to stimulate sound learning practices and the development of critical thinking in the history class? What modes of evaluation are appropriate to the processes we wish to encourage? What teaching methodology should be encouraged and which discouraged? How are claims for the inclusion or exclusion of content validated? What process is appropriate to the selection of content? How much freedom is to be given to the teacher or the school in selecting the syllabus content? How do we weigh the call for community history (however defined) against the need for history in schools which underwrites the goals of building a new nation? How much influence will we give to historians in defining the future curriculum?

All these questions and many more have informed a number of discussions between members of the HEG in Cape Town, the History Workshop in Johannesburg, and the Natal History Teachers' Society in Durban. These discussions culminated in a meeting at the Kenton–Katberg Education Conference at the end of October 1991 where it was decided that we should examine the possibility of holding a number of workshops during 1992 to promote discussion of these issues. We also raised the same questions with the NEPI Curriculum Studies Group, and the ANC Education Department. All are in broad agreement that we should launch an initiative to promote a public debate in this area as soon as possible, and proceed with the development of research related to the formulation of curriculum development procedures and the production of resources for future classroom use.

In order to address these questions a number of workshops on History Education were held at centres like Johannesburg, Cape Town and Durban. In this way we hope to open a new chapter in the development of school history in South Africa, and ensure that the richness of our historiographical heritage, as outlined in the first part of this chapter, comes to inform history in the schools, thus finally moving us away from our colonial past and the domination of Afrikaner nationalist ideology.

Notes

INTRODUCTION

1   Saner L. Gilman, *Difference and Pathology: Stereotypes of Sexuality, Race and Madness*, (1985), (Ithaca and London: Cornell University Press, 1985), p. 239.
2   Stephen Ball, 'Imperialism, social control and the colonial curriculum in Africa,', *Journal of Curriculum Studies*, (1983) 25: 237–63; Chris Mullard, 'Racism in society and schools: history, policy and practice', Occasional Paper of the London University of Education, (1979); Kevin Lillis, 'Africanising the school literature curriculum in Kenya: a case study of curriculum dependency', *Journal of Curriculum Studies*, (1986), 18: 63–85; amd J.A. Mangan, 'Ethics and ethnocentricity: imperial education in British Tropical Africa', in William J. Baker and James A. Mangan, *Sport in Africa: Essays in Social History*, (New York: Holms and Meier, 1987), pp. 138–71.

1 IMAGES FOR CONFIDENT CONTROL

1   Ashis Nandy, *The Intimate Enemy: Loss and Recovery of Self Under Colonialism* (Delhi: Oxford University Press, 1983), pp. x–xi.
2   Ibid., p. xi.
3   Bernard S. Cohn, *An Anthropologist Among the Historians and Other Essays*, (Delhi: Oxford University Press, 1987), p. 44.
4   Albert Memmi, *The Colonizer and the Colonized*, (New York: Orion Press, 1965), p. 71.
5   Sander L. Gilman, *Difference and Pathology: Stereotypes of Sexuality, Race and Madness* (Ithaca and London: Cornell University Press, 1985), p. 239.
6   From Mary Douglas, *Purity and Danger: An Analysis of the Concepts of Pollution and Taboo* quoted in Gilman, *Difference and Pathology*, p. 19.
7   Gilman, *Difference and Pathology*, p. 22.
8   Richard Ned Lebow, *White Britain and Black Ireland: The Influence of Stereotypes on Colonial Policy*, (Philadelphia, Institute for the Study of Human Issues, 1976), p. 103.
9   Homi K. Bhabha, 'The other question – the stereotype and colonial discourse', *Screen* (1983) 24: 23.
10 Gilman, *Difference and Pathology*, pp. 120–1.
11 Lebow, *White Britain*, p. 22.
12 Gilman *Difference and Pathology*, p. 26.
13 Raphael Samuel (ed.), *Patriotism: The Making and Unmaking of British National Identity* (volume III, National Fictions); (London: Routledge, 1989), p. xi.
14 Ibid., p. xii.

15 Ibid., p. xxviii.
16 Ivid., p.xiii.
17 Lebow, *White Britain*, p. 104.
18 Tzvetan Todorov, 'Race, writing and culture', in Henry Louis Gates, Jr (ed.), *Race, Writing and Difference* (Chicago: University of Chicago Press, 1986), p. 377.
19 Abdul R. JanMohamed, 'The economy of the Manichean allegory: the function of racial difference in colonialist literature', in Gates, *Race*, p. 79.
20 Ibid., p.82.
21 Ibid., p. 80.
22 Ibid., p. 83.
23 Ibid.
24 Ibid., p. 24.
25 Ibid., p. 81.
26 Ibid., p. 84.
27 Ibid., p. 87.
28 Ibid., p. 103.
29 Ibid., p. 91.
30 Ibid., p. 89.
31 Bhabha, 'The other question', p. 23.
32 Nandy, *The Intimate Enemy*, p. 11.
33 Ibid., p. 35.
34 Brian Stanley, *The Bible and the Flag* (London: Appollos, 1990), p. 174.
35 Bhabha, 'The other question', p. 35.
36 Ibid.
37 Dorothy Hammond and Alta Jablow, *The Africa That Never Was: Four Centuries of British Writing About Africa* (New York: Twayne Publishers, 1970), p. 183.
38 Patrick Brantlinger, 'Victorians and Africans: the genealogy of the myth of the Dark Continent', in Gates, *Race*, p. 197.
39 Edward H. Berman, *African Reactions to Missionary Education*, (New York and London: Teachers' College Press, 1975), p. 5.
40 Ibid., p. 6.
41 Stanley, *The Bible*, P. 161.
42 Ibid., p. 171.
43 Roger Bastide, 'Colour, Racism, and Christianity', *Daedalus*, (Spring, 1967) p. 315.
44 Ibid., p. 314.
45 Douglas A. Lorimer, *Colour, Class and the Victorians*, (Leicester: Leicester University Press, 1978), p. 11.
46 JanMohamed, 'Economy of the Manichean allegory', p. 269.
47 Lorimer, *Colour*, p. 14.
48 Ibid., p. 13.
49 Ibid., p. 16.
50 Ibid., p. 202.
51 Ibid., pp. 203–4.
52 Brantlinger, 'Victorians and Africans', pp. 200–1.
53 Ibid., p. 215.
54 Berman, *African Reactions*, p. 8.
55 Hammond and Jablow, *The Africa That Never Was*, p. 18.
56 Charles H. Lyons, 'The educable African: British thought and action 1835–1865', in Vincent M. Battle and Charles H. Lyons, *Essays in the History of African Education*, (New York: Teachers' College Press, 1970), p. 19.
57 Ibid., p. 13.

214   *The imperial curriculum*

58   Memmi, *The Colonizer*, p. 83.
59   Berman, *African Reactions*, pp. 10–11.
60   Battle and Lyons, *African Education*, p. 2.
61   Phillip Mason, *Patterns of Dominance* (London: Oxford University Press, 1970), p. 327.
62   Kevin M. Lillis, 'Africanising the school literature curriculum in Kenya: a case-study in curriculum dependency', *Curriculum Studies*, (1972) 18: 70.
63   Ibid., p. 70.
64   Ibid., p. 89.
65   Ibid., p. 71.
66   Ibid., p. 71.
67   Abena P. A. Busia, 'Manipulating Africa: the buccaneer as "liberator" in comtemporary fiction', in David Dabydeen (ed.), *The Black Presence in English Literature*, (Manchester: Manchester University Press, 1985), p. 171.
68   Ibid., p. 173.
69   Hammond and Jablow, *The Africa That Never Was*, p. 197.
70   Nandy, *The Intimate Enemy*, p. 38.
71   Ibid., pp. 38–9.
72   Frances M. Mannsaker, 'The dog that didn't bark: the subject races in imperial fiction at the turn of the century' in Dabydeen, *The Black Presence*, p. 121.
72   Ibid., p. 127.
73   Ibid., p. 132.
74   Hammond and Jablow, *The Africa That Never Was*, preface.
75   Frank Musgrove, 'Curriculum, culture and ideology', *Journal of Curriculum Studies* (1978) 10: 102.
76   Ibid., p. 105.
77   Ivor F. Goodson (ed.), *Social Histories of the Secondary Curriculum: Subjects for Study*, (London: Falmer Press, 1985), p. 363.
78   Ivor F. Goodson, *The Making of Curriculum*, (London: Falmer Press), 1988, p. 10.
79   Musgrove, 'Curriculum' p.102.
80   John M. MacKenzie, *Propaganda and Empire*, (Manchester: Manchester University Press, 1984), p. 174.
81   Ibid., p. 178.
82   Ibid.
83   Ibid., p. 181.
84   Ibid.
85   Ibid.
86   Ibid., p. 184.
87   Ibid., p. 190.
88   Ibid., p. 193.
89   Memmi, *The Colonizer*, p. xx.
90   Goodson, *Social Histories*, p. 11.
91   Stephen J. Ball, 'Imperialism, social control and the colonial curriculum in Africa', *Journal of Curriculum Studies*, (1983) 15: 237–8.
92   Ibid., p.258.
93   Berman, *African Reactions*, pp. 24–30.
94   Ibid., p. 30.
95   Ibid.
96   Ibid., p. 33.
97   Ibid., p.8.
98   Ibid., p.43.
99   Bhabha, 'The other question', p. 19.

100 Brantlinger, 'Victorians and Africans', pp. 186–6.
101 Ibid., p. 217.
102 Ibid.
103 Ibid., p. 185.
104 Ibid.
105 Ibid., p. 218.
106 James W. Fernandez, 'Fang, representations under acculturation' in Philip D. Curtin (ed.). *Africa and the West* (Wisconsin: University of Wisconsin Press, 1974), p. 5.
107 M.J. Ashley, 'Universes in collision: Xhosa, missionaries and education in nineteenth century South Africa', *Journal of Theology for Southern Africa*, (1980) 36:28.
108 Ibid., p. 35.
109 M.J. Ashley, 'Features of mediocrity: missionaries and education in South Africa, 1850–1900', *Journal of Theology for Southern Africa*, (1982) 38:49.
110 Ibid., p.49.
111 Ibid., p. 58.
112 Abdul R. JanMohammed, *Manichean Aesthetics: The Politics of Literature in Colonial Africa* (Massachusetts: University of Massachusetts Press, 1989) p. 5.
113 Ashley, 'Features of mediocrity: missionaries and education in South Africa', p. 58.
114 Rosemary Gordon, *Sterotype of Imagery and Belief as an Ego Defence*, (Cambridge: Cambridge University Press, 1962), p. 6.

2 THE IMPERIAL INDIAN

1 H.E. Cooper, British education, public and private, and the British Empire, 1830–1950, unpublished PhD thesis, (Edinburgh, 1979); John MacKenzie, *Propaganda and Empire*, (Manchester, 1985); John Springhall, *Youth, Empire and Society*, (London, 1977); J.R. Gillis, *Youth and History* (London, 1981), p. 141–6; K.A. Castle, 'Attitudes toward non-Europeans in British school history textbooks and children's periodicals, 1890–1914' unpublished PhD., (CNAA, 1986).
2 The Earl of Meath, *Essays on Duty and Discipline* (London 1910), p. 59.
3 W.H. Webb, 'History, patriotism, and the child' *History* (1913) 2:53.
4 Board of Education, 'Suggestions for the Consideration of Teachers and others concerned in the work of Public Elementary Schools' (London, 1914), 5.
5 J.W. Duckworth, 'The Evolution of the History syllabus in English schools', unpublished M.Phil. thesis, (London, 1972), p. 24; M. Sturt , *The Education of the People*, (London, 1967), p. 397–415; F. Glendenning, 'The evolution of history teaching in British and French schools with special reference to attitudes to race and colonial history in history textbooks', unpublished PhD., (Keele, 1975), chap. 2; R. Aldrich, 'Imperialism in the study and teaching of history', in J. Mangan (ed.). *Benefits Bestowed? Education and British Imperialism* (Manchester, 1988).
6 S.R. Gardiner, *A Students History of England* (London, 1892), Preface.
7 Gardiner, *A Students History*, p. 859, 728;*Macmillan History Readers* (London, 1891–95), p. 224; R. Walker and G. Carter (eds.), *Local Examination History of England*, (London, 1905). pp. 1,103; A. Innes, *History of England* (Cambridge, 1907), p. vi.

8   R. Preiswerk, 'Ethnocentric images in history books and their effect on racism', Appendix I: List of criteria for the evaluation of racism in children's books and guidelines for the production of anti- and non-racist books, in R. Preiswerk (ed.) *The Slant of the Pen* (Geneva, 1980), pp. 131–48.

9   P. Murrell, 'The imperial idea in children's literature, 1840–1902', unpublished PhD thesis (Swansea, 1975); P. Dunae, 'Boys' literature and the idea of empire', *Victorian Studies*, (1980) 24(1): 105–22; J.S. Bratton, *The Impact of Victorian Children's Fiction* (London, 1981), pp. 28–9.

10   J.W. Duckworth, 'The evolution of the history syllabus in English Schools, 1900–25', (unpublished M.Phil, London, 1972), pp. 24, 122; *London Matriculation Test Papers*, (Cambridge, 1902); *Oxford and Cambridge Examination Papers* (London, 1891); *Oxford Higher Local Examination Papers* (Oxford, 1902–1914).

11   *Special Examiners Reports*, (Oxford, 1908), p. 41.

12   M.F. Thwaite, *From Primer to Pleasure*, (London 1963), p. 181.

13   F. Glendenning, 'School history textbooks and racial attitudes, 1804–1911', *Journal of Educational Administration and History* (1973) v: 40–1.

14   G. Carter, *History of England* (London, 1899), p. 84.

15   J.R. Green, *A Short History of the English People*, (London, 1894), p. 1659; M. Keatinge and N. Frazer, *A History of England for Schools*, (London, 1911), p. 506; F. York-Powell and T. Tout, *History of England*, (London, 1900), p. 785.

16   Airy, O, *Textbook of English History* (Longmans, 1893) p. 496.

17   G. Warner and C.H.K. Marten, *Groundwork of British History*, (London, 1912), p. 467.

18   F. York-Powell and T. Tout, *History of England*, p. 995.

19   Warner and Marten, *Groundwork*, p. 466.

20   York-Powell and Tout, *History of England*, pp. 785, 995; Carter, *History of England*, p. 84; Warner and Marten *Groundwork*, p. 466; C.L.R. Fletcher, *Introductory History of England* (London, 1909), pp. 110, 112; R.S. Rait, *School History of England*, (Oxford, 1911), p. 92.

21   M.E. Chamberlain, *Britain and India*, (Newton Abbot, 1974), pp. 52–4; P. Mason, *Patterns of Dominance*, (London, 1970), p. 95. *Macmillan History Readers*, p. 31; *Avon Historical Readers* (London, 1895), p. 85.

22   Warner and Marten, *Groundwork*, p. 466; P. Mudford, *Birds of a Different Plumage* (London, 1974), pp. 143–58.

23   J.F. Bright, *A History of England for Public Schools*, (London, 1887–1901), p. 799; Gardiner, *A Students History*, p. 859; J.M.D and M.J.C Meiklejohn, *A School History of England* (London, 1901), p. 451; Sir C. and M. Oman, *A Junior History of England*, (London, 1904), p. 239.

24   York-Powell and Tout, *History of England*, p. 1001. See also Green, *A Short History*, p. 1712; Gardiner, *A Students History*, p. 758; Carter, *History of England*, p. 118; M.O. Davis, *The Story of England*, (Oxford, 1912), p. 283.

25   Airy, *Textbook of English History*, p. 494.

26   Warner and Marten, *History of England*, p. 688.

27   V.G. Kiernan, *The Lords of Human Kind* (London, 1972), p. 55; Bright, *Public Schools History*, p. 293; Carter, *History of England*, p. 217; A. Hassall, *A Class Book of English History* (London, 1901), p. 548; Innes, *History of England*, p. 542; Keatinge and Frazer, *History for Schools*, p. 514.

28   Gardiner, *A Students History*, p. 954.

29   Innes, *History of England*, p. 373; Gardiner, *A Students History*, p. 804; Chancellor, *History for their Masters*, (Bath, 1970), p. 38–66.

30   Board of Education, *Suggestions for the Consideration of Teachers and Others Concerned in the Work of Public Elementary Schools*, (London, 1914), p. 9.

31 A. Hassall, *The Making of the British Empire* (London, 1896), p. 52; J.C. Curtis, *Outlines of English History* (London, 1901), p. 58; G. Bosworth, *A History of the British Empire*, (London, 1905), p. 228; Rait, *School History*, p. 95; Green, *A Short History*, p. 1710; Carter, *History of England*, p. 84; Meiklejohn, *A School History* p. 379.

32 Meiklejohn, *A School History*, p. 379; Warner and Marten, *Groundwork*, p. 469; Green, *A Short History*, p. 1648; York-Powell and Tout, *History of England*, p. 998; Gardiner, *A Students History*, p. 802; Carter, *History of England*, p. 88.

33 Gardiner, *A Students History*, p. 802; Innes, *History of England*, p. 400.

34 Mudford, *Different Plumage*, p. 153; Mason, *Patterns of Dominance*, p. 95; Chamberlain, *Britain and India*, p. 101.

35 Glendenning, 'School history textbooks', pp. 41–2.

36 Letter of J.Z. Holwell, reprinted in T. Charles-Edwardes and B. Richardson, *They Saw it Happen* (Oxford, 1974), pp. 278–85; S. Wolpert, *A New History of India* (Oxford, 1989), pp. 179–80; Chamberlain, *Britain and India*, p. 45.

37 Avon *Historical Reader*, p. 77; Rait, *School History*, p. 95; Warner and Marten, *Groundwork*, p. 471; Davis, *The Story*, p. 283.

38 *Macmillan History Readers*, p. 54; Carter, *History of England*, p. 86; Meiklejohn, *A School History*, p. 358; Bright, *Public Schools History*, p. 1118; Oman, *A Junior History*, p. 253.

39 *Avon Historical Readers*, pp. 78–9.

40 Chamberlain, *Britain and India*, p. 94.

41 Gardiner, *A Students History*, p. 953; Airy, *Textbook of English History*, p. 498; Keatinge and Frazer, *History for Schools*, p. 514; Rait, *School History*, p. 171.

42 *Macmillan History Readers*, p. 35. *Avon Historical Readers*, p. 96; T. Livesey and B. Thorp, *History of England* (London, 1908), p. 93; A Buckley, *History of England for Beginners* (London, 1904), p. 351; *Jacks Historical Readers* (London, 1905), p. 141.

43 Warner and Marten, *Groundwork*, p. 692.

44 Meiklejohn, *A School History*, p. 449; Bright, *Public Schools History*, p. 233; H. Egerton, *Oxford Survey of the British Empire* (Oxford, 1914), p. 305; E. Hawke, *The British Empire and its History* (London 1911), p. 315; Hassall, *Making of Empire*, p. 593; Rait, *School History*, p. 171.

45 C. Bolt, *Victorian Attitudes to Race* (London, 1971), p. 192; Bright, *Public Schools History*, p. 233; York-Powell & Tout, *History of England*, p. 1019; Oman, *A Junior History*, p. 734; Warner and Marten. *Groundwork*, p. 698.

46 Bolt, *Victorian Attitudes*, pp. 157–80.

47 'The Indian Mutiny in fiction' (anon.) *Blackwoods Magazine*, (1897), CLXI; 218–31; Bright, *Public Schools History*, p. 292. R. Pringle, *Local Exam History* (London, 1899),p. 138; Warner and Marten, *Groundwork*, p. 692.

48 Bright, *Public Schools History*, pp. 292–8.

49 *Macmillan History Readers*, p. 182; C. Yonge, *Westminster Readers* (London, 1890), p. 98.

50 Gardiner, *A Students History*, p. 952; Airy, *Textbook of English History*, p. 498; Bright, *Public Schools History*, p. 295. Carter, *History of England*, p. 215.

51 York-Powell and Tout, *History of England*, p. 1015; Carter, *History of England*, p. 216; Hassall, *Making of Empire*, p. 558; Meiklejohn, *A School History*, p. 428; Oman, *A Junior History*, p. 242; Innes, *History of England*, p. 483.

52 Warner and Marten, *Groundwork*, p. 690; Bosworth, *History of the Empire*, p. 281. Hasall, *Making of Empire*, p. 558.

53 Airy, *Textbook of England History*, p. 498; Gardiner, *A Students History*, p. 952; Oman, *A Junior History*, p. 244; Keatinge and Frazer, *History for Schools*, p. 513.

54 Hawke, *The British Empire*, p. 3.
55 Egerton, *Oxford Survey*, p. 173.
56 Mudford, *Different Plumage*, p. 208.
57 Rait, *School History*, p. 171.
58 D. Gordon, *The Moment of Power* (Englewood Cliffs, N.J., 1970), pp. 116–17; R. Faber, *The Vision and the Need* (London, 1966), pp. 87–99.
59 C. Bolt, *Victorian Attitudes;* V. Chancellor, *History for their Masters*.
60 Glendenning, 'School history textbooks', 41; D. Kuya, 'Racism in children's books in Britain', in R. Preiswerk (ed.), *The Slant of the Pen* (Geneva, 1980), pp. 26–45.
61 Sir C. Oman, *A History of England* (London, 1895), p. 734.
62 A.J. Greenberger, *The British Image of India* (Oxford, 1969), pp. 42–3. Meiklejohn, *A School History*, p. 450.
63 York-Powell and Tout, *History of England*, p. 1021; Hawke, *The British Empire*, p. 318; Carter, *History of England*, p. 218; Bosworth, *History of the Empire*, p. 138; Warner and Marten, *Groundwork*, p. 697–8; Rait, *School History*, p. 171; Keatinge and Frazer, *History for Schools*, p. 276.
64 Geography texts did deal with the economic aspects of Empire. See MacKenzie, *Propaganda*, p. 186.
65 J.H. Plumb, *The Death of the Past* (London, 1969), p. 32; A. Sandison, *The Wheel of Empire* (London, 1967), p. 18; J.S. Bratton, *The Impact of Victorian Children's Fiction* (London, 1981), p. 29; A.P. Thornton, *The Imperial Idea and its Enemies* (London, 1959),p. 94.

3 THE BLACK AFRICAN IN SOUTHERN AFRICA

1 W.E. Marsden, 'Continuity and change in geography textbooks: perspectives from the 1930s to the 1960s', *Geography* (October 1988) 73 (4): 327–43.
2 Ibid., p. 328.
3 J. Fletcher, 'Report on the day schools of the British and Foreign School Society, Minutes of Committee of Council in Education', (London: HMSO 1846) II: 100–1. The reference is to J. Cornwell, *A School Geography* London, (Simplon, Marshall, 1846).
4 W.D. Jordan, 'First impressions: initial English confrontations with Africans', in C. Husband (ed.) *Race in Britain*, London: Hutchinson, 1982), pp. 42–58.
5 J. Walvin, 'Black caricature: the roots of racialism', in *Race in Britain*, pp. 59–72.
6 T. Bankes, *A System of Universal Geography*, (London: C. Cooke, 1787).
7 Ibid., p. 317.
8 J. Bygott, *A Regional Geography of the World* (London: University Tutorial Press, 1932), p. 197.
9 C. Bird, *A School Geography*, (London: Whittacker, 1898), p. 197.
10 R. Miller, *Africa*, (London: Nelson, p. 227).
11 The reminiscences of Thomas Dunning, quoted in 'Transactions of the Lancashire and Cheshire Antiquarian Society', W.H. Chaloner (ed.), (1948) LIX: 89–90.
12 The African Association had evolved into the Royal Geographical Society and they, like their predecessors, supported expeditions into Africa.
13 1851 Census: 'Great Britain: reports and tables, parliamentary papers 1852–3' XC cxxxii, quoted in J.J. Hurt, *Elementary Schooling and the Working Class*, (London: Routledge and Kegan Paul, 1979), p. 28.
14 Fletcher, 'Report on the day schools', p. 100.
15 African Association, 'First Report', H. Beaufoy (ed.), 1790, quoted in C. Hibbert, *Africa Explored 1769–1889*, (London: Penguin, 1984), p. 216.

16 G. Shepperson, 'David Livingstone 1813–1873', *The Geographical Journal* (June 1973) 139 (2): 211.

17 Livingstone, quoted in Shepperson, ibid., p. 211.

18 Hibbert, *Africa Explored*, p. 209.

19 H.M. Stanley, 'Through the Dark Continent, 1878', *In Darkest Africa*, vols I & II (Sampson Low, Marston & Co., 1890). The latter sold 150,000 copies.

20 Stanley, *In Darkest Africa*, II: 40–1.

21 A. Wallace, 'The origin of human races and the antiquity of man deduced for the theory of natural selection', *Journal of the Anthropological Society*, (1864) 2: clviii–clxx, reproduced in M.D. Biddis, *Images of Race* (Leicester, 1979), p. 48.

22 C. Mackay, 'The Negro and Negrophilists', *Blackwood's Edinburgh Magazine* (1866) 99: 581–97 in Biddis, *Images of Race*, pp. 89–112.

23 H.L. Duff, *Nyasaland Under the Foreign Office*, (London: Bell, 1903) p. 230.

24 Anon., *Manual of Geography*, (London: Allman, 1891) p. 278.

25 Bird, *A School Geography*, p. 197.

26 J.M.D. Meiklejohn, *A New Geography* (27th edn) (London: A.M. Holden, 1902), p. 364.

27 W. Hughes, *Class Book of Modern Geography*, (London: Philip, 1893), p. 263.

28 Anon., *The World at Home*, (London: Nelson, 1887), p. 34.

29 Anon., *Manual of Geography*, p. 278.

30 J.H. Stembridge, *The Southern Continents*, (London: Oxford University Press, 1963), p. 3.

31 A.W. Coysh and M.E. Tomlinson, *Africa*, (London: University Tutorial Press, 1970), pp. 17–19.

32 G. Hickman, *The New Africa*, (London: Hodder, 1976) pp. 143–4.

33 R. White, *Africa*, (London: Heinemann, 1978).

34 Van Riebeck quoted in de Kiewet, *A History of South Africa*, (London: Oxford University Press, 1941), p. 20.

35 J. Cornwell, *A School Geography* (7th edn) (London: Simplon, Marshall, 1850), p. 246.

36 W.L. Bunting and H.L. Collen, *A Geography of the British Empire*, (Cambridge: Cambridge University Press, 1935) p. 134.

37 G.B. Redmore, *Under the Southern Cross* (London: John Murray, 1971), p. 153.

38 L. Hughes, *The First Book of Africa* (1st British edn) (London: Mayflower, 1961), p. 60.

39 H.R. Sweeting, *The British Empire* (London: Nisbet, 1930), p. 179.

40 H.M. Spink and R.P. Brady, *The Southern Lands*, (London: Schofield, 1966), p. 14.

41 For modern usage of these terms see H. Ngubane, *Zulus of Southern Africa*, (Hove: Wayland, 1986). However in the same series, 'Original Peoples', the text specific to these peoples is entitled 'Bushman of the Kalahari'.

42 J. Thomas, *Explorer Geography*, (London: Bell, 1923), p. 103.

43 R.W. and E.M. Steel, *Africa*, (London: Longman, 1974) p. 36.

44 For an account of the writing of B. Hemyng see M. Anglo, *Penny Dreadfuls*, (London: Jupiter, 1977). Representation of Africans in comics is illustrated in D. Gifford, *Victorian Comics*, (London: Allen and Unwin, 1976). In *Illustrated Chips* 361, 31 July 1897, a comic strip was captioned 'A tug-of-war then took place between niggers and animals'. Alnwick was one of the few to condemn the term, making the point that 'Nigger is a term of contempt' and thereby demonstrating an early awareness of the dangers of language. See H. Alnwick, *A Geography of Africa*, (London: Harrap, 1936), p. 27.

45 V.G. Childe, *What Happened in History*, (London: Pelican, 1954), chap. 2.

46 J. Riley, *First Book of Geography. How Savages Live* (6th edn), (London: George Philip, 1932), pp. 77–80.
47 R. Miller, *Africa*, (London: Nelson, 1964) p. 236.
48 W.M. Macmillan in *Bantu, Boer and Briton*, (London: Oxford University Press, 1963), makes the point that Native with a capital N began to be accepted in the 1920s as more polite.
49 L.D. Stamp and J.N. Jamieson, *A Regional Geography of Africa and Europe*, (London: Longmans, Green, 1928), p. 13.
50 J.C. Laurence, *Race, Propaganda and South Africa*, (London: Gollancz, 1979), p. 78.
51 R. Clayton and J. Miles, *Finding Out About Geography*, (London: Rupert Hart-Davis, 1972).
52 R.C. Honeybone and B.S. Robertson; *The Southern Continents*, (London: Heinemann, 1958) p. 134.
53 Spink and Brady, *The Southern Lands*, (1958 revision), p. 15.
54 P. English, *South Africa in Pictures*, (New York: Sterling, 1968), p. 20.
55 F.E. Western, *Africa*, (London: Murray, 1933), p. 134.
56 D.A. Sherriff, *Africa*, (2nd edn) (London: Oxford University Press, 1963), p. 36.
57 Sweeting, *The British Empire*, p. 183.
58 See for example: Stembridge, *The Southern Continents*, p. 104; A.R.B. Simson, *Africa* (4th edn) (London: Bell, 1962) p. 168.
59 B.C. Wallis, *A Junior Geography of the World*, (London: Macmillan, 1917), p. 187.
60 W.H. Barker and L. Brooks, *The Peoples of the World*, (London: University of London Press, 1922), p. 62.
61 L. Brooks, *A Regional Geography of Africa and Europe*, (London: University of London Press, 1935), p. 122. H. Alnwick, *A Geography of Africa*, (London: Harrap, 1936), p. 237.
62 G.R.E. Wicks, *Africa*, (Oxford: Pergamon, 1973), p. 132.
63 J. Mack, *Zulu*, (London: Macdonald, 1980).
64 E.W. Heaton, *A Scientific Geography*, (London: Hollins, 1908), p. 98.
65 Wallis, *A Junior Geography of the World*, p. 187.
66 C.B. Thurston, *A Progressive Geography of Africa and Australia*, (London: Arnold, 1925), p. 63.
67 Ibid., p. 63.
68 S.C. Farrar and C. Matheson, *The Gateway Geography of Africa*, (London: Methuen, 1931), p. 139.
69 E.D. Laborde, *The Southern Lands*, (Cambridge: Cambridge University Press, 1931), pp. 126–7.
70 Western, *Africa*, p. 138.
71 Ibid.
72 Alnwick, *A Geography of Africa*, pp. 28–9.
73 For a vigorous rebuttal of 1930s racial theory see J. Huxley *et al.*, *We Europeans: A Survey of 'Racial' Problems*, (London: Penguin, 1939).
74 P.T. Silley, *Africa*, (London: Schofield and Sims, 1965), p. 7.
75 Miller, *Africa*, p. 226.
76 D.M. Smith, 'Inequality and conflict: the case of South Africa', in *Human Geography: A Welfare Approach*, (London: Arnold, 1977).
77 W. Fitzgerald, *Africa*, (8th edn) (London: Methuen, 1955).
78 Spink and Brady, *The Southern Lands*, p. 62.
79 Anon., *Children of the Cape*, (London: Hutchinson, 1959), p. 27.
80 D.R. Wright, 'Visual images in geography textbooks: the case of Africa', *Geography*, (July 1979): 205–10.

81 J.H. Stembridge, *Africa, Asia and Australia, Book 2*, 2nd series, (London: Oxford University Press, 1950) pp. 91–107.
82 B. Jones, 'Bias in the classroom: some suggested guidelines', *Teaching Politics* (September 1986), 15 (3): 387–401.
83 G.C. Fry, *A Text-Book of Geography*, (London: University Tutorial Press, 1911), p. 396.
84 N. Jackson and P. Penn, *The Southern Continents*, (London: George Philip, 1959), p. 131.
85 G. Hickman, *A New Africa* (4th edn) (London: Hodder and Stoughton, 1990) p. 145–63.
86 V.F. Searson and E. Evans, *The Southern Continents*, (London: Johnstone, 1937), p. 320.
87 Bunting and Collen, *A Geography of the British Empire*, p. 134.

4 THE IRISH AND OTHERS

1   David Beers Quinn, *The Elizabethans and the Irish* (Cornell University Press, 1966), p. 20.
2   Ibid., p. 21.
3   Ibid., p.26.
4   John Coolahan, 'Imperialism and the Irish National School System', in J.A. Mangan (ed.) *'Benefits Bestowed'?: Education and British Imperialism* (Manchester: Manchester University Press, 1988), pp. 76–93.
5   The author wishes to acknowledge his debt for some of the extracts used. Lorcan M. Walsh's study 'A comparative analysis of the Reading Books of the Commissioners of National Education and of the Christian brothers, 1831–1900' M.A. Thesis, University College, Dublin, 1983.
6   Commissioners of National Education, *Third Reading Book*, (1843 edn), p. 159.
7   *Second Reading Book* (1858 edn), p. 135.
8   Coolahan, *Imperialism*, pp. 84–8.
9   Richard Ned Lebow, *White Britain and Black Ireland: The Influence of Stereotypes on Colonial Policy* (Philadelphia: Institute for Study of Human Issues, 1976), p. 39.
10 Ibid., p. 40.
11 Oliver McDonagh, *Daniel O'Connell*, (1991 edn).
12 Lebow, *White Britain and Black Ireland*, p. 51.
13 F.S.L. Lyons, *Charles Stuart Parnell* (London: Collins, 1977).
14 Donal McCartney, 'James Anthony Froude: A Historiographical Controversy of the Nineteenth Century', *Historical Studies*, (1969), VII: 171–90.
15 L.P. Curtis, *Apes and Angels, the Irishman in Victorian Caricature*, (New York: Smithsonian Press, 1971, p. 13.
16 Ibid., p. 21.
17 *Fourth Reading Book*, (1861 edn), p. 56.
18 Ibid., p. 54.
19 Ibid., p. 80.
20 Ibid., p. 76.
21 Ibid., pp. 144, 145.
22 Ibid., p. 145.
23 Ibid., p. 138.
24 Ibid., pp. 154, 155.
25 Ibid., p. 153.
26 Ibid., p. 154.
27 Ibid., p. 56.

28 *Third Reading Book* 1843, p. 143.
29 Ibid., p. 167.
30 Ibid., p. 169.
31 *Supplement to the Fourth Reading Book*, (1850), p. 281.
32 *Fourth Reading Book*, (1861), p. 133.
33 *Supplement to Fourth Reading Book*, (1850), p. 281.
34 Sean P. Farragher, *Père Leman: Educator and Missionary* (Dublin and London: Paraclete Press, 1988), pp. 267–313.
35 *Third Reading Book*, 1843, p. 160.

5 RACE, EMPIRE AND THE MAORI

 1 W.F. Collier, *History of the British Empire* (London, 1875).
 2 J.M. MacKenzie, *Propaganda and Empire: the manipulation of British public opinion, 1880–1960* (Manchester, 1984), pp. 176–80.
 3 K. Sinclair, *A History of New Zealand* (Harmondsworth, rev. edn, 1980), p. 218.
 4 *School Journal* (May 1908) Part III: 102.
 5 *New Zealand Graphic Readers: Second Book* (Auckland, c. 1905), p. 78.
 6 *Public School Series, Historical Reader No. 4: History of the British Colonial Empire* (Christchurch, c. 1904) p. 11.
 7 J.A. Lee, *Early Days in New Zealand* (Martinborough, 1977), p. 93.
 8 E.K. Mulgan and A.E. Mulgan, *The New Zealand Citizen* (Auckland, rev. edn, 1919), pp. 35–6.
 9 *School Journal* (May 1909) Part III: 101.
10 *School Journal* (May 1909) Part III: 119.
11 *School Journal* (May 1908) Part III: 107.
12 *School Journal* (October 1914) Part III: 285.
13 K. Sinclair, *A Destiny Apart: New Zealand's Search for National Identity* (Wellington, 1986), p. 101.
14 M.J.B. Ward, *The Child's Geography for School and Home Tuition* (London, 1879), p. 44.
15 *Royal School Series: The Royal Star Readers: Standard III* (London, 1888), p. 170.
16 *Nelson's School Series: Royal Reader: No. VI* (London, 1874), p. 88.
17 L. Valentine, *The Victoria Geography* (London, 1872), p. 27.
18 L.W. Lyde, *Man in Many Lands* (London, 3rd edn, 1919), pp. 19–20, 145.
19 Ibid., p. 73.
20 R.F. Irvine and O.T.J. Alpers, *The Progress of New Zealand in the Nineteenth Century* (London, 1902), p. 421.
21 *The Story of New Zealand: Book III: The Growth of the Colony 1853–1906* (Auckland, c. 1925), pp. 96–7.
22 J.W. Gregory, *South Cross Geographical Readers for New Zealand Schools: Standard IV* (Christchurch, c. 1904), p. 10.
23 *Southern Cross Histories: No 3* (Christchurch, c. 1899), p. 182.
24 *New Zealand Graphic Readers: Fourth Book* (Auckland, c. 1905), p. 146.
25 J. Cornwell, *Geography for Beginners* (London, 1858), p. 92.
26 S.R. Parkin, *Round the Empire for the Use of Schools* (London, 1892), p. 109.
27 *School Journal* (May 1909) Part I: 50.
28 *Lyttelton Times*, 26 September 1907.
29 G.H. Schofield, *New Zealand in Evolution: Industrial, Commercial, Political* (London, 1916), p. 171.
30 J.J. Patterson, *A geography of New Zealand and Australia . . . (adapted to the*

requirements of the public schools of New Zealand) (Christchurch, rev. edn, 1889), p. 72.

31 A. Mackay, *Intermediate Geography* (London, 8th edn, 1882), p. 11.
32 J.W. Gregory. *The Southern Cross Geographical Readers: Standards V–VI* (Christchurch, c. 1905), p. 280.
33 *Longmans' New Zealand Readers: Book VI* (London, 1910), p. 176.
34 R. Anderson, *Modern Geography for the Use of Schools* (London, new edn, 1881), p. 200.
35 Thornton, *Longmans' Geographical Series: Book V: a Primary Physical Geography* (London, 1909) p. 101–2.
36 G.G. Chisholm, *Longmans' School Geography for Australasia* (London, 1901), p. 113.
37 J. Cornwell, *A School Geography* (London 1881), p. 330.
38 *Imperial Readers: Sixth Reader* (Christchurch, 1899), p. 83.
39 E.M. Bourke, *A Little History of New Zealand* (Melbourne, 1882), p. 2. *Syllabus of Instruction for Public Schools*, p. 31.
40 *Whitcombe's Primary History Series: Our Nation's Story: A course of British History: Standard III* (Christchurch, c. 1929), pp. 45–8.
41 *School Journal* (May 1909) Part III: 115–6.
42 *Imperial Readers: Second Reader* (Christchurch, c. 1899), p. 20.
43 J. Belich. *The New Zealand Wars and the Victorian interpretation of Racial Conflict* (Auckland, Penguin edn, 1988), pp. 311–39.
44 *Public School Series: Historical Reader No. 4: History of the British Colonial Empire* (Christchurch, c. 1904), pp. 260–67.
45 *Our Nation's Story: Standard IV*, pp. 11–12.
46 J. Belich, *The New Zealand Wars and the Victorian Interpretation of Racial Conflict*, p. 312.
47 C.M. McGeorge, 'Military training in New Zealand primary shcools 1900–1912', *Australia and New Zealand History of Education Society* (1974) III: 1–10.
48 E.P. Malone, 'The New Zealand School Journal and the imperial ideology', *New Zealand Journal of History*, (1973) VII: 12–37.
49 New Zealand Department of Education, Circular to Schools, 4 May, 1903.
50 *Lyttelton Times*, 21 October 1913.
51 R. Openshaw, 'The highest expression of devotion: New Zealand primary schools and patriotic zeal during the early 1920s', *History of Education*, (1980) IX: 333–44.
52 E.P. Malone, 'The New Zealand School Journal and the imperial ideology', *New Zealand Journal of History*, (1973) VII.
53 *New Zealand Parliamentary Debates* (1921) 191: 922.
54 *New Zealand Gazette*, 1921, p. 1582.
55 R. Openshaw, 'The highest expression of devotion'.
56 R. Openshaw, 'New Zealand state primary schools and the growth of internationalism and anti-war feeling, 1929–34', *Australia and New Zealand History of Education Society* (1980) IX: 1–14.
57 *School Journal* (August 1924) Part II: 111.
58 *School Journal* (May 1923) Part III: 111–18.
59 *School Journal* (May 1923) Part III: 12–18.
60 New Zealand Department of Education, *Syllabus of Instruction for Public Schools* (Wellington, 1929), p. 145.
61 *Our Nation's Story: Standard III, passim.*

62 New Zealand Public Broadcasting Service, *Educational Broadcasts to Schools, February–May 1938* (Wellington), pp. 18–23; 32–3. *Our Nation's Story: Standard V*, pp. 135–6.

63 *New Zealand Census of Population and Dwellings 1921: Part IV: Race Aliens*, p. 1.

64 Ibid., p. 2.

65 Ibid., p. 1.

66 Mulgan and Mulgan, *The New Zealand Citizen*, pp. 116–17.

67 N.E. Coad, *The Dominion Civics* (Auckland, 1924), p. 132.

68 *Pacific Geography: Book IV* (Christchurch, c. 1920), p. 129.

69 For the development of the great fleet story and of the 'Aryan Maori', see M.P.K. Sorrensen, *Maori Origins and Migrations: the Genesis of Some Pakeha Myths and Legends* (Auckland, 1979).

70 See, for example, *Our Nation's Story: Standard III*, pp. 22–3.

71 K. Sinclair, *A Destiny Apart*, p. 173.

6 RACIAL STEREOTYPES IN THE AUSTRALIAN CURRICULUM

1 Wray Vamplew (ed.), *Australians: Historical Statistics* (Sydney: Fairfax, Syme and Weldon, 1987), p. 340.

2 S.H. Smith, *English History Stories for Third Class. Brooks's New Australian School Series. The New Standard Histories No. 1* (Sydney: William Brooks and Company, Ltd, c. 1899), pp. 5–6.

3 *The Commonwealth School Paper for Classes V and VI* (Sydney: William Brooks and Company) [hereinafter cited as *CSP*] May 1909, pp. 141–2; March 1910, p. 126; September 1908, p. 38.

4 *CSP* June 1906, p. 171; May 1910, p. 156.

5 *The New Australian School Series Fourth Reader* (Sydney: William Brooks and Company, c. 1910), pp. 30–1.

6 *CSP* April 1907, p. 138.

7 *CSP* May 1907, p. 147.

8 *CSP* May 1905, p. 164.

9 *CSP* May 1908, pp. 156–9.

10 *CSP* February 1908, p. 108.

11 *CSP* May 1908, pp. 145–9.

12 *CSP* March 1909, pp. 111–12.

13 *CSP* December 1907, pp. 82–6.

14 Vamplew, *Australians*, pp. 4, 8.

15 *CSP* June 1905, p. 183.

16 *CSP* February 1905, pp. 120–2.

17 *New Australian School Series Fourth Reader*, 'The Song That Men Should Sing', pp. 100–103.

18 *CSP* May 1909, pp. 129–35.

19 *CSP* March 1905, pp. 135–43.

20 *CSP* February 1910, pp. 97–102.

21 E.J.M. Watts, *Stories from Australian History* (Sydney: William Brooks and Company, 2nd edn, n.d.), p. 203.

22 *Approved Readers for the Catholic Schools of Australasia Book 4* (Sydney: William Brooks and Company, c. 1908), pp. 137–8.

23 *CSP* September 1911, pp. 33–9.

24 *CSP* September 1913, pp. 40–6.

25 *New Australian School Series Fourth Reader*, p. 132; *Approved Readers for the Catholic Schools of Australasia Book 4*, p. 83.

26 S.H. Smith *English History Stories for Fourth Class* (Sydney: William Brooks and Company, c. 1899), p. 75.

27 New South Wales Department of Education, *Course of Instruction for Primary Schools 1922*, p. 97; *Courses of Study for Secondary Schools*, 5th, 6th, 7th, 8th and 9th editions (Sydney: Government Printer, 1917, 1919, 1922, 1924, 1925).

28 See for example, *Schooling, vol. X. No. 1, Sept. 1921*, pp. 10–20; P.R. Cole *The Plan of a Lesson of the Instructive Type* (Sydney: Government Printer, 1916); P.R. Cole *The Conduct of the Lesson* (Sydney: Government Printer, 1917); P.R. Cole *The Teaching of History in Secondary Schools* (Sydney: Government Printer, 1918); P.R. Cole (ed.), *The Primary School Curriculum in Australia* (Melbourne: Melbourne University Press, 1932)

29 W.J. Muller, 'History and history teaching in New South Wales schools, 1866–1939', *The Australian History Teacher* no. 5, 1978, p. 16.

30 P.R. Cole, *Great Australians: A Reader for Schools* (Sydney: Geo. B. Philip and Son, 1923), p. 36.

31 Ibid., p. 16.

32 Ibid., p. 17.

33 Ibid., p. 18.

34 Ibid., p. 20.

35 Ibid., p. 22.

36 Ibid., p. 90.

37 Ibid., p. 65.

38 C.H. Currey, *European History Since 1870* (Sydney: Teachers' College Press), pp. 101–3, 226. Currey's text was used for the Leaving Certificate history course until 1932.

39 See, for example, *A.B.C. Notes on Australian History*, (Sydney: Pelelgrini & Co., Ltd., 1936), pp. 36, 40.

40 K.R. Cramp, *A Story of the Australian People* (Sydney: Geo. B. Philip & Son, 1927), p. 9. This text was recommended reading for the Intermediate Certificate from 1927 to 1939. *Courses for study in High Schools, editions from 1927–1939*.

41 Ibid., pp. 78–80, 83, 99–100, 104–5, 159–60.

42 Ibid., p. 153.

43 Ibid., p. 186.

44 H.L. Harris, *Australia in the Making* (Sydney: Angus & Robertson, 1936), pp. 133, 136, 177, 192–3. This text was written for the Intermediate Certificate course in 1931. See *Sydney Morning Herald* 30 April 1931.

45 E. Scott, *A Short History of Australia*, 4th edn, (Melbourne, 1920), pp. 80, 92, 122, 159, 168–9; A.W. Jose, *History of Australia*, 4th edn, (Sydney, 1911), pp. 1, 23, 74–7, 205. *Courses of Study for High Schools*, edns for 1918–1939.

46 K.R. Cramp, W. Lennard and J.H. Smairl, *A Story of the English People* (Sydney: Government Printer, 1919); *Education Gazette* (Sydney), 1 March 1920, 1 August 1922.

47 Cramp, Lennard and Smairl, *A Story of the English People*, p. 380.

48 Ibid., p. 381.

49 Ibid., pp. 381–2, 385.

50 Ibid., p. 337.

51 Ibid., p. 239.

52 Ibid., p. 304–5.

53 Ibid., pp. 386, 390.

54 S.H. Roberts and C.H. Currey, *Modern British History* (Sydney: Angus and Robertson, 1932).

55 *School Magazine*, (Sydney) August 1938.
56 Cramp, Lennard and Smairl, *A Story of the English People*, p. 408.

7 RESISTANCE TO AN UNREMITTING PROCESS

1 T. Crosby, *Up and Down the North Pacific Coast by Canoe and Mission Ship* (Toronto, 1914), p. 84. and D.C. Scott, 'Indian Affairs, 1867–1912, in A. Shortt and A. Doughty (eds), *Canada and Its Provinces* (Toronto, 1914), pp. 622–3. Duncan Campbell Scott was an influential decision-maker for Indian Affairs between 1909–32. His policies affected First Nations across Canada. See also, B. Titley, *A Narrow Vision: Duncan Campbell Scott and the Administration of Indian Affairs in Canada* (Vancouver, 1986).
2 The term 'First Nations' refers to the first peoples of Canada. First Nations, a general term, is used when a number of First Nation groups are referred to. Other terms which have historically been used include 'Indian' and 'Native'. These terms will also be used in this chapter. The term 'Nation' is used to distinguish the cultural, geographic, and linguistic boundaries of the First Peoples. In British Columbia, there are 10 major First Nations language groups. More First Nation cultural groups are using their aboriginal language name, rather than the anthropological name ascribed to them. Until the 1960s, the Sto:lo were included in the anthropological ethnic division 'Coast Salish' whch encompasses a much larger geographical area (southern coastal area of BC).
3 J. Tobias, 'Protection, civilisation, assimilation: an outline history of Canada's Indian policy', in I. Getty and A. Lussier (eds) *As Long as the Sun Shines and Water Flows: A Reader in Canadian Native Studies* (Vancouver, 1983), pp. 39–55.
4 J. Kennedy, 'Roman Catholic missionary effort and Indian acculturation in the Fraser Valley 1860–1900', (unpublished BA Honours Essay, University of British Columbia, 1969), p. 50.
5 Ibid., pp. 19–20. The 'reductions' were separate church mission communities where the intent was to keep the aboriginal people away from non-native influences. The same Christianizing model was attempted in Paraguay, South America and Oregon, USA.
6 Ibid., p. 20.
7 Ibid., p. 51.
8 *Missions de la Congregation des Missionaires Oblats de Marie Immaculee* (Hereafter *Missions*), (Paris: 1863–1946), vol. iv, xxxxvi, A, Henneyer, p. 293.
9 Ibid., pp. 293–4.
10 Oblates of Mary Immaculate, 'Correspondence and records, 1841–1928' (Deschatelets Archives and Public Archives of Canada, Ottawa), letter dated 20 July 1866, New Westminster, BC.
11 L.R. Peterson, 'Indian education in British Columbia' (unpublished Master's thesis, University of British Columbia, 1959), p. 76.
12 J. Gresko, 'Creating little dominions within the dominion: early Catholic Indian schools in Saskatchewan and British Columbia', in J. Barman, Y. Hevert, and D. McCaskill (eds), *Indian Education in Canada Volume 1: The Legacy* (Vancouver, 1986), p. 98.
13 R. Knight, *Indians at work* (Vancouver, 1978).
14 'The Lucky Indians', *British Columbian*, 31 August, 1889.
15 Kennedy, 'Roman Catholic missionary effort', p. 74.
16 Ibid.
17 'Old Coqualeetza 1895', *Chilliwack Progress* (Chilliwack, BC, 1901), p. 4.
18 'Coqualeetza Institute, 1901', *Chilliwack Progress* (Chilliwack, BC, 1901), p.4.

19 H.J Vallery, 'A history of Indian education in Canada' (unpublished Master's thesis, University of British Columbia, 1942), p. 150.
20 J. Barman, Y. Hebert and D. McCaskill (eds), *Indian Education in Canada Volume 1: The Legacy* (Vancouver, 1986). Also see C. Haig-Brown, *Resistance and Renewal: Surviving the Indian Residential School* (Vancouver, 1988).
21 G. Manual and M. Posluns *The Fourth World: An Indian Reality* (Toronto, 1974), p. 65.
22 Canada, Department of Indian Affairs and Northern Development (hereafter Indian Affairs). Royal Commission on Indian Affairs. *Report of the Royal Commission on Indian Affairs for the Province of British Columbia*, 4 vols, (Victoria, 1916).
23 Indian Affairs RG 10, Central Registry System, School Files. Volume 6387, File 806-1, part 1 (Public Archives, Ottawa).
24 Ibid.
25 Ibid.
26 Ibid.
27 Ibid.
28 A. Parminter, 'The development of integral schooling for British Columbia Indian children', (unpublished Master's thesis, University of British Columbia, 1964), pp. 77–80.
29 Ibid., pp. 82–6.
30 Joint Committee of the Senate and the House of Commons on Indian Affairs. *Final Report: v: Education and Development of Human Resources* (1961), p. 610–11.
31 R. Tremblay, 'New directions in Indian affairs' notes for an address to the Indian–Eskimo Association of Canada (London, Ontario, 1964), p. 4.
32 Parminter, 'The development of integral schooling', p. 97.
33 Parminter, 'The development of integral schooling', 'Indian education in BC'.
34 H. Hawthorn, *A Survey of Contemporary Indians in Canada, Volume II* (Ottawa, 1967).
35 Peterson, 'Indian education in BC'.
36 Ibid., pp. 121–42.
37 Hawthorn, *A Survey of Comtemporary Indians*, p. 142.
38 Ibid., p. 155.
39 H. Van Brummelen, 'Shifting perspectives: early British Columbia textbooks from 1872 to 1925', in N. Sheehan, D. Wilson and D. Jones (eds) *Schools in the West: Essays in Canadian Educational History* (Calgary, 1986), pp. 28–9.
40 Ibid., p. 28.
41 Manitoba Indian Brotherhood, *The Shocking Truth About Indians in Textbooks: Textbook Evaluation* (Winnipeg, 1974).
42 W. Werner, B. Connors, T. Aoki and J. Dahlie, *Whose Culture? Whose Heritage? Ethnicity Within Canadian Social Studies Curricula* (Vancouver, 1977), p. 59.
43 Ibid., p. 27.
44 Ibid,. p. 26.
45 Ibid., p. 33.
46 National Indian Brotherhood. *Indian Control of Indian Education: Policy Paper Presented to the Ministry of Indian Affairs and Northern Development* (Ottawa, 1972).
47 Ibid., pp. 2–3.
48 Hawthorn, *A Survey of Contemporary Indians*.

8 RACISM AND AFRICAN EDUCATION

1 Stanley Aronowitz and Henry A Giroux, *Education Under Seige: The Conservative, Liberal, and Radical Debate Over Schooling* (South Hadley, MA: Bergin and Garvey, 1985), pp. 140–1.

2 John I. Goodlad, *Curriculum Inquiry: The Study of Curriculum Practice* (New York: McGraw-Hill, 1979), pp. 43–76; National Mathematics Committee, *Second International Mathematics Study: Detailed Report for the United States* (Campaign, IL: Stipes Publishing Co., December 1986), p. 6.

3 Alan A. Glatthorn, *Curriculum Leadership* (Glenview, IL: Scott, Foresman & Co., 1987), p. 21.

4 For a further discussion on this see Michael W. Apple, *Cultural and Economic Reproduction in Education: Essays on Class, Ideology and the State* (London: Routledge & Kegan Paul, 1982); Aronowitz and Giroux, *Education*; Pierre Bourdieu and Jean-Claude Passeron, *Reproduction in Education, Society and Culture* (London: Sage Publications Ltd., 1977); Martin Carnoy, *Education as Cultural Imperialism* (New York: Longman, 1974); Paulo Freire, *Pedagogy of the Oppressed* (New York: Continum Publishing, 1988).

5 A. Victor Murray, *The School in the Bush: A Critical Study in the Theory and Practice of Native Education in Africa* (New York: Barnes and Noble, 1967), pp. 152–225.

6 See Stephen J. Ball, 'Imperialism, social control and the colonial curriculum in Africa', *Journal of Curriculum Studies*, (1983), 15: 237–63; Murray, *The School in the Bush*; C. Whitehead, 'British colonial education policy: a synonym for cultural imperialism?', in J.A. Mangan (ed.), *'Benefits bestowed'? Education and British Imperialism*, (Manchester: Manchester University Press, 1988).

7 John N.B. Osogo, 'Educational developments in Kenya, 1911–1924', in Bethwell Ogot (ed.) *Hadith 3* (Nairobi: East African Publishing House, 1971), p. 113.

8 Kenneth J. King, *Pan-Africanisim and Education: A Study of Race Philanthropy and Education in the Southern States of America and East Africa* (Oxford: Clarendon Press, 1971); Donald Gilmore Schilling, 'British policy for African education in Kenya, 1895–1939' (PhD. diss., University of Wisconsin, 1972); J.R. Sheffield, *Education in Kenya: An Historical Study* (New York: Teachers College, 1973).

9 East Africa Protectorate (EAP), *Annual Report, 1906/7* (London: HMSO, 1908), p. 20.

10 EAP, *Annual Report, 1901* (London: HMSO, 1903), 20; EAP, *Annual Report, 1903/4* (London: HMSO, 1905), p. 27; EAP, *Annual Report, 1904/5* (London: HMSO, 1905), p. 21; EAP, *Annual Report. 1911/12* (London: HMSO, 1913), pp. 57, 58.

11 EAP, *Annual Report 1904/5*, p. 21; EAP, *Annual Report 1906/7*, p. 21; EAP, *Annual Report, 1917/18* (London: HMSO, 1919), p. 23.

12 Colony and Protectorate of Kenya (CPK), *Annual Report, 1924* (London: HMSO, 1926), p. 19.

13 EAP, *Annual Report, 1911/12*, pp. 57, 58; T.P. Gorman, 'The development of language policy in Kenya with particular reference to the educational system', in W.H. Whitely (ed.), *Language in Kenya*, (Nairobi: Oxford University Press, 1974) and Robert G. Gregory, 'Multiethnic education in Kenya: the language problem', forthcoming publication, 1992, deal with the language issue at length.

14 EAP, *Annual Report, 1901*, p. 22.

15 Alan J. Bishop, 'Western mathematics: the secret weapon of cultural imperialism', *Race and Class* (1990) 32(2):53.

16 For further discussion see Bishop, 'Western mathematics'; Marilyn Franken-
    stein, *Relearning Mathematics: A Different Third R – Radical Math(s)* (Lon-
    don: Free Association Books, 1989); George Ghevarughese Joseph, 'Founda-
    tions of Eurocentrism in mathematics', *Race and Class*, (1987), 28(3): 13–28;
    Michael F. D. Young, *Knowledge and Control* (London: Collier-Macmillan
    Publishers, 1971); Claudia Zaslavsky, *Africa Counts: Number and Pattern in
    African Culture* (Boston: Prindle, Weber and Schmidet, Inc., 1973).
17 Bishop, 'Western mathematics', pp. 51, 59–60. Also see A.J. Bishop,
    Mathematical Enculturation: A Cultural Perspective on Mathematics Education
    (Dordrecht, The Netherland: Kluwer Academic Publishers, 1988), pp. 20–60.
18 Bishop, 'Western mathematics', p. 55.
19 CPK, *Education Department, Annual Report, 1935*, (Nairobi: Government
    Printer, 1936), p. 36.
20 CPK, *Annual Report, 1922* (London: HMSO, 1923), p. 14.
21 Zaslavsky, *Africa Counts*, pp. 247, 252–3.
22 Ibid., p. 255.
23 See Levi Leonard Conant, *The Number Concept: Its Origin and Development*.
    (New York: Macmillan & Co., 1931) and Zaslavsky, *Africa Counts*.
24 Zaslavsky, *Africa Counts*, pp. 257–8.
25 Ibid., p. 259. Also see Conant, *The Number Concept*, 1–20 and John S. Mbiti
    African Religions and Philosophy, 2nd edn., (Oxford: Heinemann International,
    1989), pp. 19–20.
26 Zaslavsky, *Africa Counts*, p. 88.
27 Anthula Natsoulas, 'The game of mancala with reference to commonalities among
    the peoples of Ethiopia and in comparison to other African peoples: rules and
    strategies', paper presented at the eleventh annual meeting of the Ethiopian studies
    Association, April 1991, Addis Ababa, Ethiopia; Richard Pankhurst, 'Gabata
    and related board games of Ethiopia and the Horn of Africa', *Ethiopia Observer*,
    (1971),24(3); Laurence Russ, *Mancula Games* (Algonae, MI: Reference Publica-
    tions, Inc., 1984).
28 EAP, *Annual Report, 1903/3*, p. 27.
29 Ibid. EAP, *Annual Report, 1905/1906*, p. 32.
30 EAP, *Annual Report, 1910/1911*, p. 54; EAP, *Annual Report, 1912/1913*, pp.
    60–2; EAP *Annual Report, 1913/1914*, p. 60.
31 EAP, *Annual Report, 1915/1916*, pp. 21, 22.
32 Thomas Jesse Jones, *Education in East Africa. A study of East, Central, and
    South Africa by the Second African Commission Under the Auspices of the
    Phelps–Stokes Fund in Cooperation with the International Education Board* (Lon-
    don: Phelps–Stokes Fund, 1925), pp. 117–19, 124.
33 Sheffield, *Education in Kenya*, p. 21. For a discussion of the establishment of
    British education policy at this time see Schilling, *British policy for African educa-
    tion*, chapters V and VI.
34 CPK, *Department of Education, Annual Report, 1929* (Nairobi: Government
    Printer, 1930), p. 11.
35 For a full treatment of the entire issue see Robert G. Gregory, *India and East
    Africa: A History of Race Relations Within the British Empire, 1890–1939*
    (Oxford: Clarendon Press, 1971), pp. 246–8. The document in which the prin-
    ciple of 'native parmountcy' was enunciated is Parliamentary Papers (PP), *In-
    dians in Kenya: Memorandum*, cd. 1922 (London, 1923); Schilling, *British policy
    for African Education*, p. 207.
36 Schilling, 'British policy for African education', p. 221.
37 Jones, *Education in East Africa*, pp. 101, 111, 114–15.
38 Ibid., p. 136; CPK, *Education Department, Annual Report, 1925* (Nairobi: East

African Standard, 1926), p. 6; Schilling, *British policy for African education*, pp. 259–60. Separate advisory committees were established for European and Indian education.

39   Jones, *Education in East Africa*, p. 139.
40   Ibid., p. 140.
41   Ibid., p. 136.
42   Osogo, 'Educational developments in Kenya', p. 113.
43   King, *Pan-Africanism and Education*, p. 146.
44   Sheffield, *Education in Kenya*, p. 19. See the memorandum in PP, *Educational Policy in British Tropical Africa*, cmd. 2347 (London, 1925), p. 4.
45   Sheffield, *Education in Kenya*, pp. 19–20; PP, *Educational Policy*, p. 4–8.
46   CPK, *Education Department, Annual Report, 1929*, p. 7.
47   Ibid.
48   Ibid.
49   Ibid., 8.
50   Ibid.
51   Carl G. Rosberg Jr. and John Nottingham, *The Myth of 'Mau Mau': Nationalism in Kenya* (Nairobi: East African Publishing House, 1966), p. 87.
52   CPK, *Social and Economic Progress of the People of Kenya, 1932* (London: HMSO, 1933), p. 33; CPK, *Education Department, Annual Report, 1935* (Nairobi, Government Printer, 1936), p. 15; CPK, *Education Department, Annual Report, 1937* (Nairobi: Government Printer, 1938), p. 7; CPK, *Education Department, Annual Report, 1939* (Nairobi: Government Printer, 1940), p. 67.
53   CPK, *Education Department, Annual Report, 1934* (Nairobi: Government Printer, 1935), p. 9. CPK, *Education Department, Annual Report, 1937*, pp. 12–16.
54   CPK, *Education Department, Annual Report, 1937*, p. 39; CPK, *Education Department, Annual Report, 1939*, p. 11.
55   CPK, *Education Department, Annual Report, 1935*, p. 53.
56   CPK, *Education Department, Annual Report, 1929*, pp. 17–18.
57   Gorman, 'Development of language policy in Kenya', p. 418. Gorman discusses efforts to introduce English and the obstacles encountered, see especially pp. 410–21.
58   CPK, *Education Department, Annual Report, 1937*, p. 16.
59   Ibid., p. 51.
60   Ibid., p. 16.
61   Ibid., pp. 45–56.
62   Ibid., p. 48.
63   CPK, *Education Department, Annual Report, 1935*, p. 29; CPK *Education Department, Annual Report, 1937*, p. 52.
64   CPK, *Education Department, Annual Report, 1935*, p. 28.
65   CPK, *Education Department, Annual Report, 1929*, p. 7; CPK *Education Department, Annual Report, 1925*, p. 14.
66   CPK, *Education Department, Annual Report, 1937*, pp. 42, 44.
67   CPK, *Education Department, Annual Report, 1935*, pp. 14, 29; CPK, *Education Department, Annual Report, 1929*, pp. 39–41.
68   Ibid., 1929, p. 37.
69   B.E. Kipkorrir, 'Carey Francis at the A.H.S., Kikuyu, 1940–62', in B.E. Kipkorrir (ed.) *Biographical Essays on Imperialism and Collaboration in Colonial Kenya*, (Nairobi: Kenya Literature Bureau, 1980), pp. 112–59.
70   CPK, *Education Department, Annual Report, 1924* (Nairobi: East African Standard, 1925), pp. 24–5.

71 Richard D. Heyman, 'The initial years of the Jeanes School in Kenya, 1924–31', in V.M. Battle and C.H. Lyons (eds), *Essays in the History of African Education*, (New York: Teachers College Press, 1970), pp. 105–23.

72 See report on the Jeanes School by its first headmaster, James W.C. Dougall, 13 January 1926 in CPK, *Education Department, Annual Report, 1925*, 24–34. King, *Pan-Africanism and Education* discusses the Jeanes School as an experiment in 'Phelps-Stokism', pp. 150–76.

73 John Anderson, *The Struggle for the School. The Interaction of Missionary, Colonial Government and Nationalist Enterprise in the Development of Formal Education in Kenya* (London: Longman 1970), p. 122.

74 Owen W. Furley and T. Watson, *A History of Education in East Africa* (London: Zed, 1978), p. 163.

75 Theodore Natsoulas, 'The rise and fall of the Kikuyu Karing'a Education Association of Kenya, 1929–1952', *Journal of Asian and African Studies*, (1988) xxiii (3–4): 220.

76 CPK, *Education Department, Annual Report, 1929*, p.27.

77 Thomas Nganda Wangai, 'How the Orthodox Church Started', translated from the Kikuyu by Eliud Nganga Mwaura (unpublished manuscript, Nairobi, n.d.), p. 6. Wangai was an early leader of the independent school organization, the Kikuyu Karing'a Education Association. My thanks to Mr Peter Kahuho who gave me a copy of the manuscript. Kenya National Archives (KNA) District Commissioner/Fort Hall (DC/FH) 3/2, Church of Scotland (CSM) Memorandum: Prepared by the Kikuyu Council on Female Circumcision, 1 December 1931, pp. 39–57.

78 CSM memo, 49, 51. Natsoulas, 'Rise and fall of the Kikuyu Karing'a', p. 221. KNA, Provincial Commissioner/Central Province (PC/CP), 4/1/2, Annual Report/66, 1929, p. 4.

79 Natsoulas, 'Rise and fall of the Kikuyu Karing'a', p. 222.

80 KNA, PC/CP, 8/5/3, letter to Provincial Commissioner, 17 December 1929.

81 KNA, PC/CP, 8/1/1, Arthur to Director of Education, 16 January 1930.

82 CPK, *Education Department, Annual Report, 1929*.

83 Public Record Office, Colonial Office 533/422, Kikuyu Grievances: KCA Report by Johnston Kenyatta, February 1932.

84 KNA, PC/CP, 8/7/1, Fazan to PC, 24 December 1929.

85 KNA, PC/CP, 9/21/9, Maitland to Horne, 24 December 1930.

86 CSM Memo, KNA, Kiambu/22, Handing Over Report, 28 January 1930, p. 11.

87 See, for example, CPK, *Education Department, Annual Report, 1936*, p. 58 ff.

88 Information supplied by former students of the independent schools, Daniel Mariuki and Father Eleftherios Ndwuaru, July and August 1982.

89 Ibid.

90 KNA, PC/CP, 4/3/1/Annual Report, 1934.

91 Kamuya wa-Kang'ethe, 'The role of the Agikuyu religion and culture in the development of the Karing'a religio-political movement, 1900–1950 with particular reference to the Agikuyu concept of God and the Rite of Initiation' (PhD diss., University of Nairobi, 1981), pp. 382–6. Much of wa-Kang'ethe's study was based on interviews with former Karing'a members.

92 These songs were written by Kinuthia Daniel Mugia. My thanks to Dr Andreas Tillyrides in arranging for their collection and translation from the original Kikuyu.

93 Ndwuaru and Mariuki.

94 CPK, *Education Department, Annual Report, 1926*, pp. 13–15. Michele Merle, 'The Independent Schools Movement of Kenya' (Master's thesis, Teachers College, Columbia University, 1963), p. 20.

95 Corfield argues that a portion of Mau Mau leadership came from those that attended the independent schools, F.D. Corfield, *Historical Survey of the Origins and Growth of Mau Mau*, cmd. 1030 (London, HMSO, 1960), p. 40ff.

9 THE CREATION OF A DEPENDENT CULTURE

1 For details consult, for instance, R.L. Buell, *The Native Problem in Africa* (New York: Macmillan, 1928); and C. Lucas, *The Partition and Colonization of Africa* (Oxford, Clarendon Press, 1922).

2 W. Rodney, *How Europe Underdeveloped Africa*, (Washington D.C.: Howard University Press, 1981), pp. 205–80; also F. Fanon, *Black Skins, White Masks* (New York, Grove Press, 1967); F. Fanon, *The Wretched of the Earth* (New York, Grove Press: 1963); F. Fanon, *Towards the African Revolution* (New York: Monthly Review Press, 1967) are important studies that reveal the psychological aspects of enslavement and colonization of Africans in the African continent and in the Americas.

3 F.D. Lugard, *The Rise of our East African Empire*, vol. II (Edinburgh and London: William Blackwood & Sons, 1893), p. 591.

4 Sir Charles Eliot, *The East Africa Protectorate* (London: Edward Arnold, 1905), p. 24.

5 Anonymous, '*Uganda 1947*', *Colonial Annual Report* (London: HMSO, 1949); also S.R. Karugire, *A Political History of Uganda*, (Nairobi and London: Heinemann, 1980), pp. 99–122 and his *The Roots of Instability in Uganda* (Kampala: New Vision Publishers, 1988).

6 R. Mukherjee, *Uganda: An Historical Accident? Class, Nation, State Formation* (Trenton, NJ: Africa World Press, first American edn, 1985), p. 117.

7 P.G. Okoth, 'Museveni, the new generation of African leaders and the State in Uganda', *Ufahamu* (Winter 1988/78) xv(3): 7.

8 Ibid. For comparison on these views, see C. Wrigley, 'Four steps towards disaster', in H.B. Hansen and M. Twaddle, *Uganda Now: Between Decay and Development* (London: James Currey, 1988), p. 28.

9 M. Mamdani, *Imperialism and Fascism in Uganda* (Trenton, NJ: Africa World Press, 1984), p. 8.

10 M. Mamdani, *Politics and Class Formation in Uganda* (New York: Monthly Review Press, 1976), p. 40.

11 D.A. Low, *Buganda in Modern History* (London: Weidenfeld & Nicolson, 1971), p. 233.

12 For details, consult A.D. Roberts, 'The sub-imperialism of the Baganda', *Journal of African History*, (1962) III(3): 435–50; Low, *Buganda*, pp. 227–31; G. Emwanu, 'The reception of alien rule in Teso', *Uganda Journal*, (1967) 31(2): 171–82.

13 Low, *Buganda*, p. 230.

14 Okoth, 'the State in Uganda', p. 7.

15 Ibid.

16 Mukherjee, *Uganda*, p. 166.

17 Ibid., Mamdani, *Class Formation*, pp. 40–64; Mamdani, *Imperialism*, pp. 6–8; D.W. Nabudere, *Imperialism and Revolution in Uganda* (London: Onyx Press and Dar es Salaam; Tanzania Publishing House, 1980), pp. 37–96.

18 The summary of these points and their full and scholarly discussion is found in Mukherjee, *Uganda*, p. 167 and pp. 167–254, respectively.

19 For details, consult for instance, S.M.W. Lugumba and J.C. Ssekamwa, *A History of Education in East Africa 1900–1973* (Kampala: Uganda Bookshop Press, 1973).

20 For detailed study of the Mill Hill Fathers, consult H.P. Gale, *Uganda and the Mill Hill Fathers* (London: Edward Arnold 1950).

21 For details consult G.P. MacGregory, *King's College Budo: The First Sixty Years* (Kampala: Oxford University Press, 1967).

22 On Gayaza history consult A.M. Kalemera, 'Gayaza High School in History, 1905–1962', Graduating Research Paper, Department of History, Makerere University, 1975.

23 P.G. Okoth, 'A History of St Mary's College, Kisubi', Graduating Research Paper, Department of History, Makerere University, 1978; also P.G. Okoth, 'Some aspects of missionary education in Uganda', *Bulletin of the Scottish Institute of Missionary Studies*, p. 55; A. Wandira, 'Early missionary education in Uganda', Department of Education, Makerere University, Kampala, 1971.

24 J. Kenyatta, *Facing Mount Kenya* (London: Secker & Warburg, 1959), especially chapter V entitled, 'System of education prior to the advent of the European', pp. 98–129.

25 Rodney, *How Europe Underdeveloped Africa*, p. 240.

26 Ibid., p. 242.

27 E. Wamba-Dia-Wamba, 'Africanism in crisis', *Philosophy and Social Action* (1986) xii(2): 20.

28 *The Washington Post*, 16 February 1964.

29 Wamba, 'Africanism', p. 20.

30 Katebalirwe-Amooti wa Irumba, 'Culture and ideology in the struggle for liberation and independence', *Mawazo* (June 1983), 5(2): 20.

31 Ibid., p. 21.

32 For details on African traditional religions, the following are useful references: J.S. Mbiti, *African Religions and Philosophy* (New York: Doubleday, 1966); B.A. Ogot, 'On the making of sanctuary: being some thoughts on the history of the religion in Padhola (Uganda)', in T.O. Ranger and I.N. Kimambo (eds), *The Historical Study of African Religion* (Berkeley and Los Angeles: University of California Press, 1972); N. King, *Religions of Africa: A Pilgrimage into Traditional Religions* (New York: Harper & Row, 1970); E.C. Parrinder, *African Traditional Religion* (London: SPCK, 1968); B.T. Rugyema, *Philosophy and Traditional Religion of the Bakiga in South West Uganda* (Nairobi: Kenya Literature Bureau, 1983).

33 Amooti, 'Culture and ideology', p. 21.

34 Ngugi wa Thiong'o, *Barrel of a Pen: Resistance to Repression in Neo-Colonial Kenya* (Trenton, NJ: Africa World Press, 1983), p. 94.

35 Ibid.

36 Ibid, p. 95.

37 Ibid.

38 Ibid, p. 94.

39 Ngugi wa Thiong'o, *Decolonizing the Mind: The Politics of Language in African Literature* (London: James Currey; Nairobi: Heinemann; Portsmouth NH: Heinemann, Harare: Zimbabwe Publishing Press, 1986), pp. 90–95.

40 Amooti, 'Culture and ideology', p. 25.

41 Ibid.

42 Okoth, 'St Mary's College Kisubi', p. 10.

43 P.G. Okoth, 'The Genesis of St Mary's College, Kisubi', *Uganda Journal*, (forthcoming).

44 J.A. Diorio, 'Knowledge, truth and power in the curriculum', *Educational Theory* (1977) 27(2): 103–11.

45 Okoth, 'Genesis of St Mary's College, Kisubi'.

46   T.B. Kabwegyere, *The Politics of State Formation: the Nature and Effects of Colonialism in Uganda* (Nairobi: East African Literature Bureau, 1974), p. 145.
47   J.K. Nyerere, *Education for Self Reliance* (Dar es Salaam: Government Printer, 1967), p. 3.
48   Ibid., p. 25.
49   A.B.K. Kasozi, *The Crisis of Secondary School Education in Uganda*, Kampala: Longman, 1979), p. 57.
50   Karugire, *A Political History of Uganda*, p. 132.
51   Kasozi, *Crisis*, p. 62.
52   Ibid., p. 63.
53   Rodney, *How Europe Underdeveloped Africa*, p. 248.

10 RULERS AND RULED

1   M. Carnoy, *Education as Cultural Imperialism* (New York: David McKay, 1974).
2   F.C. Clatworthy, 'The formulation of British colonial education policy, 1923–48; University of Michigan Comparative Education Dissertation no. 3 (Ann Arbor, Michigan: University of Michigan, 1971); K. Watson, *Education in the Third World*, (London: Croom Helm, 1982a); C. Whitehead, 'Education in British colonial dependencies, 1919–39: a re-appraisal', *Comparative Education* (1981) 17(1): 71–80.
3   Watson, *Education in the Third World*; K. Watson, 'Educational policies in multicultural societies', *Comparative Education* (March 1979), IS(1): 17–31.
4   Fook Seng Loh, *Seeds of Separatism: Educational Policy in Malaya, 1874–1910*, (Kuala Lumpur: Oxford University Press, 1975); R. Stevenson, *Cultivators and Administrators: British Educational Policy towards the Malays, 1875–1906* (Kuala Lumpur: Oxford University Press, 1975); P.C. Wicks, 'Education, British colonialism and a plural society in West Malaysia', *History of Education Quarterly* (Summer 1980) xx(2): 179–89.
5   J. Bastin and H.J. Benda, *A History of Modern South East Asia* (New York: Prentice-Hall, 1968); D.G.E. Hall, *A History of South East Asia* (London: Macmillan, 1955); M. Collis, *Raffles* (London, Faber and Faber, 1966); Sir R. Coupland, *Raffles 1781–1826* (London: Oxford University Press, 1946).
6   V. Purcell, *The Chinese in South East Asia* (London: Royal Institute for International Affairs and Oxford University Press, 1966).
7   Sir Frank Swettenham, *British Malaya: An Account of the Origins and Progress of British Influence in Malaya* (London: Allen and Unwin, 1958).
8   Wicks, 'Education, British Colonialism', pp. 533–4.
9   J.E. Jayasuriya, *Dynamics of nation-building in Malaysia* (Colombo: Associated Educational Publishers, 1983).
10   T.G. McGee, 'Population: a preliminary analysis, in Wang Gungwu (ed.), *Malaysia* (London: Pall Mall Press, 1964), pp. 64, 71.
11   S. Arasaratnam, *Indians in Malaysia and Singapore* (Kuala Lampur: Institute of Race Relations and Oxford University Press, 1970).
12   V. Purcell, *The Memoirs of a Malayan Official* (London: Cassell, 1965); W.R. Roff, *The Origins of Malay Nationalism* (Kuala Lampur: University of Malaya Press, 1968).
13   P.L. Burns (ed.), *The Journals of J.W.W. Birch, First British Resident to Perak 1874–1875* (Kuala Lumpur: Oxford University Press, 1976); Roff, *The Origins*.
14   Loh, *Seeds*; K. Watson 'Cultural pluralism, nation building and educational policies in peninsular Malaysia', *Journal of Multilingual and Multicultural Development* (1980), 1(2): 155–74; K. Watson, 'Cultural pluralism, education

and national identity in the ASEAN countries of South East Asia', in T. Corner, (ed.), *Education in Multicultural Societies* (London: Croom Helm, 1984), pp. 197–235.

15 M.S. Sidhu, 'Chinese dominance of West Malaysian towns, 1921–70', *Geography* (1936) 61(1): 17–23.

16 Hon-Chan Chai, *Planning Education for a Plural Society* (Paris: UNESCO, International Institute for Educational Planning, 1967).

17 Jayasuriya, *Dynamics*, p. 13.

18 M.E. Chamberlain, *The New Imperialism* (London: The Historical Association, 1970), p. 39.

19 A. Mayhew, *Memorandum on Education in Malaya*, March 1929, Colonial Office, 717, vol. 67, 1929.

20 H.S. Scott, 'Educational policy in the British Colonial Empire', *Yearbook of Education* (London, Evans, 1937), pp. 411–38.

21 Loh, *Seeds*; Stevenson, *Cultivators*'; Wicks, 'Education, British Colonialism'.

22 Collis, *Raffles*; Coupland, *Raffles*.

23 R.J. Wilkinson, 'Malay customs and beliefs', *Journal of the Malayan Branch of the Royal Diatic Society*, XXX, 4 (November 1957).

24 V. Purcell, *Problems of Chinese Education* (Longman, Kegan Paul, Trench, Trubner & Co., 1936).

25 Chelliah, D.D. *A Short History of the Educational Policy of the Straits Settlements (c. 1800–1925)* (Singapore: Government Press, 1947).

26 Wilkinson, 'Malay customs', p. 46.

27 D. Saliba and G.J. Tomah, 'The great traditions: Islam', *Yearbook of Education* (London: Evans, 1959).

28 Federated Malay States, *The System of Education in the Federated Malay States* Official Report by the Federal Education Office (Kuala Lumpur, 1902).

29 Purcell, *Problems*.

30 H.R. Cheeseman, *Compulsory Education in Malaya in Overseas Education* (London: Colonial Office, 1931).

31 Chelliah, *A Short History*.

32 Federated Malay States, *System of Education*, p. 2.

33 D.F. Cooke, 'The mission schools of Malaya, 1815–1942, *Paedagogica Historica*, 6 (1966).

34 Loh, *Seeds*.

35 Mayhew, *Memorandum*.

36 Perak, Annual Report, 1890, p. 16.

37 Wicks, 'Ed. cation, British colonialism', p. 536.

38 Perak, *Annual Report 1894*.

39 Protected Malay States, *Reports on the Protected Malay States from 1896*, (1896).

40 E. Sadaka, *The Protected Malay States, 1873–1895*, (Kuala Lumpur: Oxford University Press, 1968); Stevenson, *Cultivators*.

41 Cooke, 'The mission schools'.

42 Federated Malay States, *Annual Report* (1920).

43 Cited in L.R. Wheeler, *The Modern Malay* (London: Allen and Unwin, 1928).

44 Straits Settlements, *Annual Report for Education (Straits Settlements)* (1903).

45 Kedah, *Annual Report, Kedah*, 1331 AH, 11 December 1912–30 November 1913 (1913).

46 Federated Malay States (1905) p. 9.

47 Straits Settlements, *Annual Report on Education (Straits Settlements)* (London: Colonial Office, 1921).

48 Cooke, 'The mission schools'; Watson, K. (1982b); F.H.K. Wong, 'An investigation into the work of the De La Salle Brothers in the Far East', *Paedogogica*

Historica (1976), 6: 440–54.
49   Protected Malay States, *Reports on the protected Malay States from 1896* (1892).
50   H. Clifford, 'Malaya: as it is and as it was', *Proceedings of the Royal Commonwealth Institute, XXX* (1988–9).
51   Sir F. Weld, (1883/4) 'The Straits Settlements and British Malaya', *Proceedings of the Royal Commonwealth Institute, XV* (1833–4).
52   Mayhew, *Memorandum*: Parliamentary papers, 1892; Perak, *Annual Report* (Perak, 1890).
53   Federated Malay States, *Proceedings of the Federal Council*, B66 (1915).
54   Negri Sembilan, 'Minute of the British Resident of Negri Sembilan to the Resident General, 14 June 1898', High Commissioner's Office File No. 758/1898 (1898).
55   Stevenson, *Cultivators*, p. 55.
56   Federated Malay States, *Annual Report* (1920); Straits Settlements, *Annual Report on Education (Straits Settlements)*, (London: Colonial Office, 1921); K. Watson, 'A comparative study of educational development in Thailand, Malaya and Singapore', unpublished PhD thesis, University of Reading (1973).
57   N.J. Ryan, *The Making of Modern Malaya* (Kuala Lumpur: Oxford University Press, 1967).
58   Loh, *Seeds*, pp. 23–4.
59   J. Singh and H. Muckerjee, 'Education and National Integration in Malaysia', *International Journal of Educational Development*, (1992), 12(1) (forthcoming).
60   Federated Malay States, *Annual Reports on Education for the Federated Malay States*, (London: HMSO, 1898).
61   I. Bird, *The Golden Chesonese and the Way Thither* (London, 1883, reprinted in Kuala Lumpur: Oxford University Press, 1976).
62   Sadaka, *Protected Malay States.*
63   Wicks, 'Education, British colonialism', p. 536.
64   Loh, *Seeds*; V.Purcell, *The Memoirs of a Malayan Official* (London: Cassell, 1965).
65   Federated Malay States, *Annual Reports on the Federated Malay States for 1901* (London: HMSO, 1901).
66   K. Watson, *Comparative Study*; K. Watson, 'The education of racial minorities in South East Asia with special reference to the Chinese', *Compare*, (1976), 6 (2): 14–21.
67   Arasaratnam, *Indians*, p. 173.
68   Ibid.
69   Mayhew, *Memorandum*, p. 141. Cited in Jayasuriya, *Dynamics*.
70   Watson, 'The Education'; K. Watson, 'Cultural pluralism, education and national identity in the ASEAN countries of South East Asia', pp. 197–235.
71   Colonial Office (1921).
72   V. Purcell, *The Chinese in Malaya* (London and Kuala Lumpur: Oxford University Press, 1948).
73   Wong, 'An investigation', p. 15.
74   Federation of Malaya, *Annual Education Report*. (1954).
75   Jayasuriya, *Dynamics*, p. 28.
76   Cooke, 'The mission schools'; Straits Settlements, *Annual Report on Education (Straits Settlements)* London: Colonial Office, 1921); Wong, 'An investigation'.
77   See Appendix I. Education Code, Part III, 1933.
78   Ibid. pp. 4, 9.
79   W.S. Morgan, 3rd edn, *The Story of Malaya* (Singapore: Malaya Publishing House and Exeter: A. Wheaton & Co., 1946).

80   Ibid. p. 61.
81   Ibid. p. 65.
82   Ibid. p. 67.
83   Ibid. p. 68.
84   Ibid. p. 73.
85   Ibid. p. 95.
86   N.J. Ryan, *The Making of Modern Malaya* (Kuala Lumpur: Oxford University Press, 1967).
87   Morgan, *Story of Malaya*, p. 7.
88   P.N. Nazareth, *The Malayan Story* (Singapore: Peter Chong and London: Macmillan, 1956).
89   Ibid., p. 11.
90   Morgan, *Story of Malaya*, pp. 97–9.
91   Singapore, *Syllabus for Civics in Secondary Schools*, Ministry of Education (1957); *Right Conduct: Syllabus for Primary English Schools*, Ministry of Education (1958).
92   Singapore, *Passages for School Assemblies: An Anthology*, Ministry of Education (1959).
93   Ryan, *Modern Malaya*, p. 168.
94   Chai, *Planning Education*, p. 243.
95   Awang Had Sellah, *Malay Secular Education and Teacher Training in British Malaya* (Kuala Lumpur: Dewan Bahasa dan Pustaka, 1979).
96   Sir R.O. Winstedt, *Education in Malaya* (Government Printer, Singapore, 1923).
97   Federated Malay States (1922).
98   Winstedt, *Education in Malaya*.
99   Ibid.
100 Federated Malay States, *Special Reports on Educational Subjects* CMD 2379, (London: Colonial Office, 1905).
101 Ibid. p. 10.
102 G. Burgess, 'A Malayan experiment in fostering rural industries', *Education in Malaya* (Being articles reprinted from '*Overseas Education*' published by the Colonial Office, 1930, 1942, 1946) (1946).
103 Sellah, *Malay Secular Education*, p. 103.
104 Harun Arminurrashid, cited in Sellah, *Malay Secular Education*, pp. 105–6.
105 Ibid., p. 133.

11 'ENGLISH IN TASTE'

1   For details about the organization of the East India Company, see P. Auber, *An Analysis of the Constitution of the East India Company* (London, 1826) and C.H. Philips, *The East India Company, 1784–1834* (Manchester, 1940).
2   T.G.P. Spear, *The Nabobs* (London, 1963), pp. 1–10.
3   Ibid., p. 11.
4. G.M. Trevelyan, *Illustrated English Social History* (London, 1949–52), III, p. 44.
5   The *Diwani* was the right to collect revenue on behalf of the Mughal Emperor. For details, see R. Muir (ed.), *The Making of British India, 1756–1858* (Manchester, 1915).

6   Suresh Chandra Ghosh, *Education Policy in India since Warren Hastings* (Calcutta, 1989), pp. 4–5.
7   Suresh Chanda Ghosh, *The Social Condition of the British Community in Bengal, 1757–1800* (Leiden, 1970), pp. 166–7.
8   David Kopf's *British Orientalism and the Bengal Renaissance* (Berkeley, Los Angeles, 1969) pays adequate attention to the role of Fort William College in the development of oriental learning in India.
9   Grant wrote his *Observations* in 1792 and published it in London in 1797. The manuscript of his work still exists at the India Office Library, London and is catalogued as Mss Eur. E.93. The best biographical account of Charles Grant is by A.T. Embree, *Charles Grant and British Rule in India* (London, 1962).
10 See Introduction to Muriel Jaeger's *Before Victoria* (London, 1956), pp. ix–xi.
11 For the social consequences of the Industrial Revolution, see Elie Halevy, *Histoire du Peuple Anglais au XIX Siècle* (Paris, 1912–32), I, p. 242 *et seq.* and J.H. Plumb, *England in the Eighteenth Century* (London, 1961), p. 84 *et seq.*
12 Asa Briggs, *The Age of Improvement* (London, 1949), p. 69.
13 Ibid.
14 R. Coupland, *Wilberforce* (London, 1945), pp. 202–3.
15 J. Steven-Watson, *The Reign of George III* (Oxford, 1957), pp. 353–5.
16 D.P. Sinha, *The Educational Policy of the East India Company in Bengal to 1854* (Calcutta, 1964), pp. 6–8.
17 H. Sharp (ed.), *Selections from Educational Records*(Calcutta, 1920), I, p. 22.
18 Ibid., p. 91 *et seq.*
19 G.M. Young in p. 4 of his *Victorian England* (London, 1936) states that 'in discipleship or reaction no young mind of the thirties could escape their [the Utilitarians'] influence. Bentham's alliance with James Mill, Mill's friendship with Malthus and Ricardo, had created a party, almost a sect, with formularies as compact as the Evangelical theology and conclusions no less exorable.'
20 Quoted in K.K. Chatterjee, *English Education in India: Issues and Opinions* (Delhi, 1976), p. 15.
21 G.M. Young (ed.), *Macaulay, Prose and Poetry* (London, 1967), pp. 717–18.
22 H. Sharp, *Selections*, pp. 107–17.
23 Ibid., pp. 117–29.
24 Ibid., pp. 130–31.
25 T.G.P. Spear, 'Bentinck and education', *Cambridge Historical Journal*, (1938) VI, 78–104.
26 K.A. Ballhatchet, 'The home government and Bentinck's educational policy', *Cambridge Historical Journal*, (1951)VI: 224–9.
27 In a farewell dinner at Grole's house, just on the eve of his departure for India as Governor-General in December 1827, he had said to James Mill, 'I am going to British India but I shall not be Governor-General. It is you, that will be Governor-General'. Quoted in J. Bowring (ed.), *The Works of Jeremy Bentham* (London, 1843), X, pp. 576–7.
28 A. Mayhew, *The Education of India* (London, 1926), p.18.
29 Suresh Chandra Ghosh, 'Formation of an educational policy of the British Raj between 1757 and 1857', in W. Frijhoff (ed.), *The Supply of Schooling* (Paris, 1983), pp. 43–56.
30 Government of India, *Report of the Indian Education Commission, 1881–82* (Calcutta, 1883), p. 18.
31 University of Calcutta, *Hundred Years of the University of Calcutta* (Calcutta, 1957), p. 127.
32 Appendix M, Statement 3 in Government of India, *Report of the Public Service Commission*, 1886–87 (*Calcutta*, 1988),p. 81.

33 Ibid.
34 Ibid.
35 Ibid.
36 Ibid., Appendix M, Statement 4, p.82.
37 J. Strachey, *India* (London, 1903), p. 187.
38 For details about the courses, see J.A. Richey (ed.), *Selection from Educational Records* (Calcutta, 1922), II, p. 371 *et seq.*
39 Richard Temple, *Men and Events of My Time in India*, (London, 1882), pp. 432–3.
40 *Indian Mirror*, Calcutta, 13 February 1878.
41 For the origin of the elite service, see Suresh Chandra Ghosh, *The Social Condition of the British Community in Bengal, 1757–1800* (Leiden, 1971), Chapter II.
42 B.B. Misra, *The Central Administration of the East India Company* (London, 1959), p. 404 *et seq.*
43 See Appendix I to Government of India, *Report of the Public Service Commission 1886–87*, pp. 51–5.
44 J.P. Naik and Suresh Chandra Ghosh, (eds), *Development of Educational Service 1859–79* (Delhi, 1976), pp. xxix–xxx, 361–70.
45 Anil Seal, *The Emergence of Indian Nationalism* (Cambridge, 1968), ch. 3, pp. 114–30.
46 'Wretched pettifogger' – this is how the Bengali lawyers were described by the *Pioneer* in July 1888. See Prem Narain, *Press and Politics in India* (Delhi, 1976), p. 196.
47 *Friend of India*, Calcutta, 1 December 1856.
48 Extract from the Minute by the Lieutenant-Governor of Bengal on 5 January 1877 in *Report on the Administration of Bengal, 1857–77*, (Calcutta, 1877), p. 59.
49 *Journal of the East India Association*, XIV, 1882, pp. 171–2.
50 Subordinate Collector, normally held by an Indian.
51 *Indian Spectator*, Bombay, 27 May 1883.
52 *Englishman*, Calcutta, 28 February 1870.
53 All the three were Bengalees. They were Ramesh Chandra Dutta, Bihari Lal Gupta and Surendra Nath Banerjea. See Joges C. Bose, *Surendra Nath Banerjea* (Dacca, 1939), p. 20 and L.S.S., O'Malley, *The Indian Civil Service* (London, 1931), pp. 204–10.
54 Supplement to the *Gazetteer of India*, 7 May 1870 pp. 715–17.
55 Surendra Nath Banerjea, *A Nation in Making* (Calcutta, 1925), p. 40 *et seq.*
56 *The Times of India*, Bombay, 24 December 1877.
57 Hamilton to Curzon, 20 September 1899. *Hamilton Papers*, Reel No. 1 (*Hamilton Papers* on microfilm in the National Archives of India, New Delhi).
58 James Johnston, *Our Educational Policy in India* (Edinburgh, 1880), introduction. Also quoted in University of Calcutta, *Hundred Years*, p. 15.
59 Government of India, *Report of the Indian Education Commission, 1881–82* (Calcutta, 1883). Also quoted in Haridas Mukherjee and Uma, *The Growth of Nationalism in India* (Calcutta, 1957), p. 125.
60 For details, see Government of India, *Report of the Indian Education Commission, 1881–82* (Calcutta, 1883).
61 Quoted in University of Calcutta, *Hundred Years*, p. 152.
62 See Briton Martin Jr., *New India, 1885* (Bombay, 1970) for the birth of the Indian National Congress.
63 See p. 59 in the *Report of the Proceedings of the Sixteenth Indian National Congress* at Bombay on 28 December 1900 when Surendra Nath Banerjea referred to it in his speech on that day.
64 See *Reports of the Proceedings of the Indian National Congress since 1885.*

65 See *Report of the Proceedings of the Sixteenth Indian National Congress* at Bombay on 28 December 1900, pp. 61–2.
66 See Sir Alfred C. Lyall's Introduction to Valentine Chirol's *Indian Unrest* (London, 1910), pp. xiii–xvi.
67 See Curzon's inaugural speech at the Conference at Simla on 2 September 1901 in National Archives (New Delhi) unpublished records: Home Education A Progs., October, 1901, No. 19, Appendix A.
68 Quoted in ibid., p. 12.

12 HISTORICAL DISCOURSES

1 The linkage between ideology and bias in school history education has provided an important area of interest for educationalists throughout this century as the linkages between nationalism, racism and ideology have gained significance in the understanding of political forces, though it can hardly be said that the research has often been more than descriptive. Key standard references in this area are: J.A. Lauwerys *History Textbooks and International Understanding* (Paris: UNESCO, 1953); E.H. Dance, *History the Betrayer* (Westport Conn: Greenwood, 1960); S.A. Smith, *Towards World Understanding: Bias in History Textbooks and Teaching* (London: The Library Assn, 1962); N. Glazer and R. Ueda, *Ethnic Groups in History Textbooks* (Washington DC: Ethics and Public Policy Centre, 1983).
2 G. Frederickson, *White Supremacy: A Comparative Study in America and South Africa*(Oxford: OUF, 1980); C.T. Loram, *The Education of the South African Native* (London: Longman Green, 1917).
3 Writers in this tradition have included J.C. Smuts, *A Century of Wrong* (1899); Gustav Preller, *Dagboek van Louis Trichardt* (1917) and *Piet Retief* (1920); C.M. van den Heever, *Hertzog* (1946); D.W. Kruger, *The Age of the Generals* (1958) and *Paul Kruger* (1961); and F.A. van Jaarsveld, *The Awakening of Afrikaner Nationalism* (1961) and *The Afrikaner's Interpretation of South African History* (1964), the last two being of particular significance in the apartheid era.
4 Examples found in the library were: C. de Fowler, K. and G.J.J. Smit, (1933) *New Senior History Course* (Cape Town: Maskew Millar); *Senior History* (1973) (Ninth Impression) (Cape Town: Maskew Millar).
5 C. Saunders, *The Making of the South African Past: Major Historians on Race and Class* (Cape Town: D Philip, 1988).
6 A sample of the long list of published materials, mostly based on doctoral dissertations on this topic, is listed below: Shula Marks, *Reluctant Rebellion* (1970), Philip Bonner, *Kings, Commoners and Concessionaires: the evolution and dissolution of the Swazi State* (1983), Peter Delius, *The Land Belongs to Us* (Pedi History (1983), Wiliam Beinart, *The Political Economy of Pondoland* (1982), Jeff Guy, *The Destruction of the Zulu Kingdom* (1979) and Jeff Peires, *The House of Phalo* (A history of the Xhosa) (1981) and *The Dead Will Speak: Nonggawuse and the Great Xhosa Cattle-Killing Movement of 1856–7* (1989).
7 Gail Gerhart, *Black Power in South Africa: The Evolution of an Ideology* (1978); B.M. Magubane, *The Political Economy of Race and Class in South Africa*(1978); Tom Lodge, *African Politics since 1945*(1984).
8 *Radical History Review* 46/7 (1990); 189–212.
9 C. Bundy, *The Rise and Fall of a South African Peasantry* (1979); Tim Keegan, *Rural Transformations in Industrializing South Africa* (1986).
10 M. Legassick, R. Johnstone and H. Wollope *Race, Class and Gold; A Study of Class Relations and Racial Discrimination in South Africa* (1976).
11 Shula Marks and A. Atmore (eds), *Economy and Society in Pre-Industrial South*

Africa (1980); S. Marks and S. Trapido, *The Politics of Race, Class and Nationalism in Twentieth Century South Africa* (1987).

12   C. van Onselen, *Studies in the Social and Economic History of the Witwatersrand: 1886–1914*: vol. I *New Babylon*; vol. II *New Nineveh* (1982). Also see the various published papers of the History Workshop conferences. This tradition was also not without its critics, see M. Morris, 'Social history and the transition to capitalism in the South African countryside', *Africa Perspective* New Series (December 1987) (5–6): 7–24.

13   *The Power of Prejudice in South African Schools* (Cape Town, 1965).

14   R.B. Mulholland, 'The evolution of history teaching in South Africa: A study of the relationship between modes of political organisation and the history taught in schools', (unpublished MEd dissertation, University of the Witwatersrand, 1981).

15   M. Cornevin, *Apartheid Power and Historical Falsification*(Paris: UNESCO, 1980) E. Dean *et al.*, *History in Black and White* (Paris: UNESCO, 1983).

16   See A.K. Dickenson and P.J. Lee, *History Teaching and Historical Understanding* (London: Heinemann, 1978); J. Fines, *Teaching History* (London: Holmes McDougall, 1983).

17   P. Kallaway (ed.), *History Alive 9* and *History Alive 10* (Pietermaritzburg, Shuter & Shooter 1986 and 1987 respectively).

18   Examples are: C.J. Joubert, *History for Std 10* (Johannesburg, Perskor, 1975 – fourteen impressions by 1985); H.A. Lambrechts *et al.*, *History 10* (Goodwood: Nasou, 1986); F.P.I. Lintvelt *et al.*, *Timelines 10* (Cape Town: Maskew Millar/Longman).

19   NECC, *What is History?* (Johannesburg: NECC, 1988).

20   See Part Four of P. Kallaway (ed.), *Apartheid and Education* (Johannesburg: Raven Press).

21   HSRC Working Group on *Report on History Education in the RSA* (HSRC 1992); Kallaway, P. (1991) 'Education and nation-building in South Africa in the 1990s: Reforming history education for the post-apartheid era', unpublished conference paper presented at the Comparative and International Education Conference, Pittsburgh, April 1991.

22   *Educational Renewal Strategy: Discussion Document* (Pretoria, Department of National Education June 1991) and the *Discussion Document: A Curriculum Model for Education in South Africa* (Committee of Heads of Education Departments, Nov 1991).

Index